The TV Director/Interpreter

Revised Edition

COLBY LEWIS and TOM GREER

COMMUNICATION ARTS BOOKS

Hastings House   Mamaroneck, New York

To Colby Lewis,
who inspired me to charge ahead
and gave me the tools to do it. My thanks to him.

TOM GREER

(Dr. Lewis passed away during the revision of this text.)

ISBN 0-8038-9318-3

Distributed to the trade by
Publishers Group West
Emeryville, CA

Printed in the United States of America

The TV Director/Interpreter

Contents

Introduction   vii

PART ONE: PRINCIPLES

1	Planning Picture Statements	3
2	Examples of Picture Statements	9
3	A Moment-by-Moment Questionnaire	21
4	Visual Clarity	23
5	Preserving Form	40
6	A Single Impression	48
7	Distractions and Discomforts	57
8	Animation or Liveliness	64
9	Expressiveness	66
10	Keeping Up with the Action	71
11	Concealing Mechanics	83
12	Spatial Relationships	90
13	Consistency	94
14	Extreme or Abrupt Shot Changes	101
15	Other Visual Transitions	109
16	The Director as Interpreter	120
17	Examples of Interpretation	132
18	Stimulating Responses	145
19	From Script to Camera Plan	155
20	"On-Location" Production	166
21	A Few Words About Editing	172
22	Don't Forget Audio	177
23	The Three *E*'s	194

PART TWO: ACCESSORY APTITUDES

24	Making Floor Plans	199
25	Efficiency	215
26	Calling the Shots	221
	Appendix—Selecting Lenses	231
	Index	240

Introduction

As a television director you are an interpreter of the program action to your audience. The audience understands the action only as you translate it through the media of your cameras and microphones. To convey to the audience the right sights and the right sounds at the right times, in order to affect your audience in the manner intended by the program—this is your chief responsibility. To make you fully aware of this responsibility and to help you to fulfill it is the purpose of this book.

This book presumes that you are either taking a course in television directing or that, although you may already be directing professionally, you are still studying how to increase your perception of the role and your proficiency at it. It further presumes that you are familiar with the tools, techniques, and terminology of television production that must be mastered before starting to learn the director's job.

In this book you will find the product of both authors' experience, including that of teaching in the classroom, actual application of on-the-job directing, supervising other directors in both commercial and educational stations, and actually owning a broadcast television station. In order to let the student maximize the opportunity to learn by doing, the authors as instructors minimized their verbal comments in favor of "handouts" to be read outside of class. From a compilation of these handouts, and the collective experience of the authors as teachers of television directing as well as actual directors, came the impetus and the material that led to this present book.

Rather than describing professional practices in the detached fashion of some other text in the field, this book is designed to talk to you directly, giving you practical principles you can put to use.

To help impress the principles upon your mind and make it easier for you to review them quickly, major statements have been given special typographical emphasis. As a help to your instructor, the statements have also been numbered. These numbers can be cited to save time and prevent ambiguity whenever your instructor finds it important to call specific principles to your attention.

Most of the principles are concerned with visual communications, because working with cameras is likely to take most of the director's time, and because students may already be familiar with audio communications from courses in radio, which generally precede those in television. Yet even those students may need to review the chapter called "Don't Forget Audio."

All of the principles are collected in Part One, which forms the major portion of the book and constitutes what might be called a kind of "grammar of the camera." Part Two provides a focus on the development of certain aptitudes (making floor plans, calling shots, and being an efficient administrator) that contribute so much to the success of the director as an interpreter.

To make this book useful for as long as possible and under the greatest variety of circumstances, an attempt has been made to stick to principles that apply regardless of the type of equipment you are using. It is impossible, however, to predict what new capabilities will be attained in present equipment or what new equipment will take over in the future. For that reason the subjects of camera and audio equipment currently in common use today have been only briefly discussed in the Appendix of this book.

Since the book had to stop somewhere—and perhaps leave room for a sequel—it is not concerned with the role of the producer or writer. It assumes that the program purpose has already been determined and that the content (what is to be said and done on the program) has already been formulated and is now waiting for you, with cameras and microphones, to interpret it accurately and effectively to your audience.

Part One: **PRINCIPLES**

Chapter 1

Planning Picture Statements

As a director you take pictures of the action that passes before your cameras. But what, of all things in sight, should a given picture include? And when is it time to change to a different picture? And by what means can you effect this change?

Some answers to these basic and important questions are provided by the picture-planning process that is outlined below:

1 Divide the action of your program into picture statements.

As a writer you would be understood only with the greatest difficulty if you were to issue an unbroken stream of words. Therefore, you communicate by making one impression at a time. To distinguish these impressions you use punctuation; you mark off your message to clarify its structure and meaning.

For the same purpose, the director uses what may be called "pictorial punctuation." As the writer divides words into sentences, the director divides the action of a program into picture statements.

1.1   A picture statement, like a sentence, has a subject.

This subject is the item (or group of related items) upon which, at a given moment you train your camera because it is important then. Your picture statement says, "See, these are the two persons who are talking together," or "This thing they are talking about," or, "Notice this man for what he is doing."

The subjects are apt to keep changing, and each new subject requires from you a new picture statement.

1.2   But just as a writer may use the same subject for a series of sentences, a director may maintain the same subject, yet take different pictures of it.

For example, the director shows a man at a table filling a glass. Then, the director shows predominantly the man's face, which is grimacing with the glass at his lips. These statements have the same subject, "man with glass," but different predicates. The first statement predicates that he "is pouring a drink," the second that he "doesn't like the taste of it."

Had the grimace been taken with the same framing as the filling of the glass, it would not have made so distinct an impression. By eliminating the table surface, which was no longer important, and contracting attention to the man's face, which had become all important, the director pointed up the man's reaction to the drink, having decided that this was sufficiently significant to warrant its own special statement.

1.3   There are then two reasons for changing picture statements:

(1) to direct attention to a new subject.

(2) to reveal a new aspect of the same subject in order to emphasize a different point about it.

2   Learn to perceive the program content as a succession of points.

At every moment of the program your picture must say to the audience, "See, this is the point!"

But before you can make your audience see the point, you must first be able to discern it yourself. You must be able to perceive your program content as a succession of changing points.

2.1   Don't wait for a television assignment to practice this discernment.

You can analyze any action you happen to witness, asking, "What points should I communicate pictorially to make what is happening intelligible to an audience?"

2.2   Example: a science lesson.

See, the instructor is challenging his students to pay close attention to the next demonstration.

See, his demonstration equipment is on the counter.

See, here is the substance on a scale.

See, the indicator on the scale is registering a certain value . . . and so on, through various other "see" statements.

2.3   Example: a twirling act.

In the example just given, each new point involves a different subject. Discerning the points is sometimes more difficult but no less important when the subject remains constant. This can be illustrated by a baton twirling act that was put on camera by a student director. The twirler was skillful, but because the director showed her stunts in one unchanging full shot, they tended to blur into one another and lose their individual effectiveness.

Then, being challenged to analyze the performance, he came to perceive it as a sequence of distinct accomplishments, each of which could be differentiated and enhanced by its own individual picture treatment. Rolling the baton around the shoulders, he decided, could be made more assertive by a chest shot, which would narrow attention to it. Throwing the baton aloft could be dramatized by a full shot from a low camera position, which would accentuate the height of the throw. The skill required to spin the baton rapidly could be played up by having the performer walk toward camera until all one saw was vibrating fingers and flashing spokes.

3   By punctuating thus, you gain several advantages.

3.1   You reveal the distinct nature of each point.

To secure this advantage, you cannot make more than one impression at a time.

For example, a program guest is presenting "The Five Rules of Water Safety." As she introduces each rule, she points to a card, shown in closeup, on which all five rules are lettered. But each time she points, other rules on the card compete for attention with the one under consideration, and since the viewers can read ahead of the speaker, they tend to listen to her with impatience.

To circumvent this difficulty one can reletter the rules one to a card—or, keeping them all on the same card, one can start with them individually concealed in some fashion and then unmask each at its proper time. Thus, each rule will make its due impression while adding to the ones previously exposed in a cumulative effect.

3.2   You keep new things happening.

In the example above, note that first only rule #1 is important, then rule #2 enters the action, then comes the turn of rule #3. Thus, new information keeps occurring.

Television is often cited as a visual medium. It should also be regarded as a temporal one, in which the maintenance of interest requires change and progression. To support this progression, a unique advantage is offered by the camera: obviously used to show things, it should also be valued for its ability not to show them until their time comes to enter the action.

Another advantage of sequential picture statements, then, is that by showing one thing at a time you can keep new things happening.

This advantage also applies to the twirling act previously cited. As originally put on camera, it tended to grow monotonous without picture changes to point up action changes and to say in effect, "Look, here is something new and different beginning!"

3.3   You clarify the structure of your material.

To mark where one unit of the action ends and another begins is important for helping the audience grasp the structure of the program material. Remember this when analyzing the points in musical material:

> Whole band for the first eight measures.
> Lead guitar for the second eight.
> Drummer for the third eight—and so on.

In this instance you are using your picture statements to establish which instruments are playing at a particular time. Your punctuation is also clarifying the musical structure, which is based on figures lasting eight measures.

In like manner, a new picture statement can be used to mark the transition between figures in a dance, stages in the development of a play, or major thought divisions in a speech. A change of picture will also support the end of a performance when it is followed by some other kind of program material. For example, it is easy to destroy the terminal impact of a song by continuing the same picture when the vocalist stops singing and begins talking to announce his or her next selection.

4   To punctuate, then, first perceive each of the points to be made.

5   Next ask, "Which visual elements in the scene are active in expressing this point?"—and make these the subject of your picture statement.

5.1   Sometimes there is but one element, sometimes more than one, and sometimes only part of one.

For example, you may have resolved a dramatic segment into the following statements:

(1) Here is the mother pleading with the father.

(2) Notice, their son is eavesdropping on their conversation with a rifle in his hands.

(3) Look at the father, how obdurate he remains.

(4) See the son's face tighten with grim resolve.

(5) Watch his fingers tighten on the rifle stock.

For #1, two elements are clearly necessary: mother and father.

For #2, besides the son, it is probably advisable to include the parents in order to establish that they are the subject of his eavesdropping.

Since #3 stresses the attitude of the father, he alone is important, and the other two characters are irrelevant. To include them would divide the viewer's attention and also make the father's expression smaller and less discernible, thus weakening the point.

The point of #4 is to convey the son's reaction as strongly as possible. Hence one concentrates on that portion of him where his reaction is most evident: his face.

In #5 the son's temptation to shoot is stressed by concentrating on another expressive part of him: his fingers. Although both face and fingers might have been shown simultaneously, they are more forceful when separated into two statements, following the principle of one impression at a time.

5.2   When the subject includes more than one element, ask, "What are their relative degrees of importance?"

In #1 above, for instance, if you decide that the mother and father are of equal importance, your picture composition should emphasize them equally, but it should make the mother dominant if you wish to emphasize her pleading.

5.3   Visualize how to arrange the elements to express their relationships.

In #1, perhaps you see the mother close to the father, but farther from camera than he is, to reveal more of her face than his. In #2, are the parents in the foreground with the son in the distance between them? Or is he behind a doorway in the foreground with them in the distance?

5.4   Visualize as compact an arrangement as possible in order to eliminate irrelevant material, which will weaken your point.

Also avoid wasting large areas of the screen with inert material (neutral background, for example) that has nothing to communicate. In the words of a once-popular song, which still deserves to be popular with directors, "Accentuate the positive, eliminate the negative."

6   After visualizing each picture statement, plan how to change from one statement to another, choosing one of the following ways:

6.1   Switch to a new shot from a different camera.

Thus, camera 1 takes a full shot of a golfer to support the point, "This is how to address the ball." Then camera 2 takes a closeup of his hands, which makes a new point, "This is the proper grip."

(Besides taking the new shot, you can, as appropriate, choose to dissolve, fade, or wipe. These alternatives, which require considerable explanation, will be considered later in the book.)

6.2 Move the camera or use the zoom lens.

For example, as each member or a row of panelists is introduced, the camera pans from one to another. Or the camera opens on an interviewer and, as he mentions the interviewee, dollies back into a two-shot. Or the camera establishes an office desk, then zooms in on a ringing telephone.

6.3 Move the subject.

Even inanimate objects can sometimes be moved. For example, the camera is trained on one face of a four-sided display board; then the board is revolved to present a new face. More frequently, however, new picture statements result for human beings entering or leaving the frame or moving around within it. A seated performer may rise, making the point, "It's time to get busy!" A teacher who has been writing on a chalkboard may turn around and walk forward, masking out the board, to begin some new topic such as "tomorrow's assignment." One of a group of actors might be placed farther from camera than his fellows so that, in facing them, his features also are revealed to the television viewer, whereas theirs, being turned away toward him, are more subordinated.

Movements such as these are often ignored by inexperienced directors as a way to make new picture statements. They tend to keep their performers stationary, thereby losing the animation and expression of human action and cheating the audience of its major interest in seeing people doing something.

6.4 Move both the subject and the camera at the same time.

For instance, the camera can start with a full shot of characters A and B, then pan with B as he moves away from A and forward into a chest shot, then pull back to widen the shot as A crosses to join B. This concerted movement of camera and performers can result in any number of changing compositions, each designed to support some new point in the evolving action. In this manner the director can help maintain visual interest for the viewer.

7 So far you have been advised to:

(1) Identify the points in the action.
(2) Visualize picture statements to support each point.
(3) Decide how to change from one statement to another.

In the next chapter, this procedure is applied to the planning of two complete program segments.

Chapter 2

Examples of Picture Statements

Example 1
The Guest Violinist

Participating in this program are a host and a guest violinist. It is planned that the host will have a few remarks for his viewers before introducing his guest. After chatting briefly with the guest, the host will suggest inspecting the guest's violin, which was made by a notable craftsman. Then the guest will accept the host's invitation to play a selection. This is prefaced by a short piano introduction and consists of two sections: the first *andante* (moderately slow and flowing), the second *allegro* (brisk and lively). Following this, the host will thank the guest, inform the audience about the feature on his next program, and conclude.

In some circumstances, particularly when there is a standardized setting and a routine with which the program host and the production people are familiar, the director might be expected to improvise his or her camerawork, punctuating the action as best he or she can on the spur of the moment. Here, however, it is assumed that the director has an opportunity to preplan.

The first stage of the planning is presented below. Here are the points as the director perceives them, the pictures he or she visualizes to support these points, and some comments to explain how the decisions were made:

THE POINTS	WHAT THE AUDIENCE SHOULD SEE

The host is welcoming the audience to his program. — HOST, SEEN FROM CHEST UP.

The host should be close enough to make good contact with his audience. His face is the part of him which carries the expression of welcome. A view of the guest at this moment would be irrelevant and distracting, tending to break the bond between the viewer's eyes and those of the host.

The host has a guest with him. — THE PICTURE WIDENS TO REVEAL THE GUEST, SEATED CLOSE TO THE HOST.

Now is the time for the guest to enter the action and, consequently, enter the picture. The host should also be seen, however, to establish his location in relation to the guest.

This is the kind of person the guest is. — GUEST ALONE, SHOWN FROM CHEST UP.

A closer, isolating shot will give the guest his due importance as the new center of interest when he first speaks. It will also give the audience a more intimate impression of him.

The host and guest are conversing. — SAME TWO-SHOT AS BEFORE, WITH EMPHASIS EQUAL BETWEEN THEM.

The shot should be compact enough to permit easy reading of their faces.

They are going to inspect the violin. — BOTH, RISING AND MOVING, FRAMED MORE AND MORE CLOSELY SO THAT ON REACHING THE VIOLIN THEY ARE SEEN ONLY FROM THE WAIST UP.

Placing the violin apart keeps it out of sight until it enters the action. This also introduces variety through movement to a new location. Narrowing framing during the move will make the violin large enough when it enters the picture to promote its prominence as the new center of interest.

This is what the violin looks like. — VIOLIN (HELD BY GUEST) FRAMED CLOSE WITH BACKGROUND DE-FOCUSED.

Taking the closeup and defocusing the background both serve to eliminate irrelevant material.

The host is inviting the guest to play.	BOTH PERFORMERS AS BEFORE THE VIOLIN CLOSEUP.

No explanation seems necessary for this picture.

The guest prepares to play while the pianist plays the introduction.	GUEST STEPS AWAY FROM HOST AND FORWARD TO WHERE ACCOMPANIST CAN BE SEEN IN BACKGROUND.

This eliminates the host, who is no longer significant, and reveals the presence of the piano and the accompanist, keeping them subordinated, however, to the guest. The picture change also marks the beginning of the guest's musical performance, a new major section of the program.

The guest is playing an andante *passage.*	GUEST PLAYING, VIEWED FROM ABOUT WAIST UP (PIANIST ELIMINATED).

Now all that matters is the violinist's performance. Although the truly active elements in this performance are his face, arms, and violin, it would not be advisable to frame them too closely at first, since closer framing will be needed to support the next passage of the music.

He is changing to an allegro *passage.*	GUEST PLAYING, VIEWED FROM ANOTHER AND CLOSER ANGLE.

Pictorial punctuation is used to clarify a change in the pattern of the music. The closer shot should reinforce the more animated performance that results from the increased tempo; the active elements (face, arms, violin) will now make a stronger impression since they have been enlarged and given exclusive command of the frame.

He finishes the performance.	CONTINUING THE SAME SHOT, THE PICTURE WIDENS AS THE MUSIC ENDS.

The sense of completion is reinforced by a withdrawal from the performers and a progressive reentry of the environment, creating anticipatory space for the host's reentry. This withdrawal should also provide activity during the brief auditory pause, which seems desirable here to let the spell of the music linger somewhat before the host speaks.

The host thanks the guest.   GUEST AND HOST—THE HOST SEEN
                                            FIRST IN THE REAR OF THE PICTURE,
                                            THEN MOVING UP TO THE GUEST.

Cutting from the guest alone to a two-shot of him and the host makes a more pronounced change between the musical performance and the ensuing talk than were the host to walk into the concluding shot of the performance.

The host announces the feature for the next   HOST LEAVES GUEST (CAMERA PAN-
program and concludes the show.   NING   WITH   HIM)   AND   MOVES
                                                 CLOSER TO CAMERA TO MAKE HIS
                                                 CLOSING ANNOUNCEMENT.

Since the guest's part is over, he is eliminated from the picture. To take leave of him by panning away from him seems more polite than to cut abruptly to a one-shot of the host. Having the host move nearer to the camera for the program closing will help to reestablish the host with the viewers.

                                            CLOSING   TITLES   AND   FADE   TO
                                            BLACK.

This, of course, is not the only way to visualize the sequence. But however the director does conceive his or her pictures, there should be a reason for each of them, based on the points of the program.

Planning the actual camera treatment

Now comes the last stage of the planning process: the visualized pictures must be realized in actual camera shots. To this end, the director takes pencil and paper to work out at reduced scale actual physical locations for the performers and cameras and to test which focal lengths on the camera lenses he or she will use for each particular shot.[1]

As shown in *Figure 2/1*, the director starts with the host and guest seated in adjacent chairs, and places camera 1 for its opening shot of the host. Using a camera with $2/3$-inch pickup tubes, the director chooses to shoot at 25mm for this shot. Then, when zoomed back to 12mm, the guest can easily be included in the shot.[2] (See *Figure 2/2*)

---

[1] For the process of planning shots on paper at a reduced scale, see Chapter 24, "Making Floor Plans."
[2] Information concerning lens focal lengths, field of view, and the effect of different diameter camera pickup tubes is discussed in Chapter 24 of this text.

Fig. 2/1

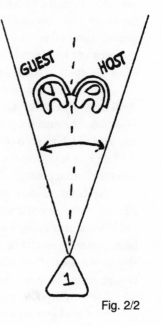

Fig. 2/2

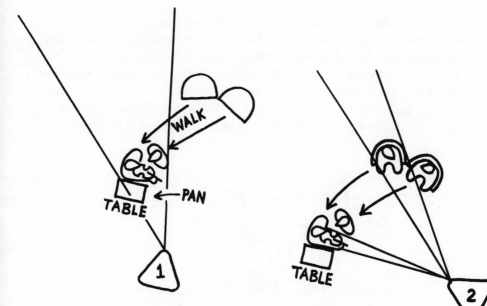

Fig. 2/3

Fig. 2/4

Having determined the field of view at the end of the zoom, the director can now determine where the host and guest will stand after walking over to inspect the violin. Here the director plans to have camera 1 pan them to this location. Since the violin is not wanted in camera 1's shot of the men while they are seated, the director knows that the small table on which the instrument is to be placed must be stationed off to one side of this shot. The guest's side is logical, since this will allow the guest to reach for the violin without crossing in front of the host.

The shot of the men inspecting the violin should be closer than the one of them seated in order to make the image of the violin as large as possible. Therefore, the men must end their walk at a place where camera 1's lens angle is narrow enough to accomplish the closer framing. Having located this place with the help of a lens template, the director sets the table where it will guide the men into the desired position. (*Figure 2/3*)

Next, the director seeks a basic location for camera 2, which is needed for a closeup of the seated guest when he is introduced, and later for a closeup of the violin when it is being inspected. Since the guest is seated to camera left of the host, camera 2 should be on the right so that it can command an adequately full shot of the guest's face while he is looking toward the host. Also, it should be far enough from the guest in his standing position so that, when the lens is zoomed into a more telephoto position, the depth of field will be reduced, creating a defocused background in the closeup of the violin. So Camera 2 is placed as in *Figure 2/4*.

During the piano introduction to his selection, the guest can keep some visual activity going by advancing in front of the table. Meanwhile, to avoid being seen during the selection, the host can return to his chair. Camera 2 is assigned to the piano introduction, panning with the guest to his playing position, where the pianist is seen to his right in the background. By using the lens template to spot the guest and pianist within a 35mm lens angle projected from camera 2's location on the floor plan, the location of the piano can be determined, as in *Figure 2/5*.

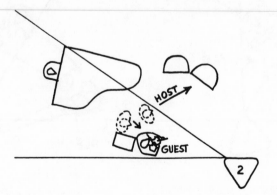

Fig. 2/5

The furniture and basic camera positions are now established. In relation to these, a drape background can also be established and the remaining shots and movements calculated.

Figure 2/6 shows locations during the violinist's performance. Camera 1 takes the *andante* passage. Meanwhile, camera 2 (between shots) zooms in on the violin. In this closeup view it takes the *allegro* passage, at the conclusion of which (while still feeding program) it zooms back to its original wider shot.

During the *allegro* passage, as shown in *Figure 2/7*, camera 1 moves left to a place from which it can show the host moving forward from his chair to thank the guest at the end of the selection. As soon as camera 1 is taken for this shot, camera 2, its mission accomplished, withdraws in order to avoid getting in the picture when the host, panned on camera 1, moves away from the guest and forward to deliver his closing remarks.

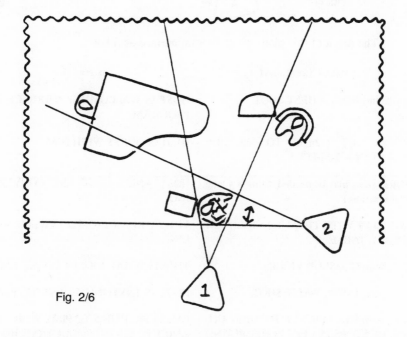

Fig. 2/6

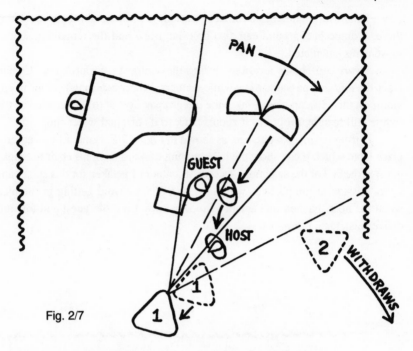

Fig. 2/7

The result of this plotting can be summarized as follows:

CAMERA TREATMENT	THE POINTS
1 (25mm) HOST, CHEST SHOT.	HOST IS WELCOMING AUDIENCE TO PROGRAM.
ZOOM OUT (12mm) TO INCLUDE GUEST IN A 2-SHOT.	HE HAS GUEST WITH HIM.
(Other shots may be needed if this is a long conversation.)	HOST AND GUEST ARE CONVERSING.
PAN LEFT WITH THEM TO VIOLIN ON SMALL TABLE.	THEY ARE GOING TO INSPECT VIOLIN.
2 (75mm) CLOSEUP VIOLIN.	THIS IS WHAT VIOLIN LOOKS LIKE.
1 (25mm) BOTH, WAIST SHOT.	HOST IS INVITING GUEST TO PLAY.
2 (25mm) PAN LEFT WITH GUEST UNTIL HE STOPS IN LEFT FOREGROUND OF SHOT WITH PIANIST IN RIGHT BACKGROUND.	GUEST PREPARES TO PLAY WHILE PIANIST PLAYS INTRODUCTION. HOST, OFF CAMERA, RETURNS TO HIS CHAIR.

1 (25mm) GUEST, WAIST SHOT.	GUEST IS PLAYING *ANDANTE* PASSAGE.
(2 ZOOM IN CLOSER (75mm) FOR NEXT SHOT OF GUEST).	
2 (75mm) GUEST, CHEST SPOT.	GUEST IS PLAYING *ALLEGRO* PASSAGE.
ZOOM OUT TO INCLUDE PIANIST.	GUEST IS FINISHING PERFORMANCE.
(1 HAS MOVED LEFT AND BACK SOMEWHAT FOR NEXT SHOT)	
1 (25mm) BOTH, WITH HOST ADVANCING FROM RIGHT REAR.	HOST MOVES UP TO THANK GUEST.
(2 WITHDRAWS)	
PAN WITH HOST AS HE LEAVES GUEST AND APPROACHES CAMERA.	HOST ANNOUNCES NEXT FEATURE AND CLOSES PROGRAM.

With this planning accomplished, the director is ready to actually shoot the program, with reasonable assurance that the pictures the audience sees will enhance its understanding of the structure and meaning of the program, thus accomplishing the goal of pictorial punctuation.

Example 2
Jean Learns a New Dance

In this sequence, Jean, the program host, is to learn the fundamentals of a new dance step from a guest named Bill.

From a conference with Jean, the director learns that the dance involves the entire body, requiring full shots rather than closeups of the feet. Over opening music, Bill will dance briefly, after which Jean will ask her viewers, "Wouldn't you like to learn how this is done?" Bill will proceed to demonstrate the basic movement with Jean beside him, trying to follow his instructions. Then Jean will watch him perform two variations, trying after each to do it herself. To close, Jean will thank Bill, then invite his viewers to try the dance themselves.

As shown in *Figure 2/8*, the director decides to base the cameras about 90° apart so they can take reverse angle shots, one favoring Jean, the other Bill, at a distance sufficient to allow full-length shots with their widest lenses. A corner is chosen for the playing area where the studio drapes meet at right angles. With the attention on moving bodies, there is no need for elaborate scenery.

For audio pickup the director will need either a boom or wireless lavalier microphones. There should be no cables trailing from the performers to impede their action and look unsightly in long shots.

Following these decisions, the director works out the sequence of picture statements below.

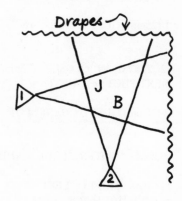

Fig. 2/8

BILL BRIEFLY DEMONSTRATES
THE DANCE.

Bill is the dominant subject and is seen full length because his dance involves the total body. Jean is shown, too, because it's her show and because her location should be established before cutting to a one-shot of her. She has been subordinated, however, by being placed in the distance. Perched on a stool, she contrasts with Bill's standing figure. To motivate a cut to her, she applauds Bill's performance, and he turns toward her in acknowledgment.

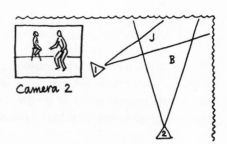

JEAN ORIENTS THE AUDIENCE.

"That was the (name of dance). Like to learn it? Let's ask Bill to show us how." The shot should be close enough to give Jean eye contact with her viewers, but not too abrupt a change in scale from the preceding long shot. The zoom lens setting depends not only on the initial framing of Jean by herself, but also on the framing of her with Bill after the camera has panned with her to him.

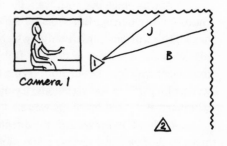

BILL WILL GLADLY TEACH HER.

This framing should favor Bill and be close enough to show his face clearly. After a few sentences, Bill invites Jean to stand beside him. Her move to do so cues the next shot.

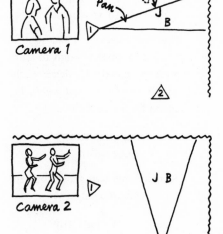

JEAN LEARNS THE
FUNDAMENTALS.

This is a full shot of both performers, equidistant from the camera since interest should be distributed equally between them.

BILL DEMONSTRATES
VARIATION #1.

Attention should center now on Bill. Hence, have him move away from Jean and face her, taking him with the camera that favors him. A full view is still needed of him, but not of her.

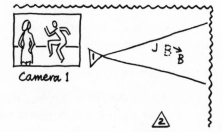

JEAN TRIES THE VARIATION.

Take the other camera as interest now passes to her.

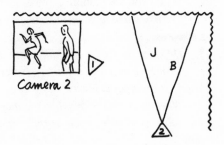

BILL DEMONSTRATES VARIATION #2
and
JEAN TRIES IT.

These shots are the same as for the first variation.

JEAN MOVES IN TO THANK
BILL, WHO IN TURN
CONGRATULATES HER.

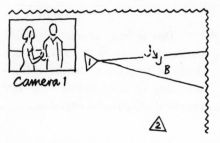

Camera 1

Pan with Jean into a two-shot favoring Bill and close enough to show
his expressions clearly. He deserves the
major emphasis as the guest who is being thanked for his performance.

JEAN REACTS TO HIS
COMPLIMENT.

A matching two-shot from the
other camera favors Jean.

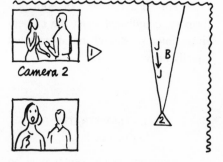

Camera 2

JEAN ADDRESSES THE
AUDIENCE.

"If *I* can do it, *you* can, so why
not try it?" To mark her shift of attention from Bill to the audience, have her
walk closer to the camera. This will
give her dominance over Bill, who remains in the background.

END OF SEQUENCE

Aided by the two examples you have just read and by the chapter that
preceded them, you should be able to start planning television picture statements
that will interpret accurately the structure and meaning of your program to its
audience.

While you are planning, remember:

*From moment to moment throughout the program there are different points to
be conveyed.*

Different points involve different visual subjects.

*To make each point definitely, frame prominently the relevant subject, or part
thereof, or group of subjects.*

*When more than one subject is included in the frame, reveal and emphasize
these subjects in proportion to their relative importance in making the point at
hand.*

The resultant arrangement is your picture statement.

When a new point is to be made, change to a new picture statement.

Chapter 3

A Moment-by-Moment
Questionnaire

At every moment the picture you show should make the point to be made at that moment. To assess how well it will do so, it is helpful to ask a number of critical questions. Three of these should already be evident from your reading of the preceding chapters:

Am I conscious of the point?
What visual subjects convey it?
Are they included in my picture?

But there are six more useful questions to be asked:

Can the subjects be seen clearly?
Do they preserve their natural and characteristic form?
Does my picture make a single, dominant impression?
Is it free of distractions and discomforts?
Is it sufficiently animated?
Does it make the point expressively?

You should ask these questions throughout the whole production process, during your planning, as well as while you are watching the control-room monitors. The questions are useful for evaluating every factor of your pictorial composition: the relation of your subject to its background and to the camera, the effect of the video control adjustments, the choice of the angle of a lens and of its aperture, the design of the setting, the action of the performers, and even the selection of their wearing apparel.

Each of the next six chapters will be devoted to one of the questions and to the production conditions that must be achieved in order to answer the question affirmatively. Although some of these conditions may be familiar to you under such categories as lighting, staging, performing, and camera operation, you will find them classified here rather differently—not by crafts, but by communication purposes that the crafts should serve. This may help you to evaluate the crafts in a new and useful light.

It should also help to accustom you to a director's way of looking, for a director is concerned not with one craft at a time, but with the interrelationship of all of them. When deciding where a performer will stand, for instance, the director may take into account the need for backlight, the color and pattern of the background, the elevation of the camera, and what visual elements will be in focus on a particular lens at a certain distance and with a given intensity of illumination. When viewing a picture or planning one, the director evaluates more or less simultaneously all of the various factors that combine to make up its appearance.

In conducting such an evaluation, you will find it useful to apply the Moment-by-Moment Questionnaire.

Chapter 4

Visual Clarity

To communicate, whatever has meaning must be clearly perceived by the audience. Evident as this requirement may seem, it cannot be achieved without conscious effort. Cameras must be aimed from revealing angles. Subjects must be related to the proper cameras and kept in frame and focus. They must be framed closely enough to reveal their significant details. Their form must be brought out by proper brightness levels and not obscured by other elements of the picture.

As a director, you are responsible for seeing that these conditions are achieved. Therefore:

1 Aim your cameras from revealing angles.

Relate the positions of camera and subject so as to reveal the most communicative aspect of the subject. Nine times out of ten with human subjects, it is important to reveal facial expressions.

1.1 When performers are interacting with each other, cross your cameras.

Don't shoot as in *Figure 4/1*, using the camera on the right side to take the person on the right and the camera on the left to take the person on the left, for when the performers are looking toward each other, these shots will take only profiles. And one eye, one eyebrow, one nostril, and only half a mouth are liable to reveal only half of what a face is communicating. Therefore, cross your cameras: right camera on left performer, left camera on right performer.

1.2 Remember the need to show faces when devising your floor plan.

Even with the cameras crossed, the setting in *Figure 4/2* is so narrow and deep that the cameras cannot spread far enough apart to take much more than

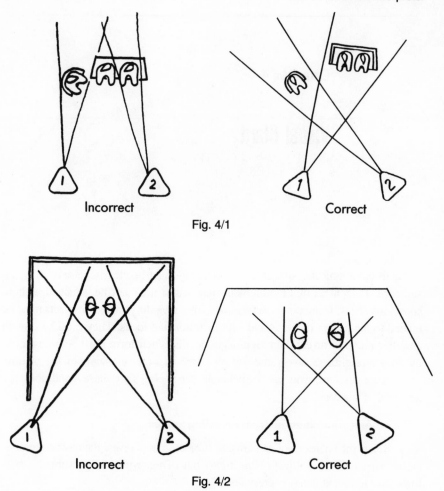

Fig. 4/1

Fig. 4/2

profiles. More advantageous camera angles are provided by a wedge- or L-shaped setting. Occasionally, directors also design openings in the walls through which cameras can shoot without being noticed, or employ "wild walls," which can be moved aside for certain shots.

How do you cover the conference setup in *Figure 4/3* if you are allowed only two cameras? With this arrangement it is impossible to reveal clearly the faces of all participants. As the cameras are stationed in the diagram, each covers one side of the table adequately, but neither will show the face of the person at the end of the table.

In the kitchen set in *Figure 4/4*, there are no stations from which cameras can reveal more than profiles of the performers when they are using the counters, sink,

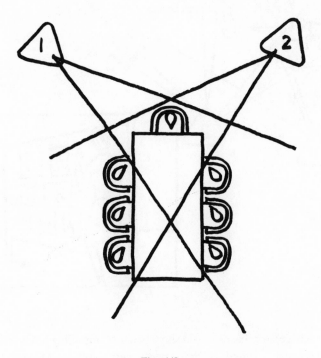

Fig. 4/3

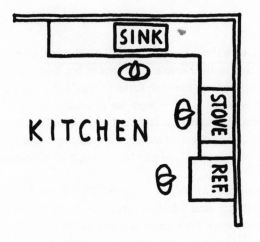

Fig. 4/4

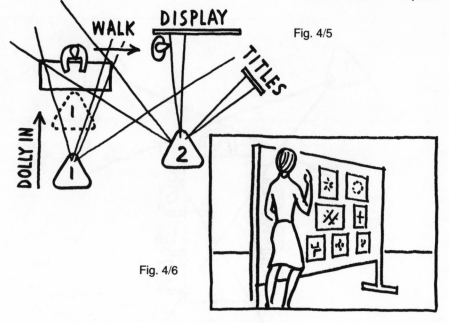

Fig. 4/5

Fig. 4/6

stove, and refrigerator. Faces would show better by installing kitchen facilities in an "island counter," behind which the performers could stand facing the camera.

1.3   Work for the most revealing camera angles when planning your shot alterations.

Figure 4/5 shows how a student director planned a demonstration of potato printing.

Camera 2 took the opening title on an easel. Next, camera 1 established the teacher at the table, dollied in to a chest shot of her, then tilted down to her hands working with materials on the table surface. This shot of the hands was alternated with wider shots of the teacher taken by camera 2. Just before the end of the sequence at the table, camera 1 (between shots) zoomed out to its starting position. From there it panned with the teacher to the display board and remained on her there as she showed examples of finished prints, which were taken in closeup by camera 2.

This treatment was deficient in clarity. When the wide-angle lens, needed on camera 1's first shot to establish the teacher, was zoomed in and tilted down for the closeup on the tabletop, the camera was too far from the table and the resulting angle down on the table was too low to reveal any detail in the demonstration. Also, as shown in *Figure 4/6*, camera 1's pan with the teacher to the display board

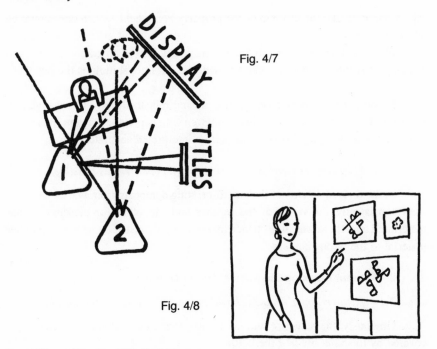

Fig. 4/7

Fig. 4/8

showed the teacher, back to the camera, with the display board sloping so much into the distance that the display seemed to be presented to some offstage observer rather than to the television viewer.

An improved treatment is diagrammed in *Figure 4/7*. Here, camera 2 takes all the wide shots of the teacher, both at the table and at the display board. As can be seen by comparing *Figures 4/6* and *4/8*, the revised framing of the display board is clearer, not only because the teacher is closer, but also because she is turned toward the audience. Camera 1 takes all closeups, of both the displayed prints and the table demonstration, getting a closer, hence clearer view of the latter because its lens and camera angle can be selected solely for that purpose.

The improved version could have been devised on paper before bringing the program into the studio, where time is too precious to waste on needless revisions.

2 Relate the action to the proper camera.

The best-planned camera treatment can be defeated by a performer who plays to the wrong camera.

2.1 Be sure that performers understand their relation to the camera.

Although it's inadvisable to burden a performer with unnecessary information, provide the basic information that needs to be known about the cameras—

which one will take the closeup of the property being held, which one should be addressed, and so on.

If the performer is new to television, you will need to communicate even elementary points, such as the camera with the red light shining is the one that's "on."

If you change a performer's action during rehearsal, have the change performed so that you know it is understood. Even with experienced talent, it is rarely safe to assume that your instructions will be interpreted accurately.

2.2   Keep your camera plan as simple and consistent as possible.

In the revised version of the potato-printing demonstration, one camera was used consistently for views of the teacher and the other for closeups of her material. Thus, there was little chance that she would present either her face or her material to the wrong camera.

3   Prevent masking the subject from camera.

3.1   The performer's hands should not mask essential information.

Obviously, the audience will not be able to read the label on a bottle if it is covered by the hand holding the bottle.

It is frustrating when hands that are writing on chalkboards or other vertical surfaces cover the letters as they are being formed. A long-handled chalk holder or felt pen will keep the hand below the line of writing—or the performer can be taught, as in *Figure 4/9*, to work from the camera right side of the board (assuming that the performer is right-handed). This also

Fig. 4/9

opens his or her face and body to the camera, which in turn will help to pick up the voice on a boom microphone, since there will be no room to get the microphone in front of the performer if he or she is facing close to the vertical surface.

3.2   Keep the performers from covering other performers who ought to be seen.

Even when they have rehearsed their positions, inexperienced performers may fail to duplicate these positions in performance. It may help, during rehearsal, to have them sight coordinates by which they can orient themselves. ("I'm in front of the right end of the sofa and just opposite the window in the left wall.")

Sometimes you can direct them in relation to the furniture. ("Stand beside the armchair, then cross to behind the desk.") Critical locations can be marked on the floor with chalk, water paint, or masking tape.

Even when they hit their marks, performers may be covered or be covering someone else because the camera is off its position. Hence, critical camera positions may also need to be marked.

4 Keep the subject in frame.

4.1 When framing, keep important elements away from the edges of the picture.

Although visible on control-room monitors, these elements may not appear on less carefully adjusted home receivers.

Lettering on cards that are to be taken by studio cameras should be indented at least one-sixth of the height and width of the framed area, as shown in *Figure 4/10*. Outside this area there should be a margin to keep the camera from accidentally shooting off the edge of the card.

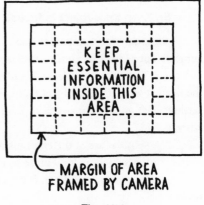

Fig. 4/10

4.2 Work with performers on keeping in frame.

Caution inexperienced performers against making abrupt and unevenly paced movements unless these have been successfully rehearsed on camera. Otherwise, they may walk out of frame before the camera can pan with them, or rise and decapitate themselves, so to speak, before the camera can tilt up.

In ad-libbed situations, performers can signal their intentions of moving. They can do this either verbally ("Now, over on the workbench we have . . .") or visually, as when placing their hands on the arms of their chair and shifting their weight before rising.

Performers who are handling small objects should be taught not to gesture broadly with them or pick them up suddenly. It may be advisable for beginners to keep an object in constant contact with a table surface to inhibit the object's being waved around at random.

4.3 Framing also depends on the camerawork.

Rapidly moving objects are difficult to keep framed properly when they are followed in too tight a shot. Frame them rather loosely if your camera operators are not expert.

When panning laterally moving subjects, it is customary to "lead" them, allowing more space ahead than behind them. While partly for compositional balance, as will be explained later, this also helps to prevent the subject from nosing out of the frame during unexpected spurts.

When two or more performers move at once, as do the host and guest approaching the violin in Chapter 2, they may separate beyond the limits of the frame. Instead of trying to contain them both, it is preferable to frame the leader acceptably and let the follower reenter the frame at destination.

5 Keep the subject in focus.

Although you sometimes want the background out of focus to stand your subjects out against it, almost invariably you want the subjects themselves sharp and clear. Their being so depends on the depth of field, i.e., the distance between the nearest and farthest subject that will appear acceptably focused at a given lens setting. The greater the depth of field, the less focusing problem you will have when:

. . . subjects are at different distances from the lens.

. . . the subject is very close to the lens.

. . . the camera must pan from a near subject to a more distant one, or vice versa.

. . . the distance between camera and subject is altered either by the camera or the subject moving forward or back.

Here are some suggestions to apply to such conditions:

5.1 Consider the illumination.

Adding more light to the scene will permit the lens to be stopped down. The smaller the diaphragm opening, the greater the depth of field.

5.2 Consider the focal length of the lens.

You can attain greater depth of field by zooming out to a wider lens angle, but only if you accept the consequently wider framing. If you move the camera closer to approximate the framing as it was before the zoom, the depth of field will be reduced again.

It does pay, however, to use a wide lens angle when either the subject or the camera is moving in or out. In fact, don't expect inexperienced camera operators to maintain focus while dollying on anything longer than the wide-angle setting on their zoom lenses.

When a subject can be brought no closer to the lens without going out of focus, try using a wider lens angle. The wider the lens angle, the closer the subject can be focused. But there is a catch to this: unless the subject is flat and perpendicular to the camera's axis of vision, it will appear increasingly distorted the closer it comes to the lens.

5.3   Consider the camera angle.

Occasionally, as when shooting a chessboard, you may have difficulty getting equal focus on small objects (such as the chessmen), which lie at different distances from the lens. By shooting at a steeper downward angle, you can diminish the span between the nearest and farthest subject over which the focus has to be distributed.

5.4   Help inexperienced camera operators to improve their focusing ability.

When depth of field is shallow and you need equal focus on two subjects at unequal distances from the camera, your camera operators may need to learn that, to split the focus, they should focus not halfway between the subjects but at roughly one-third of the distance from the nearest to the farthest.

To let the operators give utmost attention to following focus during straight dolly movements, you can sometimes suggest that they lock unneeded mobile parts, such as the pedestal elevating device, horizontal pan head, or tripod wheels. If jurisdictional rules permit, you can also enlist assistants to move the camera mounts, thus freeing the camera operators to use one hand for focusing and the other (if need be) for panning or tilting.

When it is necessary to pan between a close and distant subject, you may need to allow your camera operators some practice time. During this, if they will note and remember how much they had to adjust their focusing devices, they should be able to change focus while panning without waiting for the new subject to come into view.

6   Frame closely enough to reveal the important details.

Loosely framed subjects can be indistinct because they are too small on the screen and spread over too few scanning lines to be resolved with sufficient definition. Hence:

6.1   Generally restrict wide shots to:

. . . framing broad physical movement, as in dance or sports, where interest is on movement rather than facial expressions.

. . . establishing an overall situation by showing the presence and relative locations of its participants.

. . . showing the total environment in which the action occurs.

6.2   Otherwise, rely mainly on medium shots and closeups, framing only what is meaningful at the moment.

Constantly ask whether you are shooting close enough. Is reference being made to the whole piano or merely to its keyboard? How close does the master of ceremonies have to be before you feel that he is really talking to you?

6.3   For shooting close, will you move the camera in, or zoom the lens in to a longer focal length?

Using the long focal length allows you to keep the camera at a distance where the lens will have more framing possibilities for subsequent shots. For example, a camera that is too close to its subject may lack the ability to gain a wide shot necessary to cover, for instance, the relationship between a speaker and the audience. It may also interfere with another camera's shot, or disturb the performer's concentration.

6.4   When a camera mount is stopped from coming close enough, as by the front side of a desk or counter:

. . . see whether the distance between camera and subject can be lessened by revolving the base of the tripod or pedestal to present a flat side to the furniture, or

. . . consider substituting furniture with an opening into which the base of the camera mount can penetrate.

6.5   When closeups are to be taken, make the subjects conveniently large if you can control their size.

The smaller the subject, the more difficult it is to frame closely. Musical notation, snapshot photographs, diagrams occupying partial pages of books, and the like will benefit from enlargement if they are to be taken by a studio camera. As appropriate, you can have them redrawn, or get photographic blowups made of them, or convert them to slides for rear-screen projection.

6.6   Closeups of miniature subjects are more easily shot in limbo.

When closeups are needed of miniature subjects (coins, stamps, watch dials, etcetera) being used by the performers, you can try to get duplicates of the items to be shot in limbo (i.e., in some convenient place outside the playing area) by a camera that has sufficient opportunity to frame and focus them properly from as close a distance as necessary. It will also allow the camera operator to move close enough to the subject to use an extreme wide-angle lens or the macro position, if the lens is so equipped. Since depth of field in this case is particularly shallow, however, the subject must be such that all visible parts of it are approximately equidistant from the lens. Furthermore, special care must be taken to prevent a shadow of the camera from obscuring the subject.

6.7 Closeups of small, static subjects can be photographed in advance and used as slides on the film chain.

This avoids having to divert a studio camera from the main action for the length of time it may take to frame and focus the subject properly.

6.8 Proportion your subject, when possible, to a 3 × 4 ratio.

Although sufficiently large in actuality, some subjects may not appear large enough on the screen because their proportions do not suit the 3 × 4 aspect ratio of the screen. When they are tall and narrow or low and broad, and must be shown in entirety, the camera may have to move back so far to encompass them that their details will be illegible. Therefore, any graphic material which is to be framed as a whole in closeup should be prepared in a 3 × 4 ratio. The teacher who is putting a long sentence on the chalkboard should be asked to write it in several short lines rather than a single extended one. And the chorus in two rows of twelve persons should be regrouped into four rows of six persons, if it can still sing well in this arrangement.

6.9 Restrict the number of elements per line.

The more elements that must appear side by side in the picture, the wider the framing must be, hence the smaller and less distinct the elements will appear. Therefore, one should restrict the number of characters per line in printed titles and captions. For the same reason, groups of singers or dancers who were originally constituted to fill the breadth of a theater stage may need, for television, to be reduced in membership and reorganized more compactly.

6.10 Bring performers as close together as possible.

The nearer performers play to each other, the more closely the camera can frame them. It is surprising how close they can be to each other without appearing unnatural on the screen.

6.11 Shoot wide subjects from a side angle.

When persons need to be separated by the requirements of the action yet still need to be included in the same frame, the screen distance between them can be reduced by shooting them from the side, as camera 2 is doing in *Figure 4/11*. Notice how much more discernible the features will be in camera 2's shots than in camera 1's. Similarly, an angled shot can be used to enlarge the screen size of the members of large groups such as vocal choruses.

The side angle is useful not only with stationary groupings, but also for movements that carry persons away from each other. If taken from the front, dancers who separate widely can cause problems: the camera may not be able to zoom out as quickly as they separate; yet if it pans with only one of them, the choreographic relationship between dancers will be lost. An angle shot, however, will contain the entire movement.

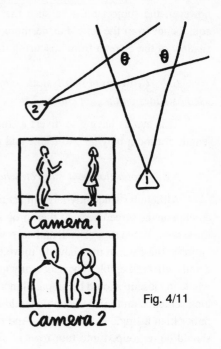

Camera 1

Camera 2

Fig. 4/11

6.12   Deploy your subjects in depth.

The movement of the dancers in the angle shot just cited will tend to be more parallel than perpendicular to the camera's line of vision. This illustrates a difference between blocking action for television and for the stage. Since a theater stage extends across the spectators' line of vision, the axis for movement and placement of characters on it tends to run from side to side. The television "stage," however, is the angle embraced by the camera lens, a truncated pyramid of space widening away from the lens, which invites the placement and movement of subjects in depth. Such deployment, as already demonstrated, helps to reduce needless screen distance between the subjects.

6.13   Place small subjects closer to the lens, big ones farther from it.

Within the camera's expanding angle, a small subject close to the lens can fill the entire screen. As distance from the lens increases, it takes more subjects or larger subjects to fill the screen. Applications of this fact are illustrated in *Figures 4/12* and *4/13*. In *Figure 4/12* the telephone, as principal subject, has been placed in the foreground, where its screen size exceeds that of the two persons behind it.

In *Figure 4/13* three subjects of different size have been arranged so that they
can be panned by a single camera and
command equal size on the screen. This
principle of arrangement should be kept
in mind when blocking a one-camera
program or any sequence where changing the zoom lens focal length would
happen too rapidly for accurate refram-
ing and focus.

Fig. 4/12

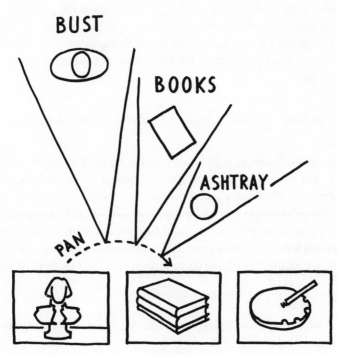

Fig. 4/13

7   Bring out clarity of form by proper brightness levels.

The form of subjects on the television screen is rendered by phosphorescent particles glowing at various degrees of brightness. In order for these brightness differences to define the subjects clearly, production people—under the ultimate supervision of the director—must present to the camera visual material that the electronic system is capable of reproducing faithfully. One of the requirements for satisfactory reproduction is proper lighting.

7.1   See that there is sufficient light on the subject.

Too little light will obscure the picture with vibrating specks called "snow" or "noise," and will damage color fidelity.

Directors sometimes cause problems of insufficient illumination by prescribing an effect that the system cannot reproduce. For example, if you want dark tones to simulate night or to create a somber mood, do not expect all of the light sources to be reduced uniformly. Although the instruments providing general illumination can be dimmed, some of the highlight sources should be left undimmed. The highlights are needed both to satisfy engineering requirements and because, without them for contrast, the other areas of the screen will not appear sufficiently dark.

7.2   Provide enough brightness difference to establish the form of your subjects.

Brightness differences depend not only on the tonal gradations inherent in the subjects, but also on how the subjects are lighted. If faces and background are placed under equal illumination, there may not be enough tonal separation to keep the subjects from vanishing into the background. To better distinguish the subjects from their background, it is recommended that you put more illumination on the performers and less on the background. To do this, however, you must keep the background far enough behind the performers so that light on them will not spill onto it.

7.3   In color TV, use differences in hue to enhance contrast between subjects in the scene.

In monochrome television, a red tulip, for example, can appear to be about the same shade of gray as the green lawn behind it, hence disappearing into its background. In color television, however, subjects can be distinguished from each other when they are of different hues.

7.4 Do not exceed the contrast range of which the system is capable.

There is a limit to the range of brightness the system can reproduce, just as with any other medium of reproduction. In a pencil drawing, for instance, the darkest tone achievable is governed by the blackness of the lead, and the lightest by the tone of the paper. Television likewise has restrictions; it cannot reproduce extremely dark and extremely bright elements with the same lens setting. If the lens is opened to expose gradations in the darkest tones, very light gradations such as those in the performers' faces are liable to be washed out. Or when the lens is stopped down to expose the faces properly, gradations in the darker tones are liable to appear uniformly black on the screen.

Therefore, avoid including extremely light and dark elements in the same scene. Expect to cause the video engineer and lighting person some trouble if you let your performers wear starchy white shirts with very dark suits. If you intend to stage a scene cameo-style in pools of light against blackness, be sure that enough time is allotted for adjusting the illumination and the camera control settings.

7.5 Be careful about panning or zooming between very bright and very dark subjects.

Unless the lens opening can be adjusted remotely or automatically, don't expect to pan with a person as he or she moves from a dim interior into bright sunlight, or to zoom in from a predominantly light poster to a predominantly dark photograph included in it.

7.6 When there is a wide inherent brightness contrast in the subject, hold down the lighting contrast.

Suppose, for example, that under even illumination the lightest area of the subject is ten times brighter than the darkest—a ratio of 10:1. Then you apply four times as much light to one side of the subject as to the other—a ratio of 4:1. Multiplying these ratios gives a total contrast ratio of 40:1, meaning that the lightest area is now forty times brighter than the darkest. A 30:1 contrast ratio pushes the extremes of video camera reproduction. For a typical interview program, a 3:1 or 4:1 contrast ratio might be more appropriate.

7.7 Avoid extreme changes of illumination.

These result not only from turning lights on and off and moving them up and down, but also if you:

. . . have a performer walk toward the source of a horizontal light beam, thus becoming subject to the "inverse square law"—having covered half the distance to the source, he or she becomes not twice but approximately four times as bright.

... call for the follow-spot that has been lighting the vocal quartet to be focused down on the soloist who comes next, thus taking light which has been spread over four persons and concentrating it all on one.

7.8 Supply film and slides that do not vary inconsistently in density.

What has been said about extreme brightness differences in the scene applies also to changes in the density of projected materials. Film shots that vary from differences in exposure can be evened out at the laboratory during printing. When slides vary, the video engineer can make shading adjustments if enough time has been allowed to see and work on them before they are switched into the program. If they are all on the same camera chain, however, and taken in direct succession, the engineer cannot see them before they are switched; hence the shading adjustments will be seen by the audience. Loading the slides alternately on two camera chains will prevent this difficulty, provided that the director does not take them in such quick succession that the shading cannot be accomplished between takes.

It is true that some television camera chains are equipped with automatic brightness compensators. These are corrective devices, however, and do not alter the desirability of having film and slides properly exposed in the first place.

7.9 Cooperate with the lighting crew.

Give them advance information about the positions of your performers, scenic elements, cameras, and overhead microphones. Give them ample time to set their instruments and illumination levels. It will not help if you dry rehearse during lighting setup, occupying places where the crew needs to walk or place ladders.

7.10 Cooperate with the video engineer.

Be willing to listen to the engineer's recommendations. If there is but one intercommunication system, avoid using it during times when the engineer needs to talk through it about camera alignment. Avoid retaining the cameras for rehearsal just before air or taping time if they are needed then for rebalancing. When rehearsal time is limited, spare some of it to show the video engineer any parts of your program containing sudden or wide variations in brightness; and if there is no rehearsal, at least provide some forewarning about these parts so that the engineer can be ready to try to compensate for them with shading adjustments. In obliging your engineer, you are obliging yourself; it's the clarity of your program that's at stake.

8 Don't mix up the image of a principal subject with other pictorial elements.

8.1 Avoid scrambled superimposures.

Don't super or key the guest's name right across his or her face. Don't allow ghosted hands on a keyboard to claw at the pianist's face.

When setting up a super, have the detail in the frame of one camera coincide with plain area in the frame of the other camera. Be sure that each camera operator knows the precise composition of his or her shot, making guide marks for it, if necessary, on the camera viewfinder. If your system permits, preview the super before using it.

8.2 Don't let the contour of your subject blend into a visual element that it is overlapping.

Don't let the boiled egg get lost in the slice of bread behind it, or the face of the girl on the sofa get confused with the peonies in the bowl on the table behind her.

9 Avoid visuals that are rendered in needlessly fine detail.

The 525-line system used for broadcasting in the United States is not particularly noted for its ability to resolve fine detail, nor do television viewers ordinarily have much time to scrutinize a complicated image before it disappears from the screen. For sufficient clarity, therefore, make your visuals as bold and simple as possible. For example, since the thin lines of many standard maps are less than satisfactory on camera, it is advisable to have the maps redrawn, simplifying their complexity and rendering them in bolder lines and masses.

Chapter 5

Preserving Form

Do the subjects as pictured on the screen look natural and acceptable to the viewers? Despite the images' artificiality, viewers should be able to recognize what they represent, find them looking as they expect them to look, and believe in them. To help viewers do so, follow these recommendations:

1 Choose your camera angles with regard for the normal and natural appearance of the subject.

1.1 Shoot from the angle that promotes most ready recognition.

Neither a shoe nor a shoe brush can be readily recognized from an end view at the lens level. A potter's wheel and a plate of hors d'oeuvres are more easily identified from a downward than a horizontal line of view. And a box, to read as a box, should present three planes to the camera (top and two sides) instead of only two planes or one.

1.2 Normally avoid upward or downward angles toward the human face.

It is usually advisable to show things as your viewer is accustomed to picture them. Unless you aim for intentional distortion, avoid inclined angles up or down when shooting the human face. A camera on a tripod is usually fixed at a height above the faces of seated persons and below those of standing ones. Hence, the closer it comes, the more it will have to tilt either up or down, showing either too much chin or too much pate and, if the lens has a short focal length, foreshortening the subjects' heads unnaturally. By pulling the camera back and using a longer lens, you can minimize the angle of tilt and show the faces from a more favorable level.

1.3 Avoid angled closeups of rectangular subjects such as title cards or pictures mounted on vertical surfaces.

The viewer expects to see these looking foursquare, not "keystoned," i.e., with two opposite sides tapering as on the keystone of an arch. To avoid keystoning them, be sure that your cameras aim perpendicularly at the rectangles' centers. When they are mounted in a row on a flat surface and are to be viewed one after another, do not pan them unless the camera is sufficiently far back to make its angle toward either end of the row almost unnoticeable. Instead, if the row is vertical, pedestal or boom up or down; or if horizontal, truck from one subject to another. Another solution, which eliminates the trucking and pedestaling, is to mount the cards on a curved surface of a "pan board," which is concentric with the arc traveled by the panning or tilting lens.

When the subjects are to be taken in limbo, it is sometimes easier, rather than moving the camera or panning the subjects, to move the subjects past the camera by mounting them on a sliding strip.

2 Avoid distortion from extreme-angle lenses.

An extreme wide-angle lens, used too close, will make the nearer portions of the subject look abnormally larger than the more distant portions, resulting in huge noses or in enormous hands and feet when these are extended toward the lens. Unless you intend such distortion, pull the camera back and use a narrower lens.

Quite an opposite effect is produced by a telephoto or extreme narrow-angle lens. When this is used for a close shot from a great distance, spatial depth seems to be flattened out, lacking the diminishing effect of normal perspective. Thus, a shot from a theater balcony can make the keyboard of a piano onstage look compressed and rectangular, or a shot from the bleachers behind home plate at a baseball game can make the pitcher look as large as the batter.

Time as well as space seems to be altered with extreme-angle lenses. Because the pitcher seems close to the batter on a telephoto shot, he will seem to take abnormally long to walk between his mound and home plate. With the wide-angle lens, on the other hand, forward and backward movements seem unusually rapid, with the moving subjects swiftly enlarging or diminishing. Hence, this lens can be used intentionally to add force to a boxer's punch, speed to an oncoming train, or shock when an assailant attacks the hero from behind.

3 Create an illusion of three-dimensional form.

Since television is viewed on a two-dimensional surface, an illusion of space and form must be created by artificial means. Some of these means are as follows:

3.1 Shoot the action from a variety of angles.

Take the opportunity offered by multiple and mobile cameras to shoot the action from various sides. Action in television does not have to be viewed from only one direction, as in the theater. Your cameras can get right on the stage, as it were, and move around the scene, shooting from enough directions to make the environment really seem to surround the action instead of backing it up from one side.

3.2   Move your performers.

You can create more awareness of space by moving your performers through space than by keeping them stationary. Unlike actors on a proscenium stage, who have to favor the auditorium, television performers can face and move naturally in many directions. Don't be reluctant to show their backs occasionally; you can get them head-on from another camera when you need to.

3.3   Use moving camera shots.

Dollying in past performers and scenic objects gives a sense of penetrating space. Camera motion also makes one aware of space by creating shifting planes. When the camera dollies in, foreground elements enlarge and rise more than background elements. When the camera trucks across a scene, the foreground elements pass by more quickly than the background elements, an effect you have probably also observed from a moving car or train.

3.4   Use the zoom lens.

The zoom effect, unlike the effect of the dolly, enlarges the foreground and background elements equally. The zoom also lets you cover space in a hurry and cross hedges and streams that would obviously limit the use of the dolly.

3.5   Show receding planes.

It is common for beginning directors to line up a desk or counter parallel to the background and shoot it from front and center. This makes the background surface and the frontal plane of the furniture extend in height and breadth but not in depth, so that the composition is largely two-dimensional.

For a more vigorous sense of three dimensions, show receding planes. Take angle shots of walls and furniture to make them slant back in space and show their intersecting planes. Instead of lining up performers across the camera's line of vision, let them turn their bodies at angles to the camera and group in receding lines and triangles. Don't hesitate, when occasion offers, to let them overlap one another; this permits closer shots and stimulates depth perception by emphasizing that one is in front of the other. In wide shots it is often effective to stress the receding plane of the floor as the base on which your spatial composition is deployed. This can be done by using rugs on it, throwing shadows on it, and by patterning it with paint or masking tape.

3.6 Emphasize volume and space in your settings.

Settings look more three-dimensional when they contain receding elements, openings through which vistas can be seen, recesses to create pockets of space, and volumes projecting out into space or totally surrounded by it. Objects in the foreground, besides helping to create an illusion that the action is enclosed on four sides, also provide a frontal frame of reference against which to measure the recession in depth or other scenic elements.

3.7 Make foreground elements stand out against their background.

On the two-dimensional screen, things which are actually at different distances may seem to be in the same plane unless artificial means are used to reinforce their separation. One means is to focus more sharply on the near subjects than the far ones. Thus, performers can be stood out against their background, provided that the background is far enough behind them to lie beyond the limit of the depth of field.

With ample distance between performers and background it also becomes possible to stand the performers out by means of lighting. As previously explained, light can be concentrated on the playing area without spilling onto the background, allowing the latter to be lighted independently to whatever degree seems desirable. Furthermore, use can be made of backlight—light slanted down toward the performers from the side opposite the camera, to rim their heads and shoulders with a bright outline. If the background is too close, this light will fall too steeply, becoming toplight rather than backlight and producing unattractive shadows.

Color can also be used to make subjects stand out through the use of advancing and receding hues. The "warm" hues (reds, oranges, and yellows) seem to advance closer to the beholder than the "cool" ones (blues and greens). This is true at least if other dimensions of the colors are equal.

A color can vary in three dimensions. "Hue" distinguishes it as red, green, blue, or whatever. "Saturation" distinguishes between a vivid color and a duller, grayed-down, "desaturated" one. "Brightness" refers to whether the color is light (a tint) or dark (a shade).

Assuming their saturation and brightness to be the same, then, a warm hue will seem to advance more than a cool one. Otherwise, a lighter or a more saturated color may seem to advance more than a darker or less-saturated one.

Whatever the case, you should keep the color of the background from seeming to be closer to the viewer than the persons who are playing in front of it.

3.8 Bring out form with modeling light.

The form of three-dimensional subjects can be enhanced by modeling light—light coming sufficiently from one side of the camera to produce on the subject visible highlights and shadows. The contrast between highlight and shadow should be restrained unless some dramatic effect is intended, and even then should be kept within a tolerable contrast range for video reproduction.

3.9   Use spotlights rather than sources of flat illumination.

If modeling light is minimized, the frontlighting (that aimed from the direction of the camera) should be such as to produce advancing highlights on the bridge of the nose and the high spots of forehead, cheekbones, and chin. Such highlights are produced by spotlight beams rather than by the diffuse illumination emitted from scoops, broads, or soft lights.

For all ways to enhance form and space by lighting, spotlights, indeed, are the instruments to use. Because their light can be concentrated into beams, they produce sharper rim lighting when used as backlights. Because the beams can be aimed in specific directions, they can be kept from spilling undesired light on backgrounds and, when used for modeling, they will produce more discernible shadows. Instruments without lenses, such as scoops, are needed to lighten excessive shadows and even out unwanted irregularities in the lighting distribution, but if used exclusively, will flatten out space and form rather than enhance them.

4   Promote conditions of achieving color fidelity.

Except for stylized effects, the colors in television must appear as natural as possible—particularly those of human flesh and of commercial products, for which the audience has ready standards of comparison. To help ensure color fidelity in your productions, it is desirable to understand the factors that affect the appearance of color in television.

4.1   The color of the subject is affected by the color of the illumination.

Color is a sensation produced in the brain, normally as a result of light striking the retina of the eye. According to a prevalent and useful theory, light travels in waves of different lengths, each length producing a different hue sensation and ranging from 400 millimicrons for blue to somewhat over 700 for red. White light is a mixture of all wavelengths within this range.

Wavelengths figure in the theory of selective absorption, which provides a physical explanation for the appearance of colored material. Under white light, the material will absorb certain wavelengths from that light and reflect others which, reaching an observer, will stimulate his or her sensation of a particular hue. Thus, "red" material is so structured that it absorbs all but the wavelengths around 700 millimicrons, which are the "red" wavelengths.

For the material to appear red, however, the light must contain red wavelengths to be reflected. It will look red under red light and under white light (which has red wavelengths in it), but under pure green or blue light it will look black.

A "black" material absorbs all wavelengths, therefore reflecting none. A "white" material reflects all the wavelengths it receives, looking white under white light, red under red light, and so on.

This is the theory. In practice, colored light is rarely restricted to a single wavelength, and materials rarely reflect only one wavelength or a narrowly confined band of wavelengths; hence the results are not so easily predictable. Caucasian flesh under green light, for example, will go dark but not black and, reflecting some green, will take on a quite unwholesome appearance.

The essential thing to remember is that the color of a subject will be altered under light of different wavelengths than those it is structured to reflect. For this reason, television performers are usually lighted without the use of color filters over the light sources except for intentionally stylized effects.

4.2 The color of the subject is affected by the balancing of primary colors in the television system.

To understand more about the appearance of colors on television, it is useful to know something about the principle of additive color mixture, on which current television reproduction is based. You have probably observed that, when passed through a prism, white light separates into a rainbowlike spectrum of component hues. Vice versa, hues can be added together to constitute white light.

One way to do this is to use the three "light primaries," red, green, and blue. When red, green, and blue lights are added together, they will produce not only white light, but also (by varying their proportions) virtually every other hue. Therefore, they are used in the present color television system, both at the camera and the receiver end. The light entering the camera from the scene is separated into its component red, green, and blue wavelengths, each component being directed to a separate pickup tube or other imaging device.[1] In most television receivers there are three electron beams, one to respond to the output of each camera pickup tube. On the face of the receiver picture tube are particles called "phosphores," grouped in triads—one phosphore in each triad glowing red, another green, and another blue when activated by the relevant electron beam. Each triad combines the light from its phosphores to produce a bit of color corresponding to a tiny segment of the original scene.

[1] While there have been many different types of image-recording tubes used in television cameras since they were first developed, the two most common pickup tubes used in today's broadcast-quality cameras are the saticon and the plumnicon. The newest development in the technology of video camera imaging devices has been in the area of the tubeless camera, using the charge-coupled device (CCD) in place of tubes. This computer chip technology has made it possible to create an even more rugged and compact camera.

The camera must be matched as closely as possible to the eye's relative sensitivity to various wavelengths. The eye is more sensitive to the yellow and green regions of the spectrum than to the red and blue regions. Adjusting the response of the camera to that of the eye is accomplished by proportioning or "balancing" the outputs of the red, green, and blue pickup tubes, often termed camera "white balance." As a director, you must understand the need for this balancing and wait for it to be accomplished, sometimes allowing time for re-balancing just prior to the actual performance.

4.3   The color of the subject is affected by the camera's response to color temperature.

Camera balancing must take into account the "color temperature," a term used to describe the relative proportion of the wavelengths in the illumination falling on the scene. In interior shots, for example, the blue tube output is increased to compensate for the relatively low blue content of incandescent light. If, mean-while, another camera on the program is being used outdoors where there are more blue wavelengths in the natural light, it would require a different balance than the indoor camera. When these relative balances are accomplished, takes can be made between the two cameras without inconsistencies of color in successive shots.

Artificial light sources may differ in color temperature. Incandescent and fluorescent sources are too different in this respect to be mixed on the same subject without unpredictable results. Furthermore, color temperature changes when in-candescent lights are dimmed, the filaments yielding progressively less blue and making skin tones brown, which leads some studios to set limits below which their lights should not be dimmed.

Natural light also varies in its constitution, being yellowish and reddish early and late in the day, blue in shade and overcast, and white in noon sunshine. As such changes occur, a filter can be used to change the quality of the light striking the pickup tubes to match that for which they are balanced. This adjustment may be needed during an outdoor remote that you are directing.

4.4   The color of the subject is adversely affected by too little illumination.

An insufficiently lighted subject will not only fail to reveal its true color, but may also be mottled by spurious hues. For low key scenes (those in which dark tones predominate), light on the background must be kept relatively high.

4.5   The color of the subject is adversely affected by excessive contrast range.

For example, a camera takes a predominantly dark scene of three fashion models in royal blue ensembles, then zooms in to a closeup of a white bag which one of them is holding. As the iris (remotely controlled by the video engineer) is closed down to prevent overexposing the closeup, one can see the royal blue clothing darken to navy blue.

4.6   The color of the subject is affected by its reflective characteristics.

Thus, a wool and a satin may look different although colored by the same dye. Having a harder, smoother surface, the satin reflects some wavelengths that the wool absorbs and, acting more like a mirror, tends to reflect light beams in specific directions rather than to diffuse them, thus producing white highlights.

4.7   The color of the subject is influenced by the color of adjacent or background areas.

Flesh can be given a dark, muddy appearance from adjacency to excessively bright areas, including very light backgrounds, starchy white clothing, and highly reflectant metals. To combat this, reflectant surfaces can be treated with a dulling spray. To darken a troublesome background, one may either move it farther from the light, angle it so that it reflects the light in a different direction, shield it from some of the light, or re-aim the lighting instrument.

Flesh tones may change as they are seen in alternate shots against differently colored backgrounds. This effect is associated with a phenomenon called "simultaneous hue contrast," whereby a color seen against some contrasting, highly saturated color will take on some of the complement of that color. In light, the complement of a given hue is the hue which, added to it, will produce white light. The hues opposite one another in *Figure 5/1* are complementary to each other. Note, for example, that the complement of yellow is blue, and that of blue-green is red. Therefore—illustrating the effect of simultaneous hue contrast—red raw beef on a yellow platter will take on blue (complement of the yellow), looking purplish and unappetizing, whereas on a blue-green platter its redness will be enhanced.

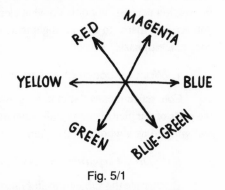

Fig. 5/1

4.8   The color of the subject may be influenced by reflected light.

A subject may be colored by light reflected from a nearby surface or filtered through some nearby translucent material. For example, a face in the shadow of a tree may be green with light reflected from or filtered through the leaves, which may be contrary to the viewer's expectations. We tend to judge colors as we expect them to look and may regard as false the camera's objectivity.

Chapter 6

A Single Impression

In television, each new situation must be comprehended promptly before another replaces it. Hence, the visual elements that portray this situation must collaborate to produce a single, readily assimilated impression. Achieving this impression depends not only on what elements you select to show, but also on how you arrange them. In this arrangement, you seek to achieve unity through coherence and emphasis.

1 Work for coherent arrangements.

Coherence means "sticking together." In a coherent pictorial composition, the parts of the picture are visually connected so that they can be readily associated and grasped as a whole. In the interests of coherence:

1.1 Do not separate subjects on opposite sides of the picture.

To separate the subjects as in *Figure 6/1* splits the eye between two divergent centers of interest and provides nothing but emptiness in the center where we would expect the interest to be concentrated. So one sees:

ONE
PERSON

ANOTHER
PERSON

Fig. 6/1

whereas one should see:

TWO PERSONS UNITED
IN A CONVERSATION

Fig. 6/2

More involvement between the persons can be promoted by pulling the camera back. By introducing more space on either side of them, the space between them is relatively lessened, but the wider shot is liable to make them too small on the screen.

In *Figure 6/2*, the composition has been improved by moving the chairs closer together and by shooting from an angle to overlap the figures somewhat so that they tend to combine into a single visual form. As indicated by the arrows, a unified circular path has been established for the viewer's eyes.

1.2   Use scenic elements and lighting to tie the composition together.

In *Figure 6/3*, the men are as widely separated as in *Figure 6/1*, but the picture has been given more coherence by filling in between the men with scenic elements and light. The coffee table and its shadow bridge between the legs. The desk top forms a tie line at waist level. The books arch across above the heads. The lamp makes a center, holding the other elements by a

Fig. 6/3

kind of centripetal attraction, and the arc of light from it bridges between the faces.

1.3   Select a few expressive shapes and lines and repeat them, varied in size and direction, throughout the picture.

Because television directors work with living, moving subjects, they cannot observe as many niceties of coherence as are practiced by the designers of still pictures. Nevertheless, for application to the relatively fixed compositions that occur in commercial displays or when performers remain stationary during a shot of appreciable duration, they will find the still-picture composers' principles worthy of study.

One of these principles is to select a few expressive shapes and lines and repeat them, varied in size and direction, throughout the picture. In *Figure 6/4* (after a photograph advertising the insulation from noise achieved by a brand of automobile body), the sleeping child is arranged to emphasize gentle curves, which repeat the curve formed by the top of the car window and suggest the caress of repose. The distribution of these curves throughout the picture gives coherence to its parts, making them work together to produce a single, overall impression.

Fig. 6/4

1.4   Similarly, in color television repeat one or more hues, varied in brightness and saturation, throughout the picture.

Perhaps you already follow this principle in coordinating your attire or the decoration of your room.

1.5   Group smaller items into larger wholes that may be more easily apprehended.

This is similar to tying a number of small items into a bundle so that they can be carried more easily. In writing, sentences are grouped into paragraphs, paragraphs into sections, and sections into chapters, so that ideas can be carried more conveniently in the mind. In pictorial composition, the separate visual elements are often grouped into embracing simple geometric shapes.

For example, to correct the split attention which is evident in *Figure 6/5*, the performers in *Figure 6/6* have been grouped into a roughly triangular position. This has been done by controlling the difference in head levels and by coordinating the slants of the guitar, the woman's left arm, the piano lid, and its supporting stick.

Fig. 6/5

Fig. 6/6

Figure 6/6 also demonstrates another means of helping the subject of the picture to make a dominant impression. This is the calculated use of emphasis and subordination.

2   Emphasize picture elements in proportion to their importance.

The point of the picture statement in *Figure 6/6* is "woman singing." In supporting this point, the pictorial elements are not of equal importance. The piano and the guitar-playing accompanist are subordinate to the woman; and the woman's figure is subordinate to her face, which expresses her emotional attitude toward the song and contains the mouth from which the singing issues. Therefore, the face should receive more emphasis than anything else in the picture. Accordingly, it has been placed at the apex of the major triangle, with various slanting lines leading the eye to it. As the brightest element in the picture, juxtaposed against the darkest, it also commands attention by being at the point of highest brightness contrast.

You will not always find it as feasible to control emphasis as in this posed situation. Nevertheless, whatever the situation, you should see that those elements which carry the most meaning at any given moment command more attention than anything else in the frame.

The rest of this chapter cites ways to accomplish this objective. Although some of the ways have been mentioned before in this book, they are worth repeating.

2.1   Frame as closely as possible around the meaningful elements.

Beginning directors are apt to frame too loosely, showing, for example, a needlessly small human figure surrounded by a mass of background which has nothing to contribute to the matter at hand. You can, of course, include a wide expanse of background when it does mean something—if, for instance, you want to contrast a small boy with the bigness of the world, or to support the lonesome mood of a ballad by surrounding the singer with empty space and shadow, or to establish the specific setting of the action.

But sometimes not even a full figure should be framed. When the announcer of a soft-drink commercial observes, while the talent is taking a drink, "You'll enjoy the clean taste," the visual expression may be confined to the actor's face and the soda can at his lips. A wider shot is justified in this instance only if something is to be gained by seeing his body in a supporting attitude of enjoyable relaxation—in which case it's up to you to make that attitude expressive enough to justify its inclusion in the picture.

2.2   When small subjects must share the screen with human beings, bring them as close as possible to the performers' faces.

Suppose that an announcer, saying, "Acme is the key to your security," holds a key at waist level, thereby requiring you to frame him in a hip shot. In this shot, the small size of the key and the number of other visual elements with which it must compete for attention does not make the key as visually assertive as it should be. By having the announcer raise the key nearer his face and extend it somewhat toward the camera, you can take a tighter shot in which the key will gain its due prominence.

When small items are being demonstrated on a table surface, there are two possible ways to bring them closer to the demonstrator's face:

. . . you can lower the person by seating him, or

. . . if he (or she) must remain standing, you can raise the table surface, choosing a waist-level counter, for example, instead of a standard-height table.

2.3   To make small subjects dominate larger ones, place them in the foreground of the shot.

Note, for example, the location of the telephone in *Figure 4/12* (page 35).

2.4   Elongated subjects may require special composition to make them dominate the picture.

When shot from front and center, a vocal chorus three tiers deep and twenty persons wide will have to compete for visual attention with large, meaningless areas of floor at the bottom of the picture or of background at the top. To make the chorus fill more of the frame, you can either:

. . . regroup them in more vertical tiers with fewer persons per row (provided that they can still sing well in this arrangement), or

. . . shoot them from an angle, which will compress its pictured width, or

. . . shoot them from above, which will make them fill more of the height of the screen by revealing more of the bodies of persons in the second and third tiers than could be seen in a lower shot.

A deck of playing cards can present similar problems. Instead of shooting it from front and center as in *Figure 6/7*, try taking it as in *Figure 6/8* from an angle

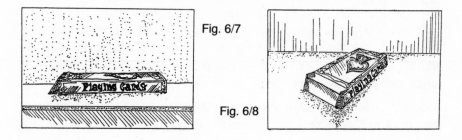

Fig. 6/7

Fig. 6/8

high enough to show its top as well as its face, also slanting it to cut across more of the vertical dimension of the frame. Projecting a shadow from it may also help to extend the influence of the deck over more of the picture area.

2.5   Contrast the important element with its environment.

Slanting the deck as in *Figure 6/8* also makes it more prominent by contrast with the rectangular alignment of the picture frame.

In *Figure 6/6*, the prominence of the vocalist was also achieved partly by contrast. Observe that her figure, as the only vertical in the picture, contrasts in direction with the other major lines. Also, as previously noted, the maximum brightness contrast is between the dark piano cover and her face.

Contrast can be useful for emphasizing a commercial product. For example, a smooth-surfaced container will be more assertive when displayed against a textured surface.

Various kinds of possible contrast are listed below:

Standing	Seated	Diagonal	Rectangular
Tall	Low	Flat	In the round
Small	Large	Alone	Together
Bright	Dark	Moving	Still
Distant	Close	Detailed	Plain
Focused	Blurred	Contrasty	Uniform
Curved	Straight	Rough	Smooth

You may also contrast warm colors with cool colors, a saturated color with a desaturated one, and a given hue with its complementary hue.

2.6   Lead toward the important elements with lines to be traveled by the eye.

In *Figure 6/6* you have already noted how various diagonals lead toward the singer's face at the apex of the major triangle. A study of many paintings and photographs will also demonstrate how the center of interest can be emphasized by placing it where prominent lines converge. In Leonardo da Vinci's *Last Supper*, for example, the head of Jesus coincides with the vanishing point of all receding lines in the composition.

In advertising layouts, lines serve not only to control the eye's path through the message, but also to keep it from wandering off into adjacent copy. Similarly, you should avoid compositions that pull your viewer's eye away from the center of interest. Avoid, for example, the arrangement in *Figure 4/6* (page 26), where attention is led back and off the screen by the perspective convergence of the display board and by the direction in which the teacher is facing. Obviously, the direction in which your performers face can and should be used to support the center of interest, as in *Figure 4/8* (page 27).

2.7   Make the important elements more visibly communicative than other elements.

When two or more performers are included in the frame, attention is likely to center on the one who is most actively communicating, whether by speech or movement. This obviously requires that sound and motion by the supporting characters be subordinated to that of the one who is leading the scene at a given moment.

In dialogue passages where no performer is particularly more active than another, attention will favor the one whose features are most clearly revealed. If two persons are facing camera at different distances from it—all else being equal—the one closer to camera is likely to be more prominent because his or her face is larger and is resolved in greater detail. If they are facing each other, however, more prominence will attach to the one farther from camera because more of his or her features are revealed.

2.8   To achieve proper emphasis, control the brightness levels.

Avoid painting or lighting the background so brightly that it dominates the persons in front of it, who, almost ten times out of ten, are more important than it is.

Avoid overhead lighting which shadows the performers' eyes, frustrating the attention that should be given to these "mirrors of the soul."

Study how artists such as Goya and Rembrandt brighten their center of interest or reinforce it with the strongest brightness contrast in their picture.

Experiment with light as a means to shift attention from one center of attention to another, either by moving performers in and out of shadow, or by dimming the light on one subject and bringing it up on another.

2.9   Simplify the environment of the important element, eliminating items that would compete with it for attention.

When a demonstrator is showing a succession of items, keep the display surface clear of items other than the one that is important at the moment. This may require an adjacent area from which the items can be procured and another to which they can be removed. Shooting downward toward the display surface will help to eliminate the body of the demonstrator from the closeup.

If several objects are to be panned in sequence, they should be spaced sufficiently apart so that only one appears on camera at a time.

Avoid busy backgrounds. These include not only the vertical surfaces of the setting, but also the clothing of demonstrators. For example, it is difficult to discern a fountain pen sufficiently if it is being held in front of a checked suit. Sometimes the demonstrator can hold the item to one side so that his or her body does not appear in the closeup at all.

3   When selecting the field of view on a lens for a given shot, consider what emphasis you desire.

Your choice of the field of view can determine how much larger one subject appears than another, and also which subjects are in focus and which ones are not.

3.1   Emphasis is affected by the depth of field.

When two subjects are at different distances from camera, you can give them equal emphasis by keeping them both in sharp focus. For this you will need ample depth of field.

But to focus more sharply on one than the other, you will need limited depth of field. When taking closeups of single items, it is usually desirable to make them stand out against a softer focused background. This is more easily achieved by using the longer focal lengths.

3.2   When two subjects are at different distances from the camera, the difference in size between them can be increased by using a shorter lens, with the camera in close.

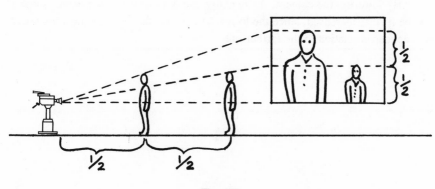

Fig. 6/9

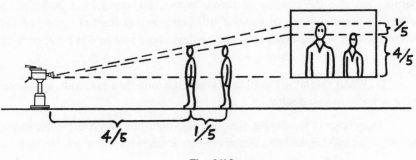

Fig. 6/10

See *Figures 6/9* and *6/10*. In *Figure 6/9* the rear subject is twice as far from the camera as the front subject; hence he looks only half as large. But in *Figure 6/10* the subjects are separated by only one-fifth of the total distance from the camera to the rear subject; hence the rear subject appears only one-fifth smaller than the one in front.

In both instances the figure in front is framed at the waist. In *Figure 6/9* this is accomplished with a short focal length wide-angle position, in *Figure 6/10* by a lens of longer focal length.

If domination by size is desired, clearly one should select a short focal length wide-angle lens, which increases the difference in scale by requiring the camera be brought in close.

By lowering the camera, incidentally, the dominance of the nearer subject can be further increased, since the lower the camera, the taller the nearer subject will appear in relation to the farther one.

Chapter 7

Distractions and
Discomforts

Viewers are less likely to heed the point of a picture statement if something about it is distracting or makes them feel uncomfortable. Therefore:

1   Take pains with your picture composition.

1.1   Pay attention to balance, particularly when your subjects are in relatively fixed positions.

The principles of balance as practiced by painters and photographers are applicable in television mainly to static situations, but there are more of such situations than one may at first realize, for the motion of performers often consists of transitions between scenes that are held for moments at a time.

When a picture is unbalanced, the elements that attract greatest attention seem to predominate on one side of it, making the other side seem wasted. High attention goes naturally to persons who are doing or saying something or to persons and things that are being talked about, but attention is also influenced by other factors, such as size, color, and contrast.

Attention factors can interact in complex ways. A tiny highlight against a dark background can balance a large mass of middle gray, or a top spinning on a bare floor can balance a whole group of boys watching it. All of the various interest values in the picture average out at some spot, which resembles a center of gravity. When this center is felt to be nearer one side of the picture than the other, the picture is unbalanced.

1.2   Place attractions of equal attention value equidistant from the center.

This is called "symmetrical balance" or symmetry. It is similar in principle to placing persons of equal weight equidistant from the fulcrum of a seesaw.

1.3   When attractions are unequal, the stronger should be nearer the center on its side of the picture.

This is "asymmetrical balance" or asymmetry. It resembles balancing a seesaw by seating the heavier person nearer the fulcrum and the lighter farther from it.

1.4   In some instances, balance for television differs from that for still pictures.

A performer looking offscreen should be framed with more room on the side toward which he or she is looking; this balances off audience interest in whatever is attracting the performer's attention. Similarly, when panning with a laterally moving subject, a camera operator customarily leads the subject, allowing more room on the side toward which the subject is moving. Although, as previously explained, this is done partly to prevent the subject from intersecting with the frame in case of an unexpected spurt, it also serves to balance off the interest that has been created in the subject's destination.

When two performers, A and B, who are conversing, are taken separately in alternate shots, it is customary to frame A with more room on the side off which B is located, and B with more room on the side off which A is located. Not only does this compensate for offscreen interest as explained above, but it also keeps the performers on the sides of the screen which they are seen to occupy when they are taken together, thus preventing a disturbing spatial disorientation.

When a picture is unbalanced, the viewer instinctively wants to see the wasted side filled with something. Capitalizing on this, a director will sometimes unbalance the composition intentionally to create anticipation for something which is about to be introduced on the empty side. Thus, actors may be moved away from a door just before the entrance of an important character; or the camera may pan a commercial product to one side of the screen, creating on the other side a kind of vacuum, which will be filled presently with an important printed message.

1.5   Prevent the following instances of faulty composition or poor framing:

There is too much headroom. The performer has sunk too low in the picture, leaving the upper part to no purpose.

There is too little headroom. The performer's head is scraping the top of the frame.

The performer is cut off at the ankles as if wading or soaking his or her feet.

The corner of a picture frame on the wall behind a performer looks as if it might puncture his or her head.

A lampshade or plant rises behind a performer's head like an exotic headdress.

In the shot of a panelist, halves of other panelists' bodies are seen moving on either side of the frame.

A very white and very unimportant piece of paper—or a red carnation in an announcer's buttonhole—is the most apparent object in the shot.

The hands of a performer are moving just below the frame so that one can't make out what they are doing.

The foregoing are only the beginning of a list to which you are urged to add to your own examples. Then you can say, as in *The Mikado*, "I've got them on the list, and they'll none of them be missed."

2 Help performers to avoid inappropriate action or unattractive appearance.

2.1 When the performer is supposed to be addressing the audience, make sure there is eye contact with the lens.

So that the performer will not have to look off-camera for a starting cue, be sure that the floor director who gives the cue is stationed beside the opening camera.

So that the performer will not be caught with an "I'm taking a cue" look when the camera dissolves to him or her, your direction should be, "Mike, cue, dissolve"—not "Mike, dissolve, cue talent."

Inexperienced performers never seem to be really talking to the audience when they are trying to read prompting devices (except, perhaps, for the kind that project the copy on a glass directly in front of the lens). Therefore, encourage such performers to speak from their own knowledge, referring frankly to notes when they come to data that the audience would not expect them to remember anyway. Unless they are able to sustain long speeches straight from their own minds, provide someone who, by asking leading questions, can prompt the information from them a little at a time. If they cannot do without a prompting device, pray that they are farsighted. This will allow you to keep the camera back from them on a narrow-angle lens, thus reducing the number of degrees through which they must move their eyes off-lens to read the copy.

Be sure the performer knows which camera to be talking to. It is not always easy for a performer to make this judgment. For example, if your talent is pointing out details in a diagram hung at eye level, both the camera taking the closeup of the diagram and the camera that includes his or her face will be aimed at approximately the same level and in approximately the same direction.

Also be sure the camera the talent is addressing is located where eye contact can be achieved conveniently. In *Figures 7/1* and *7/2*, a performer is pointing out

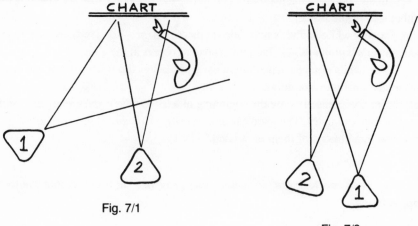

Fig. 7/1

Fig. 7/2

details in a diagram, taken in closeup by camera 2, which leaves camera 1 as the camera to take his face whenever he seeks to direct a remark to his viewers. In *Figure 7/1* he can do this conveniently—but in *Figure 7/2*, note how he can do so only by twisting his head awkwardly over his shoulder, since camera 1, unhappily, is precisely where many beginning directors are liable to locate it.

2.2   When a performer is addressing the television audience, refrain from continually changing cameras during his speech.

Otherwise, the performer's head may jerk back and forth noticeably from one camera to the other. If the change is unavoidable, the performer should be trained, when noticing the tally light go out on the first camera, to glance momentarily toward some intermediate center of attention before looking into the second camera.

2.3   Eliminate unsightly parts of the performer's body.

Closeups of tabletop demonstrations should avoid giving undue prominence to the pelvic region of the demonstrator behind the table.

It is remarkable what a confusion of angles can be assumed by the legs of a seated group of persons and how distracting this can be to the viewer. For masking these distractions, no studio should be without a coffee table.

2.4   Eliminate annoying factors about the performer's grooming and dress.

Among these are shiny tie clips, dangling earrings that sway in closeups, and sometimes open zippers.

2.5   Eliminate distasteful business.

In a student-directed commercial, a young lady serving iced tea dropped ice cubes into the glass with her fingers and then wiped the fingers on her apron. The director seemed not to notice.

2.6   Correct movements that are awkward or distracting.

As examples, some performers may keep swaying back and forth in a closeup, may keep repeating some physical mannerism, or may be ungainly when sitting and rising—possibly because the director has settled for a seat that is too low, deep, and soft.

2.7   Do what you can to prevent nervous tension.

Inexperienced performers need orientation to the studio techniques and role expected of them. They should not be expected to take cues, regulate the timing and progress of the program, sustain a lengthy presentation, perform intricate business, deliver imposed speeches requiring memorization, or, in short, do anything to which they are unaccustomed.

The director should allow all performers the freest possible exercise of their own individual faculties of communication. Find out whether they are more comfortable sitting or standing. Don't confuse them with a barrage of instructions. Don't inhibit performers with too many restrictions as to where to stand, how to hold things, which camera to play to, etcetera, until they are ready to accommodate themselves to these restrictions. A person under tension in a strange situation can take only so much at one time.

3   Be alert to correct discomforts and distractions caused by scenery, properties, and graphics.

These include:

Unpressed cloths	Amateurish lettering
Badly draped drapes	Cracks between flats
Wrinkled cycloramas	Shaking walls
Bruised or dirty surfaces	Askew pictures

4   Prevent disturbances caused by faulty lighting.

4.1   Prevent visible shadow of the microphone boom.

To do this, keep performers away from the walls of the setting as much as possible.

Provide the lighting crew with advance information about the area to be covered by your boom microphone and about the locations, facing directions, and movements of your performers and cameras.

Be willing to entertain recommendations from the lighting people regarding the best location for your boom. The more perpendicular it is to the direction of predominant spotlight beams, the less liable it will be to project vertical shadows on the walls and on the performers' bodies. Horizontal shadows are much easier to mask out than vertical ones; they can often be eliminated by lowering the top "barn door" on the spotlight causing the trouble.

4.2   Do not tolerate multiple shadows of a subject, except for a desired special effect.

These are particularly obvious and distracting when made by a moving subject.

4.3   Do not tolerate unattractive shadows on performers, such as:

. . . those that don't conform to the natural contours of the face, as when nose shadow drops onto the upper lip.

. . . those from strong toplight, which obscure the eyes and throw unnatural emphasis on the horizontal planes of the face.

. . . those from excessive backlight, which make "bibs" on the chest.

. . . those that are too dark and hard-edged, particularly on an attractive female face.

. . . those that create unmotivated dark pockets in the space through which performers move.

4.4   Prevent glare.

This results when a light beam is reflected from a bright and glossy surface directly toward the camera lens. To correct it, several remedies are possible.

The surface can be altered to provide diffuse reflection (which scatters rays in many different directions) instead of specular reflection (which reflects the beam in one primary direction). For instance, a shiny object can be sprayed with dulling spray, or matte photographs can be substituted for glossy ones.

The light falling on the surface can be made more diffuse, either by flooding out a spotlight beam, or by using a scoop instead of a spotlight, or by placing a diffusing medium in front of the instrument or by bouncing the light off some intermediate diffusing surface rather than turning it directly onto the shiny object.

The angle of the troublesome surface can be changed so that it does not reflect the beam toward the camera lens. For example, when holding glossy photographs, performers can tilt them slightly downward, thereby directing the reflected beam beneath the lens. In applying this remedy, remember the law from your physics textbook: "The angle of incidence equals the angle of reflection."

The camera can be moved out of the path of the reflected light beam.

4.5   Prevent multiple light reflections.

Large reflectant subjects such as automobiles will not look good if they reflect multiple bright images of the studio lights. Besides glaring, these multiple highlights can look unnatural, be unduly prominent, and break up the subject's unity of form. To correct them, apply some of the remedies suggested for correcting glare—or try using one or two powerful light sources instead of several weaker ones, thus producing fewer reflected beams for the camera to have to avoid.

4.6   Prevent halation or flare.

Arcs of spurious light will wash in from one edge of the picture causing lens flare when the camera faces unshielded light sources that are just outside its field of view. If, as often happens, it is the backlights that cause this problem, either raise them or use barn doors to mask off their beams from the camera lens. In back-lighted situations where the sun is the light source, try a larger lens shade or hold a black flag (or mount it on a stand) in a position that throws a shadow on the front of the lens.

5   Do what you can to eliminate poor camerawork.

It is obvious that discomfort and distraction will result from:

. . . failures to maintain focus and framing.

. . . camera movements that are not motivated by program content.

. . . jerky or wavering pans and dollies.

. . . lurching zooms.

. . . shooting off the set.

. . . showing an overhead microphone, unless its presence has been frankly acknowledged.

. . . late shots.

All of these the director must be ever watchful to correct or to prevent. You cannot always count on having expert camera operators. You may have to spend some of your directing time teaching them composition, timing, and camera-handling techniques.

Chapter 8

Animation or Liveliness

A shot can be clear, recognizable, emphatic, and free from distractions, yet fail to interest the viewer because it is visually monotonous. Therefore:

1 Provide a variety of brightness levels.

Just as you feel more alert on a sunny day than on an overcast one, your viewer will respond more alertly to a television picture with some snap in it. In television situations that lack color variety, compensate for it by adequate contrast in your lighting, including small accents of the brightest and darkest tones that the system is capable of reproducing. These accents not only liven up the picture, but also serve as reference levels that help the engineers to establish the proper gradations between the intermediate tones.

Choose colors for scenery, wearing apparel, and properties that will reproduce as clearly differentiated hues. If the colors you must work with seem too monotonous under even illumination, use modeling light to add highlights and shadows. For the snap and sparkle of highlights in eyes and on the summits of facial contours, use spotlights rather than sources of diffuse illumination.

2 Provide a variety of size and spacing.

Arrange your performers at different heights on the screen and at different distances from camera. Avoid equal spaces between them except for an intentionally formal effect.

In general, prefer asymmetrical to symmetrical compositions. Symmetry is justified when you intend a formal effect, or when you wish to give equal importance to two participants who are sharing a scene, or when you need to give equal treatment to a row of singers or dancers who are all doing the same thing. But don't cultivate the habit of shooting everything from front and center. There are more ways to shoot the news announcer than to frame him or her between balanced pictures on the background wall and balanced desk pens on the desk in front. Such regularity is trite, unimaginative, and too inanimate to reflect life as most of us experience it.

3 Use the dynamic potential of the diagonal.

Picture designers often seek to affect their viewers by the direction they give to prominent lines in their compositions. Long, horizontal lines are used to induce a feeling of repose. Diagonals, on the other hand, engender a sense of excitement and activity. In television, diagonals can be used to animate shots that lack actual motion. For example, compare *Figures 6/7* and *6/8* (page 52). It is probable that you will respond more alertly to the slanted deck of cards than the horizontal one.

4 Encourage the animation and naturalness of your performers.

Give your performers opportunity to move around a little rather than freezing them too long or too rigidly in blocked-out positions.

When they do remain in one location, let them assume as natural and informal a pose as possible, unless you have good reason for the contrary. Avoid head-on shots of seated persons with their knees pointed straight toward the camera, unless you want to make them look like ancient Egyptian statues. Let them sit with their bodies slanted to the camera. Besides looking more natural and comfortable that way, they'll fill out the width of the screen better than when forming a narrow perpendicular straight up and down the middle of it.

Chapter 9

Expressiveness

Last but not least in the Moment-by-Moment Questionnaire, you should ask: Does my picture express the meaning as effectively as it should? Does it convey the desired character and mood? To ensure that it does, ask yourself these additional questions:

1 What part of the subject should I show?

Have I restricted my shot to that part of the scene which makes the point most effectively? A common error is to show too much, to diffuse the attention over things that don't matter. Get in on what counts.

Sometimes it is better to leave something to the imagination. A student director showed his understanding of this principle (although perhaps no great originality) when, after establishing a boy overwhelming a girl with an ardent embrace, he cut away to show a flower dropping from her hand unheeded.

Details are sometimes more eloquent than generalities. Hands or feet may be more expressive than faces. And reactions may occasionally mirror an event with more impact than provided by a view of the event itself.

2 What camera angle should I use?

Shooting up from a low angle is commonly used to give the subject dominance and power; shooting down, to make it seem weak and inferior—or to identify the viewer with a superior position.

Some subjects make sense only from a high angle—for example, a bowl of soup, a phonograph record, or certain square-dance patterns. With some subjects the angle depends on your purpose: you shoot a bowl on the level when stressing its profile as characteristic of a particular art style, but from overhead if interested in its contents.

There is always a best angle from which to show such operations as working at looms, operating sewing machines, making block prints, and so on. If you have to determine the angle before actually seeing the operation, it pays to find out whether the operator is right- or left-handed; otherwise, you may have to reverse your setup completely. If the television viewers are expected to be able to copy the process being demonstrated, try to show the viewers the materials as they will face them when they try the process for themselves.

Some dramatic segments employ subjective camera angles: the camera assumes the point of view of one of the characters so that the viewer will identify more closely with that player's experience. This technique usually requires that the shooting be stopped while the camera is placed in the character's position. Hence it is feasible only when recording in segments on film or video tape, which can subsequently be edited together.

3 What framing—loose or tight?

Sometimes you need to get very close to details that make the points most strongly: glaring eyes, beads of sweat on a brow, or the flying fingers of a pianist during a nimble passage. In this latter case, the closer the fingers, the more their changing angles will contrast with the fixed margins of the frame, thus making them seem to fly even faster.

Shoot loose, however, when the environment adds meaning to the shot. An expanse of bookshelves may reinforce the authority of a learned person. The shadowy space of an empty house may add suspense. Or the space left in front of a crippled child who is walking for the first time without his crutch may add more impact to his achievement.

4 What perspective?

Perspective can be varied by your choice of lens field of view. For example, an extreme wide angle of view (wide-angle lens) can be used to:

. . . distort facial closeups for a grotesque or comic effect.

. . . increase the apparent force of a blow delivered toward camera.

. . . intensify the speed and enlargement of persons or vehicles moving toward the camera, being even more effective sometimes when used from a low camera position.

. . . increase the difference in scale between a subject in the foreground and one farther away.

. . . add apparent depth to a room or increase the apparent length of an automobile that is angled toward the camera.

. . . make a small subject in the foreground dominate a larger one in the background.

5 What focus?

Soft focus is sometimes used to disguise the lines on a face that has passed its bloom. It can help to create a romantic mood. It can dematerialize the background in a scene that depends more upon feeling or spirit than upon clear perception of physical material, such as poetry readings or a minister's sermon. By soft focusing what doesn't matter, you can make what does matter assert itself more positively.

6 What lighting quality—hard or soft?

Hard lighting, showing abrupt transitions between strongly contrasting highlights and shadows, is appropriate for action containing sudden reversals, striking surprises, intense climaxes, and boldly delineated characters. It is produced by focused spotlights, aimed at an angle to the camera, with little diffuse light to soften the shadows.

Soft lighting, used for gentler and less dramatic action, has limited contrast and gradual transitions between highlights and shadows. For this, the spotlights are flooded out, and scoops with diffusion media or soft lights are used for fill light, to dilute the shadows.

7 What lighting—high or low key?

Most programs are played in the relatively even, bright-appearing illumination known as "high key." Night scenes or somber ones use "low key," which simulates low illumination. "Simulates" is used advisedly, for, as mentioned in Chapter 4, the video engineer will object to dimming all the lights on the scene. Enough illumination is needed to prevent a noisy picture. Maintaining some highlights as "reference whites" to help the engineer establish the proper levels of other tones is also desirable.

High key is not achieved simply by turning on more and more light. As the light is increased, the lenses will have to be stopped down to keep some of it from entering the camera; and light which does not enter the camera goes wasted. Besides, the light will seem bright only when there are dark tones present to contrast with it. If the performers' faces do not seem bright enough, the solution may be not to add more light to them, but rather to gain more contrast by reducing the background illumination. This remedy will also save some electrical power.

8 What linear composition?

A model who bends her wrist and elbow in sharp angles will add little grace or salesmanship to a commercial for beauty aids, nor will a display of such products if it is composed primarily in rectangles.

Lines stimulate different responses depending on their direction and configuration. Vertical lines are generally used to denote strength and stability—or if very high, aspiration; horizontals are used for calm and repose; diagonals for activity; zigzags for excitement; plump curves for affluence; gently flowing curves for grace.

Study the use of lines in painting. For example, observe how Fragonard used curves for grace and voluptuousness in *The Bathers* and how Titian lent acuity to his sitter's character by the acute angles in his *Man with Glove.*

9 What color?

That colors can symbolize meanings and stimulate emotional reactions seems evident, but much that has been stated on this subject is speculative. The matter is complicated, since the effect will differ depending on whether a hue is dull or intense, light or dark. It will also depend on what colors are combined in a given scheme. Thus the juxtaposition of intense complementaries such as red and blue-green will be more exciting than an arrangement of analogous hues such as blue and violet; and even more sedate will be the monochromatic scheme in which a single hue is varied in saturation and brightness, as when orange is modified to produce harmonies in tan and brown. Furthermore, the effects of color vary with the sex, health, age, nationality, associations, and other characteristics of the beholder, making generalizations unreliable.

Nevertheless, many works on color assign "feelings" to the various hues. For example,

Red:	exciting, fervid, active
Orange:	lively, energetic, forceful
Yellow:	cheerful, inspiring, vital
Green:	peaceful, quieting, refreshing
Blue:	subduing, sober
Purple:	dignified, mournful
White:	pure, clean, youthful
Black:	ominous, deadly, depressing

Use such tables at your own discretion.

10 What physical relationships between the performers?

Whether characters face or shun each other, whether they are distant or close, whether one is higher than another or on the same level—such physical relationships are one of the dramatic director's principle means of expression, as you learn by consulting books about directing for the theater.

In nondramatic programs, too, the physical relationship between performers can be used to express their intellectual or emotional relationship. For example, on a public affairs program participants who represent opposing views will seem to be more in conflict if they confront each other across some separating space or person than if they are seated side by side. On a quiz show, panelists of the same team would logically be adjacent to one another and facing in the same direction, whereas the moderator would be distinguished from them by being assigned a separate location.

Chapter 10

Keeping Up with the Action

In the preceding nine chapters you have been concerned with the appearance of the television picture as if it were halted at a given moment. But a program consists of many successive moments and many changing pictures. The arrangement of pictures in time sequence is often referred to as "pictorial continuity."

Continuity means that something keeps going without interruption. The important thing to keep going without interruption is your viewers' absorption in the program. They should remain immersed in the program content, moving from one picture statement to another, with no obstacles to their concentration or understanding.

They should not be frustrated by not being shown what they want to see when they want to see it.

They should not be distracted from the content to the technical means or "mechanics" by which the content is communicated.

They should not be perplexed by failing to understand how each new picture they see is related to those which preceded it.

These last three sentences provide the subjects for the chapters that you will read next. In this chapter you are going to consider the first sentence and the rule that follows from it:

1 Show what your viewers want to see when they want to see it.

To do this, you must be ready to show each event as it happens. Hence, you must have your camera in the right place at the right time. In terms of the trade, you are "hung" when the only available camera is unable to get the shot you need. This situation may be due to any of several reasons. The camera may be in the wrong place or aimed in the wrong direction or obstructed by set elements or other cameras and time may be short to right these wrongs.

But the wrongs should never have occurred in the first place, had the camerawork been planned correctly. In this chapter, therefore, you will find a number of recommendations for keeping your cameras ready to take the action as it occurs. The first of these recommendations is:

2 Plan your shot alternation before coming to the studio.

In *Figure 10/1*, camera 1 is logically situated to take the last shot of the master of ceremonies as the director cues a dissolve into closing captions on the title cards—but camera 2 is in no position to get that next shot of the cards. To avoid such predicaments, plan your camera treatment in advance, dovetailing shots and action so that each time a particular subject needs to be shown, the camera that can show it best is always available.

Fig. 10/1

3 Remember your camera plan.

Having made your camera plan, be sure that you have it so clearly in mind that, while calling the shots, you can readily remember what's supposed to happen next and call for it without causing any delays yourself. The more you depend upon reading your script, the more liable you are to lose your place in it, and the more you must take your attention away from a critical inspection of the pictures and sound that are telling your story on the air.

4 Make sure that the camera operators and performers understand your plan.

4.1   Have them demonstrate that they do.

The best assurance that they do understand is to have them demonstrate the desired action during rehearsal. Then you'll know there is time enough for the camera to move to its new position, for instance, and that the camera operator understands what this position is to be.

4.2   When rehearsal is short, at least rehearse the more critical and difficult maneuvers.

Walk the performers through any major changes of position while the camera operators try following them. Know in advance which effects you must devote your time to and how much time to allow for each. Don't become so immersed in perfecting one of them that you rob time from the others.

4.3   If there's no rehearsal, brief the camera operators in advance.

Catch them when you can to prepare them for difficult maneuvers: "You'll be boomed down on Betsy, seated behind her desk. Then you'll boom up as she rises, dolly back diagonally to your left as she comes forward to the pedestal, ending wide enough to let in the guest and favor him; he'll be standing at the left of the pedestal. Think you can find a minute to practice it before air time?" It's likely the camera operator will, not wanting a reputation for sloppy camerawork; and even if the performers aren't present, the operator can practice in relation to the furniture.

4.4   Prepare shot sheets.

When shots promise to come too thick and fast for adequate verbal explanation during the program, you can prepare a shot sheet to be taped to the back of each camera for the camera operators to read. Here are two correlated examples:

CAMERA 1		CAMERA 2	
Shot #		Shot #	
1	Title one easel.	2	CU host (left chair) Dolly
3	CU guest (right chair)		back into 2-shot.
5	Waist shot of guest &	4	Same; pan them to pedestal.
	trophy on pedestal.	6	Both, with trophy, at pedestal.
7	CU trophy.		

. . . and so on.

4.5   Explain, when necessary, from the studio floor.

You can expedite some matters by explaining them, not from the control room, but from the studio floor, where you can actually point out locations and demonstrate positions without having to describe them through the studio intercom or though the floor director, which can sometimes be a difficult and time-wasting procedure. While working on the floor, you can ask someone back in the control room to punch up the shots for your inspection on the studio monitor.

5   Before the actual performance, make sure that things are restored to their opening positions.

Ascertain that cards are restacked in the correct order on easels, film recued, slide projectors reset, properties put back in their proper places, so that the right subject will be in the right place at the right time.

6 When shooting ad lib, keep a cover shot.

Some shows, of course, cannot be rehearsed. In a ball game or a panel show, for instance, you will know the general pattern of the action, but you cannot predict the specific sequence in which it will develop. Nevertheless, you will need some overall plan that will let you show the unexpected when it occurs.

When action is ad lib and you yourself cannot get a good view of it, you may wish to let the camera operators find their own shots, hoping thereby to catch colorful bits of human interest or unanticipated fast developments. Beware, however, lest all of your cameras get frozen on closeups so that none is available for some important occurrence elsewhere in the scene. It is prudent to reserve one camera for cover shots—shots that show the total situation. Then, when the unexpected occurs, you can take the cover shot until you have time to swing another camera over for a closer look at the situation.

Incidentally, make it clear in advance whether you do want the camera operators to find their own shots or to wait for your directions. Otherwise, they may wander off a shot that you were planning to return to and thus leave you in trouble.

7 Assign areas of responsibility.

It is sometimes advisable to assign to each camera operator a specific area of responsibility beyond which he or she should not stray. In covering a baseball game, for instance, one camera may be responsible for the pitcher's delivery to the batter, another (on a wide lens) to establish where the hit goes, and a third to take close shots of the ball being fielded, etcetera.

A similar arrangement can be made with your camera operators in studio situations, such as the round-table discussion that is diagrammed in *Figure 10/2.* Camera 1 is assigned to take the chairperson and occasional shots of the total group. Camera 2 is responsible for panelist B, and camera 3 for panelist D. When either camera 2 or 3 is not feeding program, it is responsible for panelist C. For example, D has been speaking on camera 3. If C

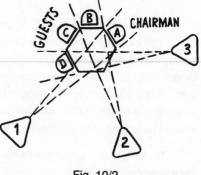

Fig. 10/2

speaks next, it is camera 2's responsibility to get the shot. On the other hand, if B has been speaking on camera 2, and then C speaks, it is camera 3's responsibility to get C. If D should then interrupt, camera 3 will pan from C to D. This pan will work with maximum efficiency if the panelists are required to signal and be acknowledged by the chairperson before speaking, thus giving the camera operators advance notice about which panelist they are to frame next.

8 Try to eliminate extra-quick shot changes.

During continuous sequences of action, it can take a substantial length of time to get the next shot ready. For example, while camera 1 is feeding its signal, the director considers the next subject, then says, "2, on the little girl's face." Then the operator of camera 2 has to find the little girl, pan to her, zoom or dolly to a closeup, adjust framing, and focus the lens. Not until then can the director say, "Take 2."

Realize, therefore, that you cannot expect to change shots as quickly as in some edited tape sequences. This is particularly true in unrehearsed productions. However, you can speed up your shot changes by observing some of the following recommendations when you are planning your camera setup.

9 Arrange for a sequence of subjects to be shot in the same location.

A camera operator can find the next shot quickly if the subjects follow one another in the same location. For demonstrations, therefore, it is often advisable to have but a single area on which the camera assigned to closeups is trained and where materials are shown one after another. Sometimes the material can be rolled past the camera on castored stands, or placed around the circumference of a round table that revolves like a "lazy Susan" past the lens.

Similarly, it is helpful to concentrate pictures, charts, and other graphics in a single area. Thus, the rectangular opening shown in *Figure 10/3* is designed to hold either a stock of opaque cards or a rear projection screen on which a series of slides can be shown. The revolving cubes in *Figure 10/4* can bring before camera four different surfaces, which may include a chalkboard, magnetic board, or cork boards for mounting picture displays.

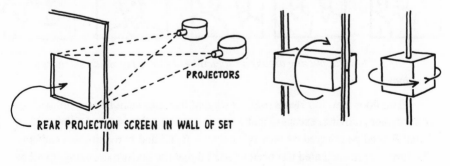

PROJECTORS

REAR PROJECTION SCREEN IN WALL OF SET

Fig. 10/3   Fig. 10/4

Such concentrated areas minimize the delays and possible errors caused by having to move the camera between shots. They also conserve studio space and restrict the area that needs to be lighted.

10 Minimize unnecessary camera movement.

10.1 Find base positions from which cameras can command a maximum variety of shots without needless adjusts.

Unless camera rehearsal time is generous, minimize camera movement except when it is necessary for an intended effect. Obviously, you may want to dolly in to support a climax, or dolly out to admit new subject matter, or pan with a moving performer. But you will not want to move your cameras unnecessarily, merely so that they can get to frame their next subject.

10.2 Find locations from which the cameras can get a variety of shots without moving.

In many situations using the zoom lens can be substituted for the dolly, thereby saving time and eliminating clumsy and noisy camera movements. With a zoom lens on the camera in *Figure 10/5*, the wide-angle zoom takes in all three persons. As it is zoomed in, the camera operator can get either B and C or A and B. Continuing to zoom in, the operator can now get a closeup of any one of them. At the most telephoto position, the lens can frame a small object displayed by any of them.

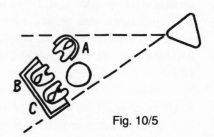

Fig. 10/5

10.3 Several playing areas can sometimes be arced around central camera locations.

The floor plan in *Figure 10/6* shows that five areas can be covered without either camera moving, except to make minor framing adjustments. Of these areas, A and E need be covered by only one camera; B, C, and D require two cameras. The furniture in each area has been so angled that the performers using it will be facing camera as much as possible when they are addressing their normal centers

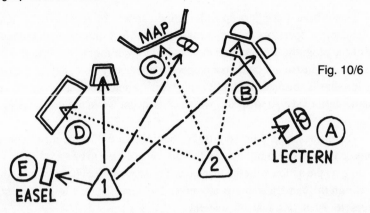

Fig. 10/6

of attention. In area B, for example, camera 2 favors the performer in the left chair behind the desk, and camera 1 the performer in the right chair. In area C, camera 1 would favor the standing performer; camera 2 would be perpendicular to the map for unforeshortened closeups of it. In area D, camera 2 would take the persons on the sofa while camera 1 covered the person in the armchair.

11 Compress your settings.

Don't disperse the playing areas of your setting so widely that to cover them requires unnecessary camera placements or needlessly long pans from one subject to another.

For example, the instructor in a program on music appreciation plays a short passage on a phonograph record, then crosses to a chalkboard to diagram the musical construction of the passage. As staged by a directing student who was used to settings that fill the whole proscenium opening of a theater, the action went like this (*Figure 10/7*):

Performer plays
record here . . . . then crosses to chalkboard here:

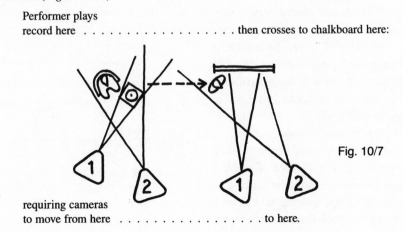

Fig. 10/7

requiring cameras
to move from here . . . . to here.

This caused a needless spread of studio area to be occupied and lighted. It put the camera operators to unnecessary work. Most important, it damaged the pace of the program. Because the student had to wait for the cameras to make the transition, the instructor could not proceed immediately from playing the music to diagramming it. Instead, he had to fill it with some needless remarks, verbally vamping until ready, so to speak, with a consequent weakening of his hold on the audience.

There was no need for so diffuse a setting, for unlike the theater, there was no proscenium frame to fill; nor did the chalkboard have to be so far away to avoid intruding on the action with the turntable. The scene in television is only what one sees within the camera frame at any given moment. Pan or tilt the camera a few degrees to what lies just outside the present frame, and you have a totally new background—or, for that matter, simply rearrange the performers within your present frame and you have a very different looking picture.

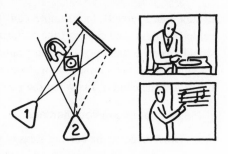

If, as in *Figure 10/8*, the chalkboard is placed quite close to the turntable, a tilt-up of both cameras as the instructor rises will effect a complete change of scene without risking the delay and chance for error that can result from trucking the cameras into new locations.

Fig. 10/8

12   Give moving cameras an orderly path.

When your cameras need to move to one subject after another, arrange the subjects so that the cameras can progress in logical and orderly paths.

Figure 10/9 shows an exhibit of paintings so arranged that, as the two commentators walk from one painting to the next, the cameras drop back in straight paths. As the discussion of each painting nears its end, camera 2 is released from a closeup of the painting to retire to its next location. Camera 1 shows the commentators advancing to the next painting, dollying back in pace with them. Since the cameras repeat

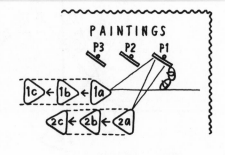

Fig. 10/9

this maneuver for every painting, there is little chance for anyone, camera operators or performers, to get confused.

An orderly path should be provided for panning as well as for dollying. *Figure 10/10* represents a tier of shelves containing items to be viewed in closeup, one after another, as each is discussed. Numerals indicate the order in which the items should be discussed so that the camera can follow the smooth and even progression traced by the arrowed dash line. Note that item #4 comes directly beneath item #3 so that the camera can tilt down to it directly rather than having to retrace awkwardly to the left end of the shelf, thus breaking the rhythm of the progression and risking a delay in keeping up with the discussion.

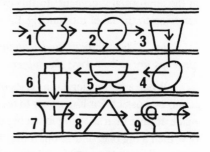

Fig. 10/10

13 Minimize changing camera positions and reframing.

Particularly on unrehearsed and unscripted programs, the time taken to reference and focus a lens may be enough to miss a shot. To guard against this:

13.1 Advise your performers to give sufficient time for changes.

For example, on a two-camera program you have used camera 1 on a wide lens to establish a performer with a number of variously sized objects that are to be discussed. Your talent begins with a large object, which you take in a closeup by camera 2. Talk about this large object by the talent will have to last long enough so that camera 1 can zoom to a narrow shot for the closeup of a much smaller object that will be referred to next.

In *Figure 10/11*, A, followed by camera 2, has just approached the counter to introduce the viewers to B, who will presently show A the label on a jug. Camera 1 is in the only good position to take a closeup of this label. First, however, it is needed for a one-shot of B, which will provide a better notion of B's appearance than the introductory view taken in profile by camera 1's two-shot. The focal length setting on camera 1's lens used for the close shot is too wide for a sufficiently close

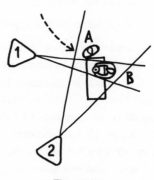

Fig. 10/11

shot of the label. Rather than having camera 1 tilt down from B's face while zooming in on the label, showing the viewer an unattractive transition of the shot across the chest of B and the top of the jar to the closeup of the label, the director returns to camera 2's two-shot. This frees camera 1 to zoom in on the label and frame it up while off the air. Then the director can cut to the close shot of the label at the appropriate moment. In this example, the director must caution B against referring to the label too quickly, thus allowing the camera to frame up the shot.

13.2   Fewer focus and framing changes are needed if, when a series of closeups are to be taken, the subjects can be grouped in relatively uniform sizes.

When a performer has a series of variously sized objects to show in closeup, it may be possible for him or her to regulate the order in which reference to them is made. Rather than showing first a big object, then a small one, then a middle-sized one, then a big one, and so on, it may be possible to show all the big ones, then all the middle-sized ones, then all the small ones.

This principle also applies to a series of pictures stacked on an easel. Ideally, such pictures should be uniformly sized so that only slight framing changes are required. If the pictures you have procured are not uniform, it may pay to have them rephotographed to identical dimensions.

14   Locate and maneuver your subjects with regard for camera location, lens focal length, and framing being used.

Besides moving your camera in relation to the subjects, remember that you can also move the subjects in relation to the camera, arranging them to suit the location for the camera and the lens it is using, thus eliminating needless zooming and camera redeployment. This can be done by applying a principle that has already been introduced to you:

14.1   Place small subjects closer to the lens, big ones farther from it.

Here are some further applications for the principle:

Example 1: Figure 10/12 diagrams the opening of an interview program. Camera 1 is assigned to the opening titles and, quickly thereafter, a closeup of B, as introduced by A. To hasten camera 1's time between these shots, the director has located the titles at the distance that will allow the operator to change only focus without having to zoom in or out to reframe for B.

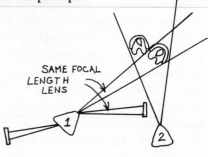

Fig. 10/12

Notice also that, in order to minimize panning time, the titles are only a few degrees off camera 1's angle toward B, rather than, for instance, at the place indicated by the dash lines.

Example 2: The principle also applies to the deployment of characters in dramatic action. Consider a sequence in which A, entering his front hall from outdoors, notices an unfamiliar hat on the hatrack and looks surprised. At the door of the living room he meets his wife, B, who tells him that they have a visitor. She takes him into the room and introduces him to the visitor, C.

Figure 10/13 shows how this sequence has been arranged for a continuous pan by a stationary camera. The hatrack is just far enough from camera 2 so that the upper part of A and the part of the rack that holds the unfamiliar hat will fill the screen when A has reached the rack. After this, A comes even closer to camera, where his surprised expression will be especially evident. Turning to enter the living room, he moves just far enough away from

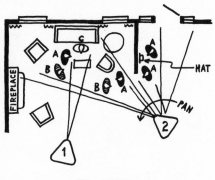

Fig. 10/13

camera to allow room for B to enter the shot. The introduction to C is staged still farther from camera, where all three characters can be framed.

The principle demonstrated here is especially recommended for productions done with one camera. For changes of framing in such productions, the only alternative is to dolly or zoom in and out, which, if done frequently and hurriedly, will make the viewer conscious of camera movement and perhaps unduly restless as well.

Even when multiple cameras are available, it may be desirable, as in the just-cited instance of A and his visitor, to sustain a sequence on one camera. The avoidance of takes to other cameras preserves the continuity of A's approach to his guest. And since takes can lose their effectiveness through needless repetition, the sustained shot also protects the impact of the next shot, which will be taken by camera 1 of the guest when he announces the purpose of his visit.

15   Let your actors do the walking—more than the camera operators.

Unrehearsed zooms and camera redeployment are liable to result in late shots, missed shots, or poor shots. For productions involving a large number and variety of shots (as dramas, for instance, often do), it is sometimes more feasible and less expensive to devote more time to dry rehearsals with the performers outside of the studio than to facilities rehearsals with the camera operators. If so, it makes sense to keep the camerawork as simple as possible, putting more obligation on the performers to be at the right distances and facing in the right directions to get the shots you need. The ultimate is attained when all the camera operators have to do is stay put and focus what unfolds before them.

Chapter 11

Concealing Mechanics

1 Don't distract your viewer's attention from the content to the technique by which the content is communicated.

Be proficient at "the art that conceals art."

1.1 This instruction does not apply if the audience accepts a device as a necessary and acknowledged part of the communication.

Students watching a televised biology lesson are likely to realize the advantage of having a television camera connected to the microscope and, seeing it thus on the screen, will subordinate their consciousness of it as an instrument to their interest in what it has to show. And if an audience has been made aware from the outset that it is watching a frankly "studio" type of program, it is not likely to resent the sight of microphones in the picture or object to a performer asking that the camera move in for a closer look at something. In a program that aims to create the illusion of action existing quite independently of television, of course, the intrusion of the tools of television would be quite out of place.

In any kind of production, however, there are other ways to distract the viewers besides showing them the tools of the trade. For example:

2 Avoid taking new shots without a reason that is evident to the viewer.

You can distract and perplex the viewers by taking a new shot without a reason that is evident to them. Although you may have your own technical reasons for getting off a camera (perhaps it must be released to set up for a subsequent shot), all the viewers see is that the subject has jumped unaccountably in size or screen location without providing any more significant visual information than they had before. So there is punctuation. Where there shouldn't be, like inserting. A period in the middle of a sentence.

2.1   The most valid reason for taking a new shot is to tell what the previous shot could not have told, or told as well.

Therefore, one changes cameras to reveal a newly significant subject or to eliminate one no longer significant—or, remaining with the same subject, to show a newly significant aspect of it, either by changing the angle of view or by altering the amount of area framed as the action expands or contracts.

2.2   Think twice about changing shots merely for visual variety.

A reason sometimes advanced for changing shots is to avoid monotony when the subject (a public speaker, for instance) must remain on the screen as the sole center of interest for minutes at a time. Hence, usually at quite arbitrary moments, the director takes a different view of the subject, which rarely reveals anything new and meaningful concerning the program content that did not appear in the previous shot.

It would appear that such a shot change provides only a superficial and not very lasting regeneration of interest. Interest would seem to come, rather, from perceiving whatever new, significant information the new shot reveals. Therefore, if constant visual interest is held to be desirable, the main problem, seemingly, is to select and develop a topic that is visually expressive. And if shot changes are wanted, the first step in making them possible is to introduce changes in the subject matter that will motivate the shot changes.

If this cannot be done, if the presentation depends mainly on speech by a single performer, one should try for a visually expressive speaker. To the extent that his or her features, gestures, and bodily attitudes are varied and meaningful, there will be less need for an arbitrary change of shot.

2.3   Sometimes frequent shot changes are not appreciated.

Although a young director may not believe it, some audiences are capable of becoming quite engrossed in what a speaker has to say to them and of being satisfied with what visual expression they can read in one's face, hands, and bodily attitude; and once in visual communion with the speaker's eyes, they can be irritated to have this contact and their mental concentration broken by an unmotivated change in their relationship with the speaker. A change of visual stimulus that calls for interpretation by their visual channel can disturb their reception through the aural channel and therefore may damage their assimilation of auditory subject matter, such as intellectual discourse, poetry, or music.

2.4 Really pay attention to the program content.

Some directors, it seems, call for new shots simply because they get restless sitting in the control room without enough to do. Their job is to call the shots, and call them they will: they are more interested in shot calling than in the nature of the program content. They do not really listen to the content or try to identify themselves with the target audience.

But you should. Then, if in your best judgment new takes are indicated, try not to make them arbitrary. By placing them between the paragraphs of a speech or the phrases of music, you can use them to clarify the structure of the communication. New shots can reinforce major changes in the development of the subject matter; and when the new shots are also closer ones, they can emphasize the arrival of a more important or more exciting part of the proceedings.

2.5 You should be able to advance a reason for every shot you take.

The reason should not derive from your own requirements, but from the content and purpose of the communication. This is the only kind of reason that will be understood by the audience and that will therefore keep the audience immersed in the program content.

3 Avoid camera movement without a reason that is evident to the viewer.

Evident reasons should exist not only for takes, but also for every other kind of picture change, including those produced by camera movement such as by panning and dollying.

3.1 Provide a lead for the camera to follow.

When a camera pans to follow a moving subject, the motivation is evident. But if a picture suddenly moves off a stationary subject without viewers knowing why, they may be startled, puzzled, and forced to think "The camera is moving," whereas they should be concentrating solely on the new pictorial information that the camera is bringing into view.

This distraction can be prevented by providing a lead for the camera to follow. The lead can be visual, as when a performer glances toward a new center of interest before the camera pans to it, or as when a demonstrator gestures along a row of items, which the camera is to traverse. The lead can also be auditory, as when a voice or noise is heard outside the frame, or a speaker within the frame directs attention to something that is out of sight. Both auditory and visual leads are supplied by the panelist who, during introduction, turns toward his neighbor, saying, "And on my left . . ." to motivate the pan.

3.2   If a camera movement continues after the reason for it has ceased, attention will go from the subject matter to the mechanics of the movement.

For example, two performers walk forward to investigate something in the foreground, the camera zooming out or dollying back as they advance. All will be well if the camera keeps pace with them so that when they stop, it stops—but if, through some need to adjust its framing, it continues to zoom out or dolly back, its movement will become noticed. The purpose of the movement was to accompany the performers to their destination. Once they have reached that destination, any further camera motion will impinge on the viewer's consciousness as an unmotivated mechanical adjustment.

3.3   Suit the pace of the camera movement to the viewer's urgency to see what it reveals.

Sometimes a camera movement may call attention to itself because its pace is inconsistent with the degree of motivation for a change of picture. A gunshot may be fired outside the frame, motivating the camera to pan rapidly toward the source of the explosion. This movement (called a "whip" or "swish pan") occurs so suddenly that it will be disturbing if not justified by the urgency of the situation. One does not use it to pan to someone who says, "I think I'd like a second lump of sugar, if you don't mind, old fellow."

Another kind of swift picture change can be achieved by the zoom-in. Thus, one may zoom in rapidly on a ringing telephone that is expected to carry a message from the governor concerning the reprieve of a condemned man. Since the matter is urgent, the speed of the zoom is justified.

Sometimes, however, a camera movement can exceed the speed limit. For example, a director may have a vocalist in long shot and wish to dolly in on her to support the climax of her rendition. This is a fairly subtle motivation, which will not strike the viewer as an urgent reason for moving closer; hence the viewer's concentration may be disturbed unless the camera creeps in ever so gradually.

Too slow can be as disturbing as too fast. The director is supposed to show his viewers what they want to see when they want to see it. It will not do to be late in panning to the product the demonstrator has started to extol, or to delay the dolly-back or zoom-out when the master of ceremonies says, "Standing beside me is a young lady I think you are going to appreciate." Tardiness of even a second is sometimes enough to blur the desired accent. The very moment your viewers perceive the need for a change, you must be ready to deliver it.

3.4   If you must make a technical adjustment, make it as imperceptible as possible.

Sometimes you must move the camera for some technical reason, which is not evident to the audience. If so, make the best of a bad bargain by keeping the movement as imperceptible as possible. Apply caution to compositional adjustment, as when the headroom is wrong or a studio card has been poorly framed and the camera must move to set things right.

4 Avoid obviously repetitive devices.

4.1 Techniques are liable to show when they are repeated in too frequent and obvious a rhythm.

The wrong way to shoot a tennis match is to station a camera off one end of the net and wag it back and forth as the ball changes courts. A poor way to take a series of close shots is to zoom in and out, in and out, in and out, and in and out. This makes the mechanics too obvious and can make some viewers queasy. The usual cause for this technique stems from the director trying to tell too much of the story with a single shot. As a director looking at such a technique, see if you can devise a way that better covers the subject in front of the camera. If you are confined to the use of one camera with a zoom lens for a sequence that requires a number of closeups, remember the advice in the preceding chapter about placing subjects for one-camera sequences.

4.2 Consciousness of camerawork can result from a monotonous repetition of the same shot sequence.

Thus, avoid a pattern of: two-shot, closeup, two-shot, closeup, two-shot, closeup, or: closeup host, closeup guest, closeup host, closeup guest, *ad infinitum*. A repetitive series of one-shots can be varied by an occasional group shot. A static situation with limited opportunities for shot variety can sometimes be improved by providing some reason and opportunity for the performers to move into different physical relationships.

The more frequently you cut from camera to camera at the opening of a sequence involving subjects in fixed position, the more quickly you can exhaust your possible number of shot combinations. These may then have to be repeated over and over, each time becoming more apparent and monotonous.

5 Restrict technical virtuosity to the proper times and places.

There comes a time in the development of some directors when they tire of conventional methods and want to express their virtuosity. This may lead them to overuse split screens, wipes, chroma key, ADO, or other new digital effects, replacing simple takes with fancy uses of wide-angle lenses and unusual camera angles to produce extremely foreshortened perspective—or to shoot from inside the fireplace, or from outside the window, or through the banister railing, or between straddled legs, or from some other vantage point where it is difficult to imagine an observer being located. Since such shots are usually out of harmony with those which have preceded them, they call attention to themselves as exploitations of technology and technique rather than as sincere and modest servants of the communication purpose. Unless the show is consistently stylized to allow such *tours de force,* they are as inappropriate as the setting for an illusionistic play that wins applause as the curtain opens.

6   Take some responsibility on yourself for inept operation by your crews.

It is obviously unfortunate when the wrong slide comes up, or cameras lurch and waver, go out of frame or focus, or are late getting their shots. Such ineptitudes not only call attention to the mechanics of production, but to faulty mechanics as well.

Although you may wish to pass the blame for such shortcomings to inexperienced crews or insufficient rehearsal time, be sure that you yourself have not failed to give sufficiently clear instructions, to allow enough time for focus changes and camera repositioning, or to have the camera on a wide enough lens that can be kept in focus while moving. If facilities rehearsal is short, have you accomplished everything you should prior to it? Have you made the most efficient use of that rehearsal? (In this connection, you may wish to read Chapter 25 on "Efficiency" in Part Two of this book.)

7   Look and listen critically, and insist on as much perfection as it is possible to achieve under the circumstances.

There is much truth in the observation that professionalism is, in general, a painstaking attention to details. An example of attention to details is provided by the following note, written to a student director about a single camera movement in one of his studio exercises:

"You ask a pedestal camera operator to make a fast dolly-in toward a standing performer. First, be sure that the camera operator is using a wide lens, which will make focusing easier and provide for the shortest possible distance to traverse with the dolly. Note that, even so, the camera goes slightly out of focus. Find the trouble: the operator doesn't keep a hand on the focus knob. Get the operator to practice and memorize how much to turn the knob, and at what speed to approach the subject. Next, notice that as the camera comes closer, the operator has to tilt up more and more, changing the angle of view for no apparent reason. Therefore, better have the operator pedestal up to put the camera lens at the subject's eye level. Then see how the camera wavers during the move. To simplify the operator's control of it, have every moving part not necessary for the move locked down: pan, tilt, and boom height. Now, observe that as the operator comes close to the subject that facial distortion is apparent. Hence, provide a framing where you want the camera operator to stop. Lastly, recognize that the dolly-in lags a little behind the action, so work to improve its timing."

All this for a single camera movement! True, it involved an inexperienced operator; but owing to job turnover, camera operators at local stations are not always experienced, and even those who can handle the mechanical aspects of the operation may need to have their esthetic standards raised. And no matter how professional the crew, there are always details to work on. It's possible to work more than an hour on a single one-minute commercial without attaining a perfection to be really proud of.

8 Don't bite off more than you can chew.

Much of the smoothness of your production may depend on how elaborate an undertaking you attempt. Laudable as their courage and optimism may be, student directors often attempt lighting and staging effects that are too ambitious to perfect with the time and resources available. Take the conditions into account—the competencies of your production crew members, how much teamwork they are capable of achieving, the amount of studio space available, the capacities of the equipment, the possible existence of other projects that will interfere with yours— and if these conditions seem unfavorable for achieving what you have conceived, either seek to improve the conditions before your time in studio, or modify your conception to what you can reasonably hope to achieve under the circumstances. A dry-ice cloud effect isn't worth it if, to make it work properly, you have to neglect more essential aspects of your production.

Chapter 12

Spatial Relationships

1 Don't perplex your viewers by failing to show them how each new picture is related to the preceding ones. It looks like rain.

The second sentence was out of context. You couldn't relate it to what you'd been reading previously. It probably startled you and puzzled you, interrupting your train of thought. The same thing can happen to your viewers if you show them a picture that they cannot immediately relate to the program content. True, your picture may not be as obviously unrelated as the sentence was to its context. Nevertheless, as this and the two following chapters will reveal, there are several ways in which new shots may fail to connect smoothly enough with the shots that have preceded them. This chapter is concerned with spatial connections.

2 The viewers must know where things are located in relation to one another.

They will know this quite certainly as long as you remain on one camera. Even when it pans and dollies, the camera traces a connecting path from one subject to another. Space in this instance is continuous. But by taking a new shot, you chop space apart. To use a term synonymous in the trade with "take," you "cut." You cut to a new location or a new subject; or if you remain with the same subject, you cut to a different position of it, or a different side of it, or a new relation between it and its environment—but when cutting these pieces, you must assemble them in an intelligible pattern.

When shooting, then, take pains to clarify the location of people and things and the physical relationships between them.

3 Show where new subjects are located with reference to those previously seen.

For example, what is wrong with the following shot series?

An interviewer, shown alone, introduces his guest.
The guest, alone.
The interviewer again, still alone.
The guest again, still alone.

The error is that the two persons are never seen together. The viewer never learns whether they are side by side or across the room from each other.

3.1 Clarify the position not only of persons but also of things:

Chest shot of a scientist (seated at a counter which is not shown).
Pan with her as she rises, moves a few steps, and stops.
Closeup of a microscope and, presently, a hand adjusting it.

Where is the microscope? Whose hand is it? Actually, the microscope is farther down the same counter at which the scientist was sitting, and the hand is her hand. . . . But from the pictures who would know it?

3.2 Clarification may also be needed when the shots are confined to the body of one person.

Consider these shots of a golf professional, who is demonstrating how to putt:

The "pro," from waist up, talking to camera.
A body, from waist down, with hands holding a golf club.

Do the two parts of the body belong to the same person? The viewer cannot be certain from this pictorial dissection.

4 Connect up space by panning, tilting, zooming, or dollying back.

To clarify relationship such as those in the examples just cited, one solution is to pan, tilt, zoom, or dolly back, depending on which of these camera movements is appropriate. In shooting the golf pro, the director could have tilted down from the upper to the lower part of his body. In the case of the interviewer and his guest, the director could have panned from the interviewer to the guest—or could have zoomed out or dollied back from the interviewer into a two-shot that included the guest. In all cases, the camera would traverse a continuous path to connect one subject with another.

5   Introduce the subject of the next shot in the present shot.

This is another way to correct the examples: you introduce the subject of the next shot in the present shot. Before taking a one-shot of the guest, you take a two-shot, which shows him with the interviewer. Before taking the shot of the pro's hands and club, you show his whole body. In the case of the scientist and her microscope, you have her rise in a shot that includes both her and the countertop. When you pan with her, using this framing, the microscope will slide into view as she nears it, and its relation to her will be evident before it is isolated in a closeup.

6   Use an establishing shot.

Each of the wider shots just recommended is an example of an establishing shot, so called because it establishes the location of a detail with reference to the total situation of which it is a part.

6.1   Although, in the examples just cited, it precedes the closer shot, it need not always do so, provided it occurs in time to forestall perplexity.

For example, it might be possible to take one-shots both of the interviewer and of his guest before taking a third shot that included them together. It is unlikely that the viewer would have worried about their spacial relationship until then.

6.2   An establishing shot is advisable at or near the beginning of any sequence involving several components in the same location.

It establishes the overall relationships so that the viewers will remain oriented when, in the shots that follow, they see the components separately or in various partial combinations. Thus, an overall shot of a dining table will prepare the way for various closer shots of the diners who are seated at it.

6.3   When the location is too wide to be easily discerned in a stationary shot, the establishing may be done with a pan.

For example, if you are shooting at the location of a wrecked train, an opening pan along the cars will prepare for a series of subsequent shots, each focusing on a different detail of the disaster.

7   Establish whatever the viewers will be bothered by not seeing.

Apart from establishing relationships with reference to subsequent shots, you need to shoot wide enough to establish what is happening in the present shot. For example, a performer who has been shown from waist up suddenly sinks down in the frame to chest level. Then his hand rises into the frame with a glass from which he drinks. Why did he sink? He was sitting down on a stool, which the director failed to show. Where did the glass come from? It was on a table, which the director also failed to show.

8 Sometimes you will need to reestablish.

8.1   Do this to remind viewers of the overall relationship.

After a fairly long series of shots that are restricted to parts of a situation, a reminding view of the ensemble will not only provide shot variety, but will also renew a sense of unity between the components.

8.2   Do this to reveal changed relationships that result from subjects moving to new locations during a scene.

It is often advisable to show these changes as they occur. Consider, for example, the following shot series:

A and B (both standing) and C (in chair).
Several shots of only A and B.
Shot including C (at piano).

What? C at the piano—how did he get there? The director knows, and probably looked through the control-room window and saw him move. But the viewer at home knows nothing except what he or she sees on the screen.

9 Use something in common to link shots of separate components.

When two components of a scene are taken in separate shots, one way to clarify their physical relationship is to keep something common to the shots of each. Thus the slanting top of a grand piano may form a mutual point of reference for relating separate shots of a singer and her accompanist. Or the mutual referent may be a person who, having appeared in the first shot, remains in view in the second.

Chapter 13

Consistency

Again you are asked to remember:

1   Don't perplex your viewers by failing to show them how each new picture is related to the preceding ones.

One way to promote the relationship between shots of the same situation is to be consistent in your pictorial treatment of them. In what follows you will learn how to do this—or, in a sense, how not to do it, for you will be reading about several types of inconsistency that the director should avoid.

2   Avoid inconsistent backgrounds.

A conversing couple is taken in reverse-angle shots that reveal alternately different backgrounds—one of drapes, perhaps, and the other of bricks in a fireplace wall; or one sharply focused and the other blurred; or one light in tone and the other dark; or one red, perhaps, and the other green. In any of these instances the conversation almost seems to be taking place in two different locations.

The discrepancy may not be bothersome if, by virtue of establishing shots, the audience has had a chance to view the overall setting and notice the variations in it. Otherwise, depending on the nature of the discrepancy, you may have to locate the performers against a more consistent background, or change the camera angles, or balance the background illumination, or match more closely the focal lengths of the lenses you are using on each camera.

3   Avoid inconsistent illumination.

When the light comes principally from one direction, but the cameras aim from widely divergent directions, the same subject may look flat and bright in one shot and dark or contrasty in another. The audience may accept this difference if it is aware of the light source and realizes that the source is directional in character. Otherwise the illumination for the two shots should be matched more evenly.

4   Avoid inconsistent variations in the light levels of slides and film fed into the film chains.

On this subject, review what was stated in Chapter 4 concerning undesirable fluctuations in scene brightness and in the density of projected materials.

5   Avoid inconsistency from shot to shot in the location of subjects on the screen.

5.1   When two subjects of similar screen size are taken in alternating shots, their headroom should be similar.

Otherwise, there will be a bobbing up-and-down effect as the shots succeed one another.

5.2   Prevent jump cuts.

A single subject will seem to jump suddenly from one screen location to another on a take between cameras that are framing the subject at similar scale, but not in identical parts of their fields. Suppose, for instance, that a punted football is picked up by a second camera when the ball is getting out of range of the first. If the ball is moving toward the right, say, and the second camera frames it more to the left than did the first camera, it will seem to jump backward on the take. A jump can also occur in a sequence taken by a single camera if the event has been recorded on videotape and a short section of the action has been removed editorially. An effect similar to a jump cut will appear when the subjects of successive shots are so similar that one expects them to be consistently aligned, yet they are not aligned. Thus, the lettering on sequential key or supertitles may seem to jump back and forth or up and down as the titles replace one another, unless the lettering has been laid out and framed uniformly.

5.3   Make it easy for your viewers to follow a subject from one shot to the next without having to hunt for it in a new part of the screen.

Example: A performer is conversing with a person on either side of him. Instead of establishing all three together, the director takes successive two-shots, first of the performer with the person on his left, then of the performer with the person on his right. On the take between these shots, the performer will jump from one side of the screen to the other.

5.4   Maintain the relative screen locations of two subjects when taking them both together in successive shots.

Two performers, A and B, are
facing each other. Camera 1 takes a
two-shot toward A over B's left shoulder. Then camera 2 also takes a two-
shot toward A, but over B's right
shoulder. On the take the relative positions of the two will be reversed. This is
illustrated by the left diagram in *Figure
13/1*. To correct the trouble, imagine a
line running through the two persons
and, as in the right diagram, keep both
of your cameras on the same side of this
line.

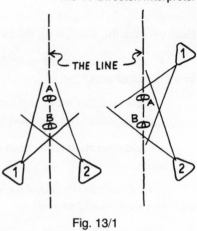

Fig. 13/1

**6   Avoid inconsistency regarding the direction in which subjects face
and move.**

6.1   Again, keep your cameras on the same side of the line.

If you shoot as in *Figure 13/2*,
although your performers are actually
facing each other, they will face in the
same direction on the screen.

Assigned to shoot the stock car
races at State Fair Park, you place one
camera inside the track to get shots of
the grandstand and the other camera
outside the track. When the races begin, you will find that, on each take,
the cars reverse direction on the screen.
In this case, the track corresponds to
the imaginary line, and you have
failed to keep your cameras on the same
side of it.

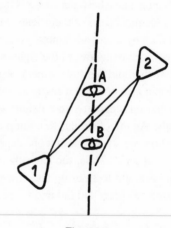

Fig. 13/2

*6.2   If you shoot toward opposite sides from a moving vehicle, the scene will
stream by in opposite directions.*

The shots that fail to match for this reason may be reconciled by separating
them with another shot, headed in the direction the vehicle is moving.

*6.3   When two persons are facing each other in conversation, successive
profiles of each taken separately should still appear to be facing each other.*

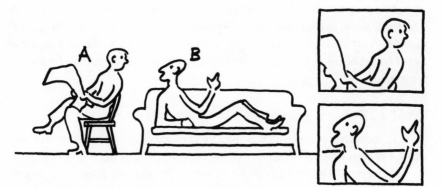

Fig. 13/3

In the framed shots of *Figure 13/3*, this is not the case. Although A's head is actually on the left of B's, it appears in the one-shot on the right side of the frame—and the same in reverse is true of B's head. Even in column I of *Figure 13/4*, where each head is center, it is not as evident that the two persons are talking to each other as it is in column II, where the heads are off-center sufficiently to correspond to their actual relationship.

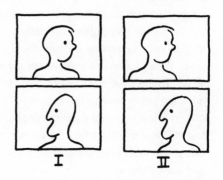

I   II

Fig. 13/4

7 Avoid inconsistent camera angles.

Unless new information is revealed by changing the point of view, it can be confusing to observe the same subject in succeeding shots from different angles.

If a speaker who is addressing the camera is taken successively in shots from widely divergent directions, the speaker's audience contact is broken, requiring him for no evident reason to shift his gaze toward the second camera. Meanwhile, the viewers, having to identify themselves unexpectedly with a new point of view, may feel as if the speaker has been forcibly and unaccountably transplanted from one seat to another.

It is also disturbing when a performer, saying, "Look at this photograph," is shown holding the photograph at a pronounced angle to the observer so that a closeup of it can be taken by another camera, which is some distance apart from the present one. To avoid this disturbance, both cameras should shoot as nearly as possible from the same direction.

In a program on how to play chess, the chessboard is viewed first from the side; then, as one of the players moves a piece, a new shot is taken over this player's shoulder. This obliges the viewers to reorient themselves to the disposition of pieces on the board, which has probably already been difficult enough for them to apprehend.

7.1   Consistency should apply also to vertical angles.

In shooting a seated couple, a director uses one camera on a pedestal mount, which has been lowered to take a two-shot from very nearly the couple's eye level. For a closeup of one of the couple, however, the director must use a tripod-mounted camera with its lens fixed at a height suitable for taking standing persons. To use this camera close to a seated subject will oblige it to angle down quite steeply in contrast to the pedestal camera's more level angle. This inconsistency can be avoided by pulling the camera back to where its declination will be more gradual and then using a longer focal length on the lens.

When there is a motivation for a change of vertical angle, of course, the sense of inconsistency will not exist. In televising a square dance, takes may seem quite logical between a camera on the studio floor to provide a normal view and a camera shooting from a gallery to show off the movement patterns of the dances. But at intermission, when the master of ceremonies interviews the square-dance caller, takes between the normal angle and the high angle will seem inexplicable and inappropriate.

7.2   Action can become confusing when it is shown from too great a variety of arbitrary angles.

The safest way to keep the audience oriented is to stick to a consistent pattern of shooting angles, avoiding the unique shot that is suddenly taken from some altogether unexpected direction (unless there is clear motivation for it). For example, having taken all of your previous shots from inside the room, don't insert a single shot from outside the window simply because you fancy it as unusual or think that it is easier to do this than to get the subject of your shot to face one of the other cameras.

The unity of an action should be reinforced by consistency of camera treatment. If a line of panelists are all looking toward the master of ceremonies, who is stationed off one end of their row, it can be quite confusing when separate shots of them are taken, to see some of them in profile and others full face. Their parallel action could be communicated better by choosing camera angles that will keep them all facing the same way on the screen. To borrow advice from a book on literary style, "one should express coordinate ideas in similar form."

8 Avoid inconsistencies of screen size.

The principle of expressing coordinate ideas in similar form should also regulate the scale of subjects on the screen. When one member of a scene expresses something of greater significance or intensity than what has come before, there is reason to reinforce this expression with a closer shot. On the other hand, there are many scenes wherein the participants make more or less equal contributions. In a sequence during which an interviewer asks the same question of three guests in turn, it would not make sense to see one guest in a chest shot, the next in a waist shot, and a third in a tight closeup. Since their functions and the weight of their remarks are coordinate, their screen scale should be likewise.

9 Avoid the inconsistency of switching between a moving and a stationary camera on the same subject.

Example: When a camera pans or trucks with a person who is moving across the scene, the person maintains a fixed position on the screen while all the stationary objects within view stream across the frame. If a cut is then made to a motionless camera, the objects halt abruptly and the person starts to move across the frame. This can be a quite noticeable and inexplicable reversal.

Example: A vocalist is singing the last measures of his selection while a camera, to support the climax, is dollying in on him from a long shot. The camera reaches his knees and is still dollying when the director takes a stationary shoulder shot. The effect of this take on a viewer is something like being catapulted forward from a moving vehicle that has suddenly stopped.

10 Avoid inconsistencies in treatment between various parts of the production.

Example: Dynamic opening titles accompanied by an exciting or grandiose musical theme introduce a mathematics lesson on quadratic equations.

11 When shooting in segments, avoid inconsistencies between one segment and another related segment.

This problem is ever present when shooting a film-style video production where action is rarely continuous for long periods. A pause after every shot may be desirable for changing the camera position, lights, field of view or other production elements. Shots may be taken over a range of weeks, at different locations, with differing conditions of light and weather, and in a sequence far different from that in which they are eventually assembled. It is possible to record two shots for the same sequence at widely separated times, yet they must correspond in lighting, audio quality, color and contrast characteristics, exposure, position of properties in the setting, appearance of the performers' hair and attire, and still other details.

11.1   One way to achieve this correspondence is to keep accurate records of all factors that must be duplicated.

These factors include the physical position of all objects in the scene, the position and dimmer settings of lighting instruments, and the f-stops and distance settings of camera lenses. Polaroid still photographs may provide useful visual records of the scene to be matched.

11.2   When a performance has been halted between shots, there is often a problem of matching action.

To make the action seem continuous, a performer's physical attitudes must appear the same at the beginning of the new shot as at the end of the previous one. One solution is to take the new shot from a different angle in order to prevent a direct comparison. Another solution is to cut during an action so pronounced that it will impel the audience's attention across the break and distract it from noticing possible discrepancies in the static elements of the two shots. It is more difficult to detect mismatches when you cut on action than when subjects sit still for comparison.

When shooting such a transition, it is advisable to record the complete action twice (both at the end of the first shot and at the beginning of the second), not only so that performers can deliver the necessary flow and follow-through, but also that the editor can cut wherever he or she finds the smoothest match between the two versions.

Electronic News Gathering (ENG) and Electronic Field Production (EFP) are two examples of one-camera production techniques that involve matching action, and a discussion on both, as well as some discussion of the editing process, follows later in the text.

Chapter 14

Extreme or Abrupt
Shot Changes

**1   A change of shot content should not be so extreme or abrupt that it
startles or puzzles (unless these reactions are intentional).**

This chapter discusses ways to avoid these reactions when they are not
intentional, thus helping to maintain the viewer's immersion in the program
content.

**2   Avoid extreme changes of scale in successive shots of the same
subject unless there is adequate motivation for them.**

Example: A full shot of a person is followed by a tight closeup. This would
be adequately motivated had the person just been singled out, for instance, as
guilty of some crime. The announcement of guilt would throw attention strongly
on the person, particularly on his or her face, where the strongest reaction would
likely be most evident. Under less dramatic circumstances, however, the change in
screen size is too extreme for the audience to adjust to readily.

*2.1   To temper such changes, insert a medium shot between the two
extremes.*

When a brook is too wide to jump without a taxing effort, one can put a
stepping stone halfway across it. The medium shot is similar in purpose to the
stone. One might also walk across a plank to the stone, then step to land from there.
Similarly, one might zoom in to the medium shot, then take the closeup.

3 Unless there is adequate motivation, avoid extreme changes of screen direction in successive shots of the same subject.

Example: A shot showing a moving subject approaching from right to left is followed by one of it approaching from left to right. At the instant of change, the audience can have difficulty appreciating that the same subject is involved in both shots—or, appreciating that, it may be uncertain whether the subject has changed or maintained its course, and if it has maintained its course, what is the reason for viewing it from a reversed direction?

3.1 To temper such changes, insert a transitional view of the subject moving directly toward or away from the camera.

As with the change in screen size, this remedy inserts an in-between step in order to accomplish the change by degrees.

4 Special techniques are usually needed when omitting a segment from a course of action involving the same subject.

Such omissions commonly used in tape editing allow one to dispense with less significant or less interesting portions of the action, jumping from one high spot to another. The jumps, however, should not seem abrupt and illogical.

Example: After showing a baseball player in the "on deck" circle, you want to show the player's turn at bat, but wish to dispense with an uneventful walk from there to home plate. Yet to cut, as the walking commences, to a shot of the player already facing the pitcher would make a disturbing jump.

4.1 In such situations you can apply out-of-frame into-frame.

Thus, you let the player walk out of the "on deck" shot and enter the shot at home plate. From this, the viewers will understand that one phase of the action is over and that another is beginning; consequently, they will not worry about the eliminated time.

4.2 For certain other cases of omitted action you can use the cutaway.

You wish to show only the highlights of a baseball game—but how can you jump coherently from a situation in one inning to a different state of affairs in a later inning? You can separate the shots that will not correspond, cutting away from the central action to insert a shot of something on the sidelines, such as the scoreboard or the spectators. By this separation of the mismatched shots you prevent a direct comparison between them.

4.3   Another technique is the cut-in.

With this, instead of departing from the central action, you insert a closeup detail of that action. Thus, suppose that you wish to shoot the erection of a brick wall without keeping the camera on the wall as it is built, brick by brick, yet juxtaposed takes of the wall at various discrete levels will make it seem to grow by leaps. Therefore, you separate these shots with cut-ins of masons' trowels being wielded and other details of the work.

4.4   To bridge between stages in a process of growth without inserting supplementary details, use the dissolve.

This would apply to the brick-wall sequence just cited. If you are not interested in showing the mason's activities, if you would prefer to say in effect, "The wall grew . . . and grew . . . and grew . . . ," you could juxtapose shots of the wall at various levels provided that you joined them, not with takes but with dissolves.

5   The dissolve is useful for accommodating the viewers to new visual circumstances for which they have not otherwise been prepared.

When a new and unexpected circumstance is introduced by a take, it hits one suddenly and therefore momentarily startles or bewilders. Since it comes immediately after the previous shot, the viewers may try to associate it with what they have just been watching. Thus, when the levels of bricks are joined by takes, viewers tend to regard them as happening within the same time continuum. In other cases, viewers are puzzled because the new shot is out of context. If this reaction lasts but an instant it is enough to interrupt the continuity. Some device is needed, therefore, to separate the new context from the old.

In writing, this is commonly accomplished by starting a new paragraph. In television, a related purpose is served by the dissolve. In a dissolve, the old picture fades out as the new picture fades in. Since this process normally lasts from one to five seconds or more, it is a separating device, accomplishing in time what the paragraph separation does in space. Also, by reason of the cross-fading, it says in effect, "Look, the present circumstance is phasing out, and a new circumstance is phasing in." Or, in the specific instance of the brick wall, "One period of time is ending, and a new one is beginning." In addition, the dissolve might be called a "get-used-to-it-gradually device." Because it develops the new picture by degrees, it allows the viewers to become accommodated to the new content, which occurs unexpectedly, before its relation to the previous context is evident.

By reason of these characteristics, the dissolve is suited to the applications discussed below. In all of these, a new visual subject is being introduced. It is unexpected at the precise time it appears. The audience has not been prepared verbally or by any other means to understand immediately the subject's relation to the present proceedings.

5.1   Dissolve between actions that occur at different periods of time.

Thus, dissolve between the shot of Mac slamming the kitchen door after an argument with his wife, and the next shot, which shows him easing his tension at the neighborhood bar.

5.2   Dissolve between actions that occur at different locations.

The example just cited includes a change of place as well as of time. But one also dissolves for a change of place when different characters are involved at the two locations.

5.3   Dissolve between sequences that are presented in different modes.

Thus, dissolve between opening titles and studio action, or between studio action and closing titles.

Dissolve between studio and taped sequences—from the news analyst in an armchair to a group of Arabs on horseback galloping across the screen—and vice versa.

5.4   Within a sequence occurring at a single place and time, dissolve to any new subject which, at the instant it appears, is not expected and cannot be immediately connected with the action in progress.

Example: You dissolve from soldiers parading down Main Street to a boy at the curb who is having difficulty with a runny ice cream cone. The audience could hardly have expected this shot. The announcer did not say, "Look at that little boy over there!" No parading soldier could be seen looking off screen and smiling to motivate a take to the source of his amusement. There was no necessary connection between the marching and the boy. Nor did the boy himself take over the action by shouting or crying or doing anything to motivate suddenly cutting from the procession to him.

Example: You have on camera an authority who is explaining advertising media. Having cited the more common media (television, newspapers, magazines, etcetera), the speaker remarks, "besides the mass media, there are a number of what we may call 'collateral media.' or 'secondary media' if you prefer. Among these, as you can see, are calendars of the sort that your local fuel company may mail to you at Christmas time. . . ."

At some point in this speech, you are expected to go from the speaker to a series of slides, beginning with one of a calendar, then of a matchbook cover, desk blotter, and other examples of the topic. Note that there is no precise cue for this transition. By the time calendars are mentioned, the first slide should already be in view. But before calendars are mentioned, the viewers have not been prepared to understand the relation between them and collateral media. Nor do they expect to see a calendar—or, indeed, any picture change at all. Hence a take to the calendar would puzzle and startle them. So you dissolve.

A like situation continues throughout the entire slide sequence: the viewers do not know what they will see next or when the change will occur. Therefore, you dissolve from one slide to another. And at the end of the slide sequence, since a return to the speaker is unanticipated at the moment it occurs, you effect it by a dissolve instead of a take.

Getting into the slide sequence would have been different had the speaker, prior to the sequence, pointed to a calendar on the wall of the set, saying, "Here's an example of what I mean." This prior establishment of the calendar precludes any need to get used to it gradually when the closeup of it appears. To introduce this closeup, therefore, it is proper to use a take.

A dissolve is sometimes used when it is desired to introduce a new shot without stressing the transition.

A take is an abrupt change. The sudden contrast that it effects between shots is likely to say, "Look, something new and important has happened!" The dissolve is a blend that eases into the new subject, softening the transition. Hence it is sometimes used for introducing a new shot without stressing the transition.

Example: A subject may remain relatively static for considerable time, providing no motivation for a change of shots, yet a change may seem desirable to combat boredom and allow inspection of the subject from some different, interesting angle. Since there is no important occurrence to be accented, a take to the new picture would arouse false expectations. Therefore, the director softens the transition by using a dissolve.

Sometimes an editor finds that there is no medium shot with which to bridge between a long shot and a closeup. Therefore, the editor uses a dissolve between these shots to soften the transition.

There are times when the dissolve does not soften as much as a director would like. This occurs when you get on the wrong camera by mistake or when, for some technical reason, you must release the present camera and substitute another for it on the same subject. Hoping that blending from one camera to the other will disguise the change, you use a dissolve instead of a take. No doubt this is making the best of a bad bargain, but the best is rarely good enough to prevent some notice of the substitution.

5.6   A dissolve is often used to link different, but similar objects into a single stream of consciousness.

A series of dissolves between beautiful flowers, trees, mountains, and other landscape might be used to effect for the viewer a theme of "summer" without the need of any narration or explanation.

6   Do not use dissolves when they are not required.

6.1   Dissolves to closeups are not required when the subject of the closeup has been visually pointed up in the previous shot and related to the matter at hand.

For example, remember the concluding discussion about the advertising calendar.

6.2   Dissolves are not needed when the subject of the new shot is verbally introduced just before or coincident with the change.

Example: (at the end of opening titles) "Now, for the latest news and views in the world of sports, here's Carl Frank!"

Example: (during a newscast) "We take you now to Philadelphia and Barbara Britt."

6.3   Dissolves are not needed to connect a sequence of brief shots which, however varied in time, place, or subject, are all evidently serving to develop a preestablished situation, action, or idea.

Example: Foreign planes releasing bombs . . . explosions shattering moored U.S. warships . . . the president addressing Congress . . . civilians being issued uniforms . . . and so on. If not evident from the shots themselves, it will be from the commentary that accompanies them, that they are all links in a single chain of action and consequence—the attack on Pearl Harbor and its aftermath. With this unity apparent to them, the viewers will be prepared to move rapidly from one shot to the next by takes.

One may cite virtually every news story on television as an example of this principle. Between news stories, however, or upon returning to the news reporter, it is advisable to dissolve, since then one is introducing the viewers to new circumstances for which they are not prepared.

7   For an extreme sense of separation between one train of thought or action and another, use the fade-out-and-fade-in.

In this device the first shot fades entirely out before the new shot begins to fade in. If the dissolve is likened to a change between paragraphs, then the fade-out-and-fade-in is like a change between chapters. So much finality, indeed, can be suggested by the complete fading out of a picture that it is ordinarily used between programs rather than within them. Within a program the blank screen following a fade-out should last only momentarily to prevent a loss of the viewers' emotional or intellectual involvement. The dissolve, on the other hand, by overlapping the sections it connects, always assures the viewers that the program is continuing.

8 For certain special effects (suggested below) transitions may be effected by the wipe.

In the wipe, the new picture progressively displaces the old, sometimes crossing straight-edged from one side to the other, sometimes expanding from one corner as an enlarging rectangle, sometimes growing from the center of the screen in the shape of a circle or diamond, or sometimes opening fanwise through a full 360° angle.

Halted partway, a wipe can split the screen to show actions occurring simultaneously in two places or to present two different aspects of the same subject. By halting the wipe that expands from a corner, one can make space in that corner for a commentator, reserving the rest of the screen for the material being talked about.

8.1 Complete wipes are used as circumstances dictate.

A lateral wipe may follow the exit of persons off one side of the screen as new ones enter from the opposite side to begin a new scene. At the end of a sequence when the subject recedes into the distance at center screen, a contracting wipe such as a closing circle can keep the subject prominent until the last moment. A wipe expanding from center may impart a feeling of growth and development to the beginning of a scene, or induce curiosity by uncovering the subject progressively. In shows of a "theatrical" nature (variety shows, for instance), the wipe may add novelty and decorative style by reason of its dynamic and geometric patterns. For more illusionistic productions, however, it may call attention to itself as a device, thereby disturbing the viewers' immersion in the story.

8.2 Avoid overusing wipes and other electronic effects.

When first provided with a special effects generator (SEG) capable of producing wipes, some directors can be so fascinated with the novelty of these effects that they overuse them and fail to consider whether they are using them appropriately. The same holds true with the continuing growth in numbers of digital optics devices such as Quantel, ADO, squeeze zoom, and chroma key that are available to the director. Care needs to be taken with any effect so that it is not overused as an excuse for uninteresting or poorly motivated program direction.

Chapter 15

Other Visual Transitions

By discussing the dissolve, fade, and wipe as the basic transitional devises, the previous chapter opened the subject of visual transitions, which will be continued in this chapter. Whereas the dissolve, fade, and wipe are controlled by the television SEG, the transitions to be considered next are produced by moving the camera. They are: the pan, the tilt, the dolly-in, the dolly-back, the truck, the arc, and (although it involves moving only the lens element within the camera) the zoom.

Most of the common uses of these devices have been listed below.

Uses of the Pan and Tilt

1 To move the eye progressively from one (usually stationary) subject to another. The pan is a horizontal movement and the tilt is a vertical movement.

Thereby the pan and tilt can be used to:

1.1 Establish a connection between the subjects.

By continuously traversing the space between the subjects, the pan establishes a greater connection, both spatial and ideological, between them than were they to be taken in separate shots. Therefore it serves to:

Reinforce such connections as action-consequence, action-reaction, and cause-effect. For example, show a closeup of tape running through the heads of a video recorder, then tilt up to a monitor that shows the image obtained from this tape.

Associate in a class a number of subjects that share something in common. For example, pan across cans containing various kinds of soup, or across a row of panelists, or from one miner's wife to another as they await news of a mine disaster, which mutually affects them.

Inspect the parts of a subject, one after another, without destroying the viewer's awareness of its unity. For example, pan from the bolt and trigger assembly of a rifle to its rear sight to its stacking swivel to its front sight, pausing to identify each in turn.

Preserve the unity of a subject, the details of which would be too small on the screen were they all included in a stationary shot. For example, pan continuously across a landscape, creating a panorama (from which the term "pan" was derived).

Follow an action, preserving its unity, as it is taken up by a succession of different subjects. For example, pan from the first to the second violinist of a string quartet as the lead in a musical passage progresses from one to the other.

Establish various other associations not precisely described above. For example, pan from a crate on the dock to the boat in the distance that is going to take it overseas.

1.2   Follow a lead initiated by one subject that creates interest in a second subject.

Example: A performer looks offscreen and the camera pans from her to the object of her attention. A performer points or gestures upward toward something and the camera tilts up from him to it.

1.3   Create anticipation when introducing a new subject.

The pan and tilt induce a feeling of moving toward something new. Whereas a take shows the new subject completely and immediately, a pan or tilt emphasizes the approach toward it, delaying its appearance and revealing it by degrees. Therefore, the pan and tilt can be used to:

Build up the importance of a new subject. It does this by delaying, just as a speaker creates emphasis by pausing before an important word or phrase. For example, pan from a master of ceremonies across the inclined piano cover to the pianist who has just been introduced. The passage across the piano cover creates anticipation for the artist one is about to see.

Create suspense, when the camera is panned or tilted slowly.

Thus used, the pan or tilt can be a movement into the unknown. For example, the camera slowly pans the attic of a "haunted" house or tilts upward from earth toward the stars.

1.4   Concentrate or expand the scope of the subject.

Example: Pan from several choir members to the face of the one nearest camera, or from one crate in a warehouse to the pile of crates stored there.

2 To follow a moving subject.

This allows one to:

2.1 Keep the subject sufficiently visible and dominant.

Example: In covering a horse race, a fixed field wide enough to contain the action may make the subjects too small and place them in competition with irrelevant details. Therefore, you close in on the leading horses and pan with them.

2.2 Maintain the unity of a movement.

Example: a dance movement, a forward pass, or the cross of an actor toward a new objective. To cut between cameras, taking successive fields through which the moving subject passes, might be difficult to do if the movement is fast, and in any case would make the action jerky and disconnected. Cuts would be justified, however, were there multiple stages of the action to be emphasized, such as 1) aiming an arrow, 2) striking the target.

2.3 Maintain the unity of a scene requiring a particularly smooth continuity.

When subjects move in such a scene, panning or tilting with them will avoid the necessity for takes, which might introduce unwarranted emphasis or excitement.

2.4 Save takes for occasions when they count.

Indiscriminate use of takes dulls their effectiveness as instruments for emphasis or excitement. The take that accentuates an important act or statement will be more effective if it has been preceded by a passage during which no takes are used. A scene in which takes are used frequently to create a sense of activity or excitement will establish its character more successfully if preceded by a scene that has been sustained on one camera.

Uses of the Dolly-in

3 To narrow the field as the area occupied by the significant action contracts.

Example: When one person exits from a three-shot, tighten to frame the two persons remaining. Or, after showing a woman raise a glass from the table to her lips, tighten to concentrate on the sip she takes and her reaction to the liquid's taste.

4 To gradually concentrate on the most significant portion of the field.

4.1 After orienting the viewers to the total environment, to narrow their attention to the active elements within it.

This may be useful at the beginning of a scene.

4.2   To increase the impact of an action by progressively closing in on the most expressive portion of it.

Example: Move in toward a performer's face, enlarging and clarifying the performer's expression, giving it command of the frame, as when supporting the climax of a solo vocal performance.

5   To follow and maintain at constant scale a subject moving to the rear.

Thus one can:

5.1   Stay with a performer as he or she moves toward some new objective.

Otherwise the performer would diminish in the distance, and whatever scenic elements were left behind would still remain in the foreground although they were no longer important.

5.2   Increase the force of the performer's move in the consciousness of the viewer.

Example: If a performer is moving aggressively toward an objective, having the camera move with the performer at the same tempo will emphatically move the viewer in as well, thus providing a subjective experience.

6   To identify the viewer subjectively with performers advancing through a terrain.

Example: To shoot through the windshield of a moving car or diving plane gives the viewer a "point of view" experience similar to that of the performer.

7   To give the viewer a sense of entering an environment.

Example: The camera moves down a street or through a crowd, which streams by on either side of the lens, giving the illusion that one is actually within the locality rather than observing it from a detached position.

8   To alter the relative dominance when two subjects are at different distances from cameras.

8.1   To increase the dominance of the foreground figure.

By dollying in with the camera lower than head height, one can increase the size and height of the closer person in relation to that of the farther one.

8.2   To increase the dominance of the background figure.

When the foreground figure is turned to face the more distant one, dollying in to shoot over the foreground figure's shoulder will give more emphasis to the distant figure.

9 To create and then satisfy anticipation.

Example: The camera reveals a new subject at a distance, then moves in closer to investigate it.

Uses of the Dolly-back

10 To include the significant action as its field expands.

Example: The present subjects move farther apart, or new subjects join those already in the shot.

11 To maintain consistent framing of a subject moving forward.

To dolly back with an advancing subject will keep its scale constant instead of letting it enlarge. When the subject is allowed to approach a stationary camera (as when moving into a closeup), more impact may be created than the subject's speech or action justifies.

To dolly back with an advancing subject will keep the same area of the subject constantly in view, whereas if the camera remains stationary, progressive amounts of the subject area will be lost from view.

12 To effect the entrance of new subject matter in the foreground.

12.1   To surprise the audience by revealing that an unsuspected subject is present.

12.2   To give adequate scale to small subjects introduced into the shot.

Example: As a person advances, the camera dollying back with him, his objective is revealed to be a telephone, which enters the frame close to the lens and is therefore large enough on the screen to make an impact consistent with its importance as a new factor in the action.

13 To accumulate actively and progressively new factors in the environment.

Example: As a character advances through a populous environment, the camera dollying back with her, a succession of persons and objects will stream into the picture from each side of the frame and accumulate in the background, making it grow in detail and activity.

14   To expand from a single subject to the context of which it is a part.

14.1   To emphasize the magnitude of the field of action by letting it grow from a small beginning.

Example: Start on a close shot of an orchestra conductor and dolly back to reveal the whole orchestra.

14.2   To provoke and satisfy curiosity progressively regarding the total nature of the subject.

Example: Start with a close shot of a gun and outstretched hand on the floor, then dolly back to show the body of the victim.

15   To emphasize the expanding significance of an event.

Example: In the example immediately above, continue to draw back as passers-by discover the body, detectives arrive, etcetera.

16   To support a climax that depends on magnitude.

Example: At the close of an instrumental musical number, dolly back to reveal the entire orchestra.

17   To create neutral space in which a new subject will presently appear.

Example: The material presently on the screen recedes and (by panning the camera during the dolly-back) moves to one side, leaving an area on the other side into which a new character may enter or over which some printed titles may be superimposed.

18   To identify the viewer subjectively with riders in a moving vehicle.

Example: One shoots backward from the getaway car toward the pursuing police.

19   To signify finality by withdrawing from the action.

This lets the subject gradually recede into the distance.

Uses of the Truck

To truck left or right is to move the camera mount sidewise, i.e., in a direction perpendicular to that in which the lens is aiming.

20 To accompany a laterally moving subject, keeping it framed at a constant scale and shown from the same constant angle.

If, instead, you pan with such a subject who is crossing from one side of the scene to the other, the subject will at first enlarge, reaching maximum scale when passing closest to the camera, and then progressively diminish. Also, the angle will reveal progressively less of the subject's front and more of his or her back. In some instances, this may be exactly what one desires—but if not, one trucks along with the subject.

21 To traverse a long subject, viewing each part of it head-on and at a constant scale.

Thus, the camera approximates the view of an officer inspecting a row of soldiers one after another, or of someone walking the length of an assembly line, inspecting each step in the process. With this technique, each element of the subject is given equal value and can be isolated in the frame for complete attention, whereas, were the subject to be panned, elements would become progressively smaller, and more and more of them would appear together in the frame because of their increasing distance from camera.

22 To view a succession of separate subjects from a consistent direction.

The subjects might be artifacts arranged in a row on a shelf, or they might be pictures hung side by side on a wall. In the latter instance, trucking along the row will preserve the four-square appearance of rectangular pictures, preventing keystoning.

Uses of the Arc

In an arcing shot, one keeps aimed at the subject while moving the camera mount in a curving path around the subject.

23 To vary the angle progressively from which a stationary subject is viewed . . .

23.1 . . . because it is interesting or informative to view it so.

Example: The subject is a statue, which has been designed to reveal a satisfying composition from many points of view.

23.2 . . . because one wishes to vary the picture on the screen to combat visual monotony without interrupting the continuity of the subject matter with a take.

Example: You may arc around a grand piano during a long, continuous passage of music.

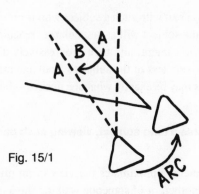

Fig. 15/1

24   To adjust the picture composition when the subjects change their physical relationship, and to do so without an abrupt change of shots.

For example, see *Figure 15/1*. Attention is on character A, who crosses in front of B in the course of a long speech. As A crosses, the camera arcs in the opposite direction to keep a favorable angle on A.

25   To direct attention gradually to a new subject without the abruptness of a change of shots.

For example, see *Figure 15/2*. A and B are gossiping. During their conversation, it becomes progressively evident that they are being overheard by C, who is the subject of their gossip.

26   To eliminate subject matter from the background.

Example: A and B are first shown conversing against the background of a crowd. As their conversation becomes more intimate, the camera gradually arcs around to show them against an inanimate background.

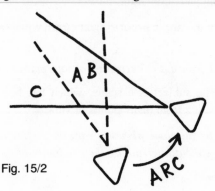

Fig. 15/2

Uses of the Zoom

The zoom may be used for approximately the same purposes as the dolly-in and dolly-back. There is one principal difference, however; in zooming, the size of the field expands and contracts, but there is no change in perspective relationships. For example, a figure in the foreground does not grow larger in proportion to a figure in the background as it would during a dolly-in. Also, because during a zoom the camera remains stationary, there is no change in the point of view. During a dolly-in, this change occurs. Thus, in *Figure 15/3*, more of the wall behind the door opening can be seen when the camera is dollied in.

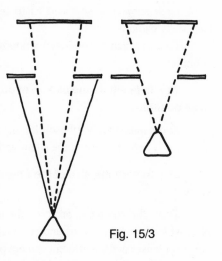

Fig. 15/3

When compared to dolly shots, the zoom offers the following unique advantages:

27   To frame a shot exactly without having to change lenses or to move the camera forward or back to adjust framing.

This can save time between shots.

28   To vary the field as the subject expands or contracts, approaches or recedes, without having to move the camera or cut to the other cameras.

Hence:

29   To do a show with one camera, either to save the cost of extra camera operators, or to maintain a consistent subjective point of view— provided that:

The camera does not have to dolly to new positions while shooting, since this may require refocusing.

The subject matter can be properly framed within the widest and narrowest extremities of the lens angle.

The action is blocked to lead the camera logically and directly from one subject to another.

There is no need for subjects to be accented as they can be when suddenly revealed by the take to a new camera.

Subjects are arranged at such distances from camera as to prevent frequent and obvious zooming in and out, which can be very distracting for the viewer.

Each subject is so faced as to be viewed from the proper angle by the stationary camera.

The lens can be operated smoothly without perceptible jerks during the zooming.

30 To facilitate the pickup of programs where cameras must remain in fixed positions.

Zoom lenses are very useful in outdoor locations or in public halls where an audience is seated between the event and the camera positions.

31 To vary the size of the field without abruptly changing the point of view.

Thus, the zoom can preserve the unity of a single action such as a football play, which rapidly expands and contracts in the field of view. To cut to wider or narrower lenses and to different camera positions during the play can damage both the viewers' orientation and the continuity of the action. In tennis matches, taken from the margin of one court, one can zoom in as the ball is driven to the far court, thus avoiding the discontinuity of takes to another camera or the wig-wagging produced when a camera off one end of the net pans back and forth from court to court.

32 To eliminate the need for correlation between different camera operators during quickly expanding and contracting action by permitting this action to be followed on one camera.

This is of obvious value during sports pickups.

33 To keep an advancing or receding subject framed at constant scale with less trouble than is sometimes encountered by a dolly-in or dolly-out.

In such instances, the zoom forestalls having to dolly over a rug or into furniture or into the field of another camera's shot.

It eliminates the need to follow focus and to risk going out of focus if the action is fast or varies in speed.

34 To alter the size of the field much more quickly than is possible by dollying.

Therefore:

34.1   To narrow attention rapidly to some detail that suddenly becomes urgently important.

The rapid zoom-in is one of the most forceful devices available to the director. Its impact can almost be that of a shock. In drama it may be used to support sudden, emotion-charged developments in the action. In hard-sell commercials it may serve to punch home some important point in the visual sales message. Quick, repeated zooming in and out has sometimes been used to induce a feeling of panic or other intense emotional excitement.

35   To keep at constant scale the subject matter framed during a pan over material that slants back obliquely in the camera field.

For example, with the camera in front of one end of a row of people, a pan down the row on a fixed focal-length lens will include progressively more people, increasingly diminished in size. By zooming in during the pan, each person can be isolated in the frame and kept at the same screen size as the other people.

36   To eliminate the exaggerated perspective that may occur when a camera dollies close to a subject on a wide-angle lens.

With a zoom, as previously explained, the perspective does not change.

37   To eliminate undesired changes in vertical angle, which may occur when a camera is dollied in close to a subject higher or lower than the level of the lens.

With a zoom, the point of view remains constant.

38   To keep a prompting device (fixed to the camera) at a constant distance from the performers.

Using a zoom lens to adjust framing obviously allows the camera to remain stationary. Hence the prompting device need not move away from the performer's range of vision as it would if the camera had to dolly back.

39   To alter the field of view when physical obstacles exist.

With the zoom lens, from a stationary position on the shore, you can keep a boat crossing from one side of a river to the other in full frame.

Chapter 16

The Director as Interpreter

1 Conform your choice and editing of shots to the meaning, mood, and form of your program material.

Preserve the nature of your material as faithfully as you can despite the fact that it must pass through your cameras and microphones in order to reach its audience. As superintendent of this translation, you must make yourself a reliable interpreter.

2 To interpret the material faithfully, you must understand its purposes and characteristics.

To accurately translate the many subjects that television brings to the screen requires a keen sensibility and broad understanding of many more aspects of human activity than any book or course in directing could ever hope to encompass. So do not limit your study to the confines of studios and stations. Seek as many experiences as possible and meet them with an inquiring mind.

3 Camera treatment must vary according to the purpose of the subject matter.

3.1 For example, the purpose of instructional television is learning, not diversion or advertising.

Directors who fail to reflect this distinction in their work have been criticized by educators for pulling against the learning process in ways such as the following:

(1) Failure to understand that the student must demonstrate competence as the result of the lesson, which can't be all effortless, spoon-fed entertainment.

Excitement values should not be confused with methods of promoting understanding and ability. Suspense about the outcome of an experiment is not the same thing as realizing the principle the experiment is intended to illustrate. Opening "teasers" and other gimmicks may not be in harmony with the purpose of the lesson. Cuts to human interest shots may interrupt the student's mental concentration.

(2) Failure to exhibit on the screen the proper learning stimulus because the director is not sufficiently knowledgeable in the subject area. Therefore, the director may include irrelevant material in the picture, or only part of the relevant material—or may introduce quite inappropriate material. For example, a director may cut to a new visual stimulus during a listening experience, thus disturbing aural concentration; or may urge the showing of pictures during the reading of a poem when the educational purpose is to develop the student's ability to cultivate his or her own images in response to verbal stimuli.

(3) Failure to exhibit the most effective learning stimuli because the director prefers to determine the shots by means of his or her own creative instincts rather than heeding the advice of learning psychologists or scientifically determining which of various visual approaches are most effective with a sample group of students.

(4) Failure to appreciate that a fast pace is not always conducive to learning. Thus the director may not keep the camera on the learning stimulus long enough to permit comprehension, analysis, or note taking. The director may ignore the need for pauses designed to elicit student reactions such as thinking, investigating, problem solving, and practicing a new learning. In so doing, the director has probably carried over from "show-business television" a notion that the lesson should be a one-way, sustained, fast-paced performance by the teacher, rather than a means whereby the teacher stimulates activity in the mind of the student.

(5) Failure to accommodate to the physical conditions of television reception in a classroom. This results in the director not making images big enough and clear enough for the back row of a class of up to thirty students who are probably sharing the same receiver.

3.2   Commercials, on the other hand, require a different treatment.

If you are shooting a hard-sell commercial where your purpose is to create desire to buy, you may need to impress the potential customers' senses and emotions with forceful shots, filled with motion and frequent changes, which sweep them along with little time to question what has (or has not) been presented to them.

Certainly, you will want to be ever conscious (as some student directors are not) that the product and the sponsor's name should be shown to best advantage.

Yet not all commercials are identical in character. One which aims to portray the feminine allure that results from using a hair conditioner should not be staged and a shot like one aiming to portray the jangled nerves that can be avoided by drinking a caffeine-free beverage.

3.3   The general purpose and character of the material should govern the treatment of the details.

For example, to create an atmosphere of feminine allure you will probably need to work with soft lighting, gentle curves, and flowing transitions, whereas to create an impression of jangled nerves would presume percussive movements, angular composition, contrast lighting, and abrupt transitions.

To make the details consistent, you first have to recognize the purpose and character of the whole.

But besides being faithful to the whole, you need to interpret the material point by point. Therefore:

4   Recognize, and support by individual picture statements, the changing points at each successive moment of the program material.

Always keep asking, "What is the point that I should be making at this moment? Then make your picture support that point and no other. Follow the advice of Andreas Feininger, writing about the still photographer's picture story:

> The simpler the subject, the more direct the impression. . . . In comparison to the eye, the lens sees too much. . . . Rather than trying to say everything in one picture, subdivide complex subjects and setups and show them in the form of a short series in which each picture clearly illustrates only a single point— as a good writer prefers several short sentences to a single long and complicated one.[1]

5   Recognize, and define by your pictorial treatment, the structural units of the material.

This applies to passages in music, figures in dance, paragraphs in speech, units in drama, plays in a sporting event, and even to the succession of stories read by a news reporter. It also applies to such changes as between ending a song and beginning to talk, or between telling a humorous story and then pointing out cold fronts on a weather map.

5.1   Reinforce changes in the structure of the material by pronounced visual changes.

[1] Andreas Feininger, *The Creative Photographer* (Englewood Cliffs, N.J.: Prentice-Hall, 1955), p. 290.

These visual changes can be accomplished by movement of the performers. Thus, to introduce a new topic, you can have performers rise or sit or cross to new locations. They can pick up properties or lay them down. They can stop moving. The performers can turn from one center of attention to another. Devices such as these are constantly employed by actors. They are also useful in instructional videos where you wish to emphasize the introduction of new ideas.

The changes can also be made by camera movements. The camera can pan decisively from one subject to another, for instance, or it can zoom out to emphasize the end of a musical selection.

Most commonly, changes of pattern are marked by shot changes. These changes will be more decisive to the degree that there is a pronounced contrast of shot content—of screen size, perhaps, or of composition, or of subject. There will be little distinction between the news segment and the commercial that follows it if, as in one student director's exercise, both the news announcer and the commercial announcer are similarly framed and similarly attired, sitting at similar desks in front of similar backgrounds.

5.2 Correlate your shot changes with changes in the pattern of the program content; do not call them at random.

Example: During a piano selection you, as the director, see that the off-air camera operator has an interesting shot of the hammers hitting the strings. You like it, so you take it. Then the camera just released gets an equally fascinating shot of the pianist's reflection in the under side of the piano cover. You cannot wait to show this to your audience, so you take this, too. Your eyes have been busy, but your ears have been shut. Such randomly timed shots as these punctuate as falsely as do the periods in the following:

> One phrase of the. Music ends and another. Begins then the selection. Finishes
> and the performer shifting. To talk announces. The title of this next selection
> he then starts. Playing again.

It sometimes helps to know the exact timing of each structural unit so that you'll be ready for a change when it occurs. When dealing with music of any appreciable length and complexity, it is advisable to follow a score on which shot changes and camera movements are marked at the appropriate measures.

5.3 Avoid breaking up the unity of a figure with unnecessary shots so that one can't see the forest through the trees.

By "figure" is meant a combination of elements (notes in music, for instance, or movements in a dance) that produces—unless you interfere with it—a single, complete, and distinct impression.

Ballet enthusiasts do not approve of the director who cuts in details of dancers' heads or feet, or changes camera angles during some figure in which a constant and consistent view of the total bodily activity should be maintained. Devotees of serious music are irritated when a director changes shots in the middle of a sustained musical phrase.

This kind of disruption is not confined to the arts. Suppose that a golf professional is demonstrating the technique of driving, which includes addressing the ball, the backswing, the downswing, and the follow-through. The director begins on a camera facing the demonstrator, but as the downswing commences, takes a camera facing in the direction of the drive. The motive, presumably, is to follow the flight of the ball down the fairway. This motive, however, is at odds with the purpose of the demonstration, which is to let viewers who are interested in improving their golfing form observe the continuity of the whole driving action. By cutting, the director has dissected this action and disoriented the observer.

To avoid taking new shots when the structure of the material fails to warrant it does not necessarily deprive you of all creative opportunity. For example, when shooting a pianist whose music lacks pronounced contrasts and changes, you can truck and dolly your camera to support crescendo and diminuendo, or merely to induce a pleasant sense of ongoing development.

5.4   If you have to change your subject during a sustained passage, use camera movement or dissolves, not takes.

As previously observed, a camera movement such as a dolly, pan, or zoom moves smoothly and continuously from one subject to another. As a sustained movement, its appropriateness for supporting a sustained passage in the subject matter should be apparent. Contrasting with this is the take (or cut), which does indeed cut shots apart, making a sudden and complete cleavage between them, and being, therefore, unsatisfactory as a unifying device.

When you need to unify two separate shots, use the dissolve. With this device, the shots overlap and intermingle, blending together much as when one chemical substance dissolves in another.

Example: During an instrumental performance, the lead in developing a musical figure passes in succession from one instrument or group of instruments to another. Rather than stressing the introduction of the new instruments, the director rightly chooses to preserve and clarify the structure of the music by sustaining the continuity of the figure. Therefore, the director pans between the instruments if they are adjacent; or if they are not adjacent, dissolves between them. Or if the passage begins on one instrument and includes progressively more instruments as it develops, the director will probably support this expansion with a zoom-out.

Another example: A lecturer on world survival observes that, despite differences, the races of mankind have many qualities in common—whereupon there appears on the screen a series of still pictures: first of a Caucasian family, then a Negroid family, then a Mongoloid family, and so on. If the pictures are on slides, the director will dissolve between them. If they are photographic enlargements mounted on easels in the studio, the director will probably truck or dolly from one to another. Whether by gliding between them or blending them, the director can help to stress their mutual association in the family of mankind. On the other hand, if the lecturer uses the sequence to emphasize differences between the races, the director should use takes to distinguish the subjects as separate entities.

6 Conform your pictorial transitions to those in the subject matter.

Because of its blending quality, the dissolve should be used to harmonize with program content that is itself marked by blended or gliding transitions. Although most kinds of program content are punctuated by changes that occur at precise instants and may therefore be appropriately accented by takes, a few evolve without marked breaks. For instance, there are the smoothly evolving movements of ice skaters, waltzers, and fashion models. There is also the pianist who drifts through a selection of reveries or nocturnes, segueing from one to another. In such material there are no precise instants of change with which a take might appropriately coincide. Dissolves, however, change in the same manner as the content changes and can help to preserve its flow.

If, on the other hand, transitions within a sequence are not blended in the manner just described, do not dissolve between them. For example, in televising a rock-and-roll singer, you wish to go from a medium shot to a closeup at the end of a musical phrase. A take in this case will make a "clean" transition. A dissolve will be "sloppy," since it begins in one phrase and ends in another.

6.1 Consider the degree to which changes occur in the material, and regulate accordingly the degree of contrast between one shot and another.

Action that is violent or that contains sudden reversals and big surprises demands pronounced contrast between shot and shot. But in a love scene where everything—girl, moonlight, and murmured words—is soft and pretty, the contrast between shots should be much more restrained.

Pertinent here is the following note to a student director: "To cut from a long shot to a closeup during a gentle, ongoing action, such as that of the guitar vocalist's melancholy refrain, is too abrupt. One needs an intermediate waist shot or a gradual dolly or zoom-in. A sudden change of scale would serve to reinforce a change of selection from dreamy ballad, say, to rock and roll, but in the content at hand all musical transitions are very gradual."

7 Reflect the degree of animation in the action by the pace of your visual changes.

The slower and more quiet the scene, the more restricted can be the performers' movements and the frequency of shot changes. Increasing animation is usually reflected by bolder, quicker, and more frequent movements by the performers. It can also be supported by increasing the rate of cutting.

8 Show by your camera treatment whether the subjects are allied or opposed.

Alliance between two subjects can be reinforced by maintaining them in the same shot with more or less equal attention on each. Thus, you would maintain a shared shot of two entertainers as they perch side by side on stools, claiming long friendship and reminiscing about their past experiences together.

Opposition can be reinforced by taking the subjects in separate one-shots or by cutting between reverse-angle shots. Such treatment is appropriate, for example, in a debate when two characters are in conflict, or in music to contrast two opposing musical statements, or in a contest show to reinforce the sense of competition.

9 Harmonize your camera treatment with any exaggerated or distorted effects in the material.

In productions of the thriller type, for instance, the characters are apt to be boldly drawn and contrasted. There are swiftly developing complications, sudden reversals of fortune, and situations that are magnified and intense. For corresponding camera treatment, the director may use unusual camera angles, sudden pans and zooms, abrupt takes between contrasting shot content, and wide-angle lenses to exaggerate the speed and force of impending danger.

10 Use your cameras to build up the increasing tension of a situation.

To create dramatic tension is to build up the dynamic potential of an event, meanwhile delaying its occurrence, thereby generating excitement in the audience but delaying its release. This technique resembles the stretching of a rubber band.

10.1 Build tension through suspense.

Keep the camera off a subject while desire to see it is being built up.

Begin by showing only part of a subject, then dolly back or zoom out to reveal it by degrees.

10.2 Build tension by using your cameras to point up in turn the forces and elements that are about to become engaged.

Thus, in a baseball game, before a crucial pitch, show the pitcher hesitating; show the runners waiting near each base, ready to steal to the next one.

Thus, in a circus act, show the high-wire artist on her aerial perch, then the height and thinness of the wire she will attempt to cross.

11   Regulate the forcefulness of your picture statements to the relative degrees of importance in the program material.

11.1   Recognize that some parts of the program are more important than others.

Special stress, for instance, is needed for the introductory appearance of subjects that are assuming a dominant role in the action. For example, the host of a children's program, saying, "Now let's see what's in our mystery box," moves away from camera toward a box in the background, which appears very small and insignificant in relation to everything else in the frame. This action does not create the desired effect. As the new center of attention, the box has received insufficient visual stress. A better effect would be created when, upon delivering the lines, the host moves toward the camera which, while dollying back, reveals the box in the foreground.

In drama, special stress is needed for key lines and actions, i.e., those which epitomize character, delineate the contending forces, or are major developments of the plot. It is also needed for crises and for the climax, where the major forces engage in a decisive encounter from which results the final state of equilibrium.

Similarly, important statements are to be found in speeches, in music, and in many other kinds of program material.

In all dynamically constructed material there is a pattern of crescendo and diminuendo, of increasing force followed by relaxation. Within a given line of development, new material must be more impressive than that which preceded it in order to maintain interest. Thus, a magic act progresses in the direction of the increasingly skillful or spectacular, and a scene in drama toward accumulated meaning or a more complicated situation or stronger assertions of action or emotion. When one line of development has reached its end, there is usually some relaxation as a new line of development begins. But overall, the various lines of development themselves mount to a climax where the program attains its highest level of importance and aims to exert the strongest impression on its audience.

Having ascertained the degrees of importance in your material, portray them with picture statements of appropriate force.

11.2   A picture statement will be more forceful to the degree that it economizes the viewer's attention.

Writing on the analogous subject of force in language, Herbert Spencer made this useful observation:

> Regarding language as an apparatus of symbols for the conveyance of thought, we may say that, as in a mechanical apparatus, the more simple and better arranged its parts, the greater will be the effect produced. In either case, whatever force is absorbed by the machine is deducted from the result. A reader or listener has at each moment but a limited amount of mental power available. To recognize and interpret the symbols presented to him requires part of this power; to arrange and combine the images suggested requires a further part; and only that part which remains can be used for realizing the thought conveyed. Hence the more time and attention it takes to receive and understand each sentence, the less time and attention can be given to the contained idea; and the less vividly will that idea be conceived.[2]

In visual communication, economy of attention can be achieved by arranging the parts of the picture to be easily read as a whole, isolated from distracting and irrelevant information.

In progressing from picture to picture, a common way to isolate a subject for more forceful attention is to move from a group shot to a one-shot of it, either by taking the one-shot or by having the subject move away from the group, with the camera following the move. For still more force, one can concentrate attention closely on the most expressive features of the subject, either by taking a closeup, by panning, dollying, or zooming into a closeup, or by having the subject itself move into a closeup.

11.3   A picture statement will be more forceful to the degree that its active content affects the viewer.

As a general rule, a speaker's words will seem more forceful to the degree they are directed toward camera. Thus, by changing from a balanced two-shot to reverse over-shoulder shots of an arguing couple, one can move the television viewer into the field of fire, so to speak, so that each character's emotion affects the viewer directly and forcefully.

The closer a subject appears to the viewer, the more forceful the subject will be. When a person is speaking directly to the camera, an especially important remark can be reinforced by having the person move closer to the camera to deliver it. Even when the audience is not being addressed directly, it is accepted in television as in the theater that the strongest move a performer can make is one directed toward the audience.

[2]Herbert Spencer, *Philosophy of Style* (New York: Pageant Press, 1959), p. 17.

11.4   A picture statement will be more forceful to the degree that anticipation has been created for it.

For instance, after the host has introduced the rock band by name, the camera pans briefly across the amplifier stacks on stage before the band comes into view. The slight delay builds anticipation, which adds importance to the musicians' appearance. Other examples of this principle have also been cited earlier in this text.

You will remember also how, in commercials, anticipation is sometimes raised by creating imbalance in the frame. The camera is panned to leave one side of the screen empty; then the blank space is filled with some important visual message.

One can also leave the new subject outside the frame until anticipation for it has been created. To have it in view before its turn to enter the action is to deny it the impact of "making an entrance."

11.5   A picture statement will be more forceful to the degree that its appearance constitutes a pronounced change from what has just preceded it.

Familiarity and sameness dull attention, but viewers will attend strongly to something different from what they have been experiencing. Hence, to impress them with the importance of a subject, introduce it by means of some pronounced visual change. Thus, have a performer rise, move, stop, or turn to deliver some important remark. Or take a new shot substantially different from the preceding one. A take has the power to say, "Look, something new and important is happening."

At least it will say this provided it follows a shot that has been sustained for some appreciable duration. Takes, like other devices, lose their force when repeated too constantly. Hence, avoid using them simply because your subjects are too far apart to be included in the same frame. Don't separate the hostess and her guest so widely that, when they are chatting over tea, you must cut to the hostess when she asks, "One lump or two?", and then to the guest when she replies, "Two, please." Save your takes for things that matter.

To bring out the force of excitement in a fast sequence of brief shots, precede them by a shot of much longer duration. To make a series of closeups effective, precede them with one or more looser shots.

A subject seen constantly on one camera is liable to lose its impact. By showing something different on the screen, if only for a few moments, impact can be restored to the subject when the camera returns to it again.

When movement is involved, either by the subject or by the camera, force increases with both the speed and the degree of the change. For example, by magnifying both speed and enlargement, a wide-angle lens increases the force of an oncoming car or train.

11.6   In applying visual force, support the climactic order.

Don't exhaust your emphatic devices through overuse before the climax has been attained.

Don't shoot in the direction of anticlimax. For example, when shooting the lead guitar player, don't start with tight closeups of his fingers picking the strings, the perspiration on his face, and the glint in his eye—and then back away into long shots. Another example: If you introduce a trio of performers by progressively zooming out from a shot of one of them, the second person, being smaller on the screen, has less impact than the first, and the third person is weaker still.

Know your objective. If you wish to pan across a line of military tanks that are passing in review, which is the more climactic direction in which to pan? By starting close on the nearest tank and widening the shot, you are stressing the vast armament the country possesses. By starting wide and panning onto the tread of the nearest tank, you are emphasizing the relentless, crushing power of this type of war machine.

11.7   Suit your force to the occasion.

By regulating the force of your visual treatment, you control the degree to which an idea or event or emotion is impressed on your viewer, and that degree should be proportionate to the significance you wish to convey. Too much force results in bombast—defined by Herbert Spencer as "a force of expression too great for the magnitude of the ideas embodied." Therefore, don't be like the director who shoots every interview in his sports program by cropping the participants at the hairline and the chin. On the other hand, as Hamlet says, "Be not too tame, neither." Don't shoot everything so loosely that your visual statements are indecisive and pointless.

12   In expressing the nature of your material, encourage and do not inhibit the expressive abilities of your performers.

As previously stated in this book, audiences do not tune in to see your camera shots, but rather to see human beings doing something. And human beings, although some directors may be reluctant to admit it, are capable of infinitely more expression than are camera shots. Particularly in televising drama, it is wise to begin by determining what human movements and relationships are natural and appropriate to the circumstances, letting these play the lead, as it were, and the cameras the accompaniment.

The more you use your performers for emphasizing points, directing attention from one to another, and changing the picture composition through their movements, the more you can save your shot changes for moments when they really count.

Chapter 17

Examples of Interpretation

This chapter contains notes written by the authors as critiques of student-directed exercises. These notes should help to illustrate and reinforce many of the principles presented in the preceding chapter.

Poetry Reading

Chris's exercise provides an example of some of the director's concerns in communicating his or her material. The exercise consisted of his sister reading excerpts from Edna St. Vincent Millay (lyric poetry, feminine, and somewhat sad), talking briefly to introduce each excerpt, then reading it from a book in her hand.

What Chris did:

He realized that mood was important and that the poetry was "de-materialized," a matter of the heart and spirit rather than of physical objects. Accordingly, he found an appropriate musical theme and used a simple, tasteful title card. He set his reader on a simple, high stool against a plain twofold flat. He wanted his shooting sequence to support the structure of the program. Therefore, he used one shot for introductions and another for reading the excerpts. He resisted cutting between the cameras during the excerpts since there was no motivation in the material for so doing and since a camera change would create in the viewers a physical awareness that could disturb their concentration on the poetry.

What the instructor suggested:

What part of the scene carries the visual expression?
In this case, it was subtle shadings of expression in the performer's face and eyes, which were too distant in Chris's shots to discern easily. Much of the physical

material he included in the frame was inert and inexpressive—also distracting (the lavalier cord and the highlighted knees seen at the bottom of the shot used for introductions). Therefore, Chris was advised to make both shots proportionately closer: a waist shot for the introductions and a shoulder shot for reading the poetry.

Is the expressive quality properly supported?

(1) The background seemed to be too sharply focused for the "dematerialized" feeling of the poetry. Thus, the instructor suggested that the background be placed farther behind the performer and that the cameras move back and then, using the zoom lens, zoom into a more telephoto shot to place the background outside the depth of field.

(2) The instructor studied the lighting. As Chris had it, the key light was frontal on the poetry reading shots, illuminating the features symmetrically and uniformly. On the introduction shots it was falling from an angle, modeling the face with soft shadow, which would have helped the mood of the poetry. Therefore, Chris was advised to reverse his shots camera for camera.

(3) Then the instructor proposed that he have his performer face a little to the side for poetry reading. This was done for several reasons. First, it improved the lighting distribution, ensuring that a triangular patch of light fell so as to illuminate the reader's right eye. Second, the informal balance seemed to make her features more attractive and the pictorial composition more in harmony with Millay's poetic style than a stiff symmetrical arrangement. And third, Chris was asked, "Where should audience attention be during the poetry reading?" Chris answered, "On the poetry." Correct, not staring into the reader's eyes.

(4) Between shots Chris was advised to use dissolves, which would let the savor of the poetry die out more slowly.

Can the performance itself be improved?

The reader puckered her brow periodically as she read—a sign of strain or a mannerism that the director should have tried to eliminate. Remember, as a director, you work on perfecting the performance as well as the shots. The performance is what the viewers notice and care about.

This was really quite a simple show, but notice how many details of expression were involved. That's why we recommend that you stick to short exercises, so there's time to work on improving them.

A Piano Pickup

Terry's piano pickup was commendably faithful to the structure of the pianist's selection.

It had unity: at the opening she had camera 1 (*Figure 17/1*) dolly out from a shot of the strings, and at the end she returned the camera to the same shot, thus signifying unmistakable finality.

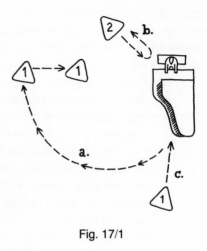

It had variety, moving out (shot "a") from the strings to the whole piano, then arcing through a varied angle. Next, shot "b" from a new angle moved from a full shot of the pianist into a closeup of his hands and back to a full shot again. Then camera 1 returned back to its opening position "c," from a reverse angle, dollied back into the

Fig. 17/1

same closeup of the strings seen at the program's beginning.

It had development: it grew and then diminished in keeping with the pattern of the music, reaching its climax some four-fifths of the way through with shot "b's" closest approach to the hands. The take from shot "a" to "b" occurred at a pronounced change in the music. The dolly-in during shot "b" accompanied a crescendo, during which the hands of the player became more active and interesting to watch. The dolly-back from these hands accompanied a musical diminuendo. The change to shot "c" also occurred at a change in the musical structure, but since it was musically a rather blended change, the camera change was a dissolve rather than a take.

All this, at least, is what Terry intended. In practice, she found that it takes time to pace camera moves to the duration of the musical passages. On the first run-through the arcing movement of shot "a" went too fast. The camera reached its destination too early; so we waited until time for shot "b" with a static picture, during which interest started to wane.

Preparing a Child's Hospital Breakfast Tray

This exercise illustrated some useful principles:

To have only one camera ever show the demonstrator's face meant that she only needed to look toward one camera. This helped to relax her by making things simple for her. It also meant a consistent visual orientation for the viewer.

Props were shown by themselves in a cleared area before being added to the other objects on the tray. Thus, they made a full impression on us, since we did not have to divide our attention between them and several other attractions in the frame.

The closeup camera and display arrangements were so related that objects were always framed at the correct size—the tray, as the largest item, being farther from camera than the area where objects were seen before being placed on the tray.

One change of placement was made. On the first run-through, the girl's arm reached up close to camera to get slices of toast, then moved backward with the bread to place them on a small plate farther from camera. As revised, the hand picked up toast from close to the demonstrator, then advanced it toward camera to place it on the plate. This was an improvement for several reasons:

(1) The strongest move is one toward camera; the approaching subject grows in size, taking more and more command of the frame, reaching a climax when the movement ceases, the subject having gained its greatest magnification. In the first run-through, the advancing movement was that of an empty hand, the climax occurring as it procured a piece of toast in the foreground; thereafter, the receding movement of the toast to the plate was in an anticlimactic direction. In the second run-through, the climax occurred as it should, at the moment of placing the toast on the plate.

(2) The first run-through required two movements of the arm, forward and back in a kind of hook pattern. The revision required only one deft, concise advance of the hand to accomplish the business. Grace comes from economy of effort. So does force. Always work to make one motion do the work for two.

(3) In the first run-through, when the arm withdrew, the plate was too small in the frame. Moving the plate closer to camera gave it the dominance it needed as the subject of the shot.

A Guitar-Playing Ballad Singer

Never having heard his vocalist's selection, Bud's problem was to work out shots and transitions that would suit its mood, which turned out to be lonesome, and its tempo, which was sustained and drifting. He discovered that close shots of the bright, evenly lighted face were less effective than those showing the shadowed sides of the figure and included a little lonely-feeling dark space around it. Takes, he found, were too abrupt for the drift of the opening and closing segments, and sudden changes from wide to tight framing fought against the rather even tenor of the piece. He also discovered that these opening and closing sections offered no interesting fingering of guitar strings to justify a closeup. As time for the exercise ran out, he was beginning to discover that there was a middle section of the song which, being stronger and brighter in feeling with more vigorous chords, might have provided a variation in camera treatment. The moral: Although a director sometimes has to shoot a number like this ad lib, the camerawork will be far more appropriate if you know the mood and structure of the music in advance.

Pantomime Face Panel Quiz

(Excerpts from the Critique)

One of the first duties in shooting a contest is to establish a sense of opposition between the contestants. In the introduction, single shots of each contestant alone would have done more to set up the contest. Remember the fight announcer's "In this corner . . . and in this corner . . ."

Simply to keep alternating between the three-shot and the pantomime face that the panelists were trying to identify did too little to promote the excitement of the contest. Intercutting between the various faces would have livened up the game—not only because of the increase in visual variety, but also because more action and interaction result from seeing elements isolated in sequence: first the stimulus, then the response; first an action, then a reaction. This method raises anticipation, then pays it off. It isolates each subject for increased concentration, thus giving it greater impact. It comes in close enough to let one appreciate the facial expressions—the perplexity, the dawning realizations, etcetera, which are strong interest factors that you can't afford to throw away. Intercutting promotes interplay, the exciting quality of give-and-take.

A Commercial for Contact Lenses

In this one, eyes were most important. The girl announcer should have been chosen for the warmth and vitality of her eyes. The lighting crew might have worked at the special task of giving her eyes a sparkle. Framing was too loose, at first; her turn into profile, saying, "You can't tell that I'm wearing contact lenses," didn't make sense since we weren't close enough to tell anyway.

The painting, which was defocused to show how blurry things can look without lenses, was done in an Impressionist technique without defined contours, and therefore continued to look rather blurred even after it had been focused back in.

Always keep asking, "What is the point I'm trying to get across at this particular moment?" (E.g., to show how much sharper things look with proper lenses; to show that one can't detect when contact lenses are being worn; to show that contact lenses preserve the natural appeal of a girl's eyes, and so on.) Then make each point as positively as you can.

Drygas Commercial

Zero in more and more on what really matters. This is particularly important at the end of a sales pitch where you want to finish off with a strong, lasting impression.

At the end of the Drygas commercial, Ted had already held up a can of Drygas in a hip shot. Then he produced a can of windshield spray from his pocket, saying, "While you're there, also get a can of . . ." and that was the finish, with both products very distant, competing for attention with a door, trees, and a bold-patterned overcoat. Result: no IMPACT! Furthermore, the cans stayed held in his hands for several seconds without anything happening to them, which meant that they were constantly getting weaker as an interest factor.

So we had Ted walk toward camera with them, holding them somewhat forward and almost at a height with his face. As he approached, more and more competing elements disappeared from the frame; the products got larger and larger; and they also got into sharp focus compared with his face, which got softer because of the narrowing depth of field. Furthermore, because Ted was bearing down on us, concentrating more and more on each of us as an individual customer, his persuasion heightened. More and more we could feel our contact with him, see the detail in his eyes which said, "I'm very earnest about this and I'm talking to you!"

Remember: action must have either crescendo or diminuendo to keep it from growing tedious. In brief and urgent messages like commercials it's usually crescendo that counts. Don't keep things so-so. Make them more so!

A Scene from *The Glass Menagerie*

Know the meaning you want to convey at each point in the action. Then visualize pictures that will best convey this meaning, and try to have the cameras in the right place to convey the meanings, one after another.

For instance, you want to convey the feeling that a boy and girl are having an awkward time together. Maybe space them apart on a longish seat, start on a shot of him and then pan across space to her, thus emphasizing their separation.

You want to point up the girl's enthusiasm about her little glass unicorn. Therefore shoot close, so that people can see the light in her eyes and the little, shining, fragile object in her hand.

You want to contrast the boy's physical energy with her shrinking, static posture. So perhaps shoot past her, seated in the foreground, to the full figure of the boy dancing by himself to the music of the café across the street.

You want to show her gathering courage to accept his invitation to dance. Maybe we could look down toward her over his shoulder, ultimately to see her rising to him.

The spell is broken when the unicorn is knocked off the table and broken. Surely a cut here will stress the abruptness of the calamity and change of mood. But if the abruptness is to be felt by the audience, you will need to have refrained from cutting for some time before this moment; otherwise the device will have been exhausted from overuse.

To mark the moment strongly, try cutting from a long shot of them dancing together to a closeup of the girl's face as she registers dismay at the sound of the breaking glass. Then cut away to his face, looking concerned. The first cut makes an extreme contrast of scale, the second, a total change of picture content. Try audio contrast also, by having the music end with the first cut and by having neither of them say anything while the two closeups are taken.

These are our visions. You, of course, may have your own interpretations; but the essential thing is that you have interpretations and that you be able to justify them from a thorough analysis of the action.

Then you realize your interpretations in terms of human movement and camera treatment. Get your characters to move. (That's life. That's the show.) And then get your cameras to follow them, panning, booming up or down, widening or narrowing the frame, changing the angle and frame content as may be necessary. As long as the characters are active, the audience will not notice what the camera is doing—as long as its moves are motivated by the action of the characters.

In this connection, ask more of your cameras than you do. In the scene just described, we tried to show what a pedestal mount could accomplish:

Camera (lens at 25mm) pedestaled down to the girl's seated level, looks past her to the boy and the lighted café sign through the window . . .

pans right to follow the boy as he dances by himself . . .

booms way up and dollies in as he comes forward, so that we look down over his shoulder to the girl, who eventually rises up toward us . . .

and into his arms—the camera meanwhile tilting up to bring more of his head into the shot . . .

then simultaneously booming down and dollying back as she tries some tentative steps with him.

As the camera is backing one way, they back the other into a long shot that shows how she lets herself go into broad motion.

Then cut as the unicorn breaks!

Note the changes in composition achieved by the characters' movements—the characters leading and the cameras playing the accompanying harmony to their movement.

Breaking the Suspect's Alibi

Tuesday evening we made considerable revisions in a little scene during which a police inspector grilled a suspect with little success until he finally produced an incriminating document which forced a confession.

In the first version there was a little physical activity to begin with when the suspect entered the office and approached the inspector's desk, but thereafter nothing happened but a monotonous succession of reverse-angle shots. Besides being dully repetitive, these shots failed to establish the changing points in the encounter and its overall construction.

Here's the structure of the piece as your instructor sees it. It starts rather slowly and deliberately with the two men first meeting and sizing up each other. Then it intensifies with an exchange of questions and answers, which gets the inspector nothing but frustration. Next comes a change: the inspector gets inspired for a new attack, which leads to his disclosure of the paper. This brings the climax: the suspect confesses.

One has to point up these changes—particularly the climax, toward which the whole action is driving. The first version failed to point up the changes for two principal reasons:

(1) There was not enough opportunity for varied expression by the performers, because they were nailed down to fixed positions.

(2) There was insufficiently varied expression in the camera treatment.

Here's how we tried to overcome these difficulties:

Reverse-angle shots were quite appropriate during the exchange of questions and answers. To restrict them to this exchange and protect their effectiveness there, we decided to have the inspector rise from his desk chair, both to emphasize his frustration and to give him more physical latitude for pressing home his winning attack. As outcome of this attack, the suspect's confession could be supported by taking a close one-shot of him, but to give this take sufficient impact we decided to precede it by a sequence sustained on one camera. So the resulting shot pattern became:

Suspect's entrance and
move to desk . . . . One camera
First round of questions
and alibis . . . . Reverse-angle shots
Inspector's frustration. . . . . A rise
Inspector's successful
attack . . . . One camera, broader movement
Suspect's confession . . . . Take to a close one-shot

Your instructor particularly welcomed being able to work with the two passages on one camera for another reason besides those already cited. To change your picture content and to make new points, most of you rely wholly on taking new shots. But new points can still be made and the composition varied even while remaining on one camera. To remind you of this, a rough storyboard of the entire camera treatment has been sketched. Read this in connection with the floor plan (*Figure 17/2*). On that plan the dash line shows the approximate path of the

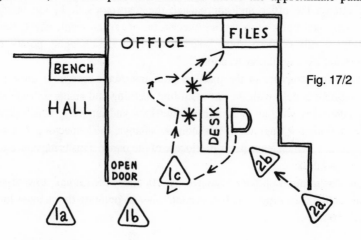

Fig. 17/2

inspector after his exasperated rise. The asterisks indicate approximate locations of the suspect after he has entered the office.

Now, here are the picture statements:

(1) Camera 1, from position 1a, shoots office door.

(2) Inspector emerges a step or two into hall, looks to camera left, and beckons, motivating camera 1 to pan left, revealing . . .

(3) the suspect, seated on bench at end of hall. Inspector exits from frame back to his desk, leaving door open.

(4) Suspect rises and moves forward toward door, thereby enlarging on screen so that we get a close look at his face. He enters office, camera 1 dollying after him until . . .

(5) it reaches a two-shot, during which inspector goes behind his desk, sits, and fires his first question. This shot is repeated a few times, alternating with . . .

(6) a reverse-angle shot taken by camera 2 from position 2a. The first take emphasizes the suspect's claim: "I don't know anything about it."

(7) Exasperated from getting nowhere with his line of questioning, inspector rises (on camera 1), moves around camera right end of desk into a closeup, which registers his inspiration for a new attack.

(8) He swoops in on suspect, camera 1 dollying after him at the same pace into position 1c. (Camera 2 can now move to position 2b in order to be ready for its next shot.)

(9) Not having received the answer he expects, inspector strides to camera left, camera 1 panning with him as he halts, turns, and swoops back right again . . .

(10) this time to confront suspect from the side.

(11) Then he moves back to filing cabinet, leaving suspect in foreground. He finds the paper he wants and . . .

(12) comes forward to wave the incriminating document under the suspect's nose, camera 1 simultaneously moving in on suspect from the opposite direction.

(13) Take 2, from position 2b, for a big closeup of suspect as he confesses.

Notice how each of the preceding picture statements makes its own definite point:

(1) tells where we are.

(2) introduces the inspector and creates suspense: he's ready for someone.

(3) pays off who the someone is to a degree, but plays on our desire to see him closer. Gives promise of some kind of interaction between the someone and the inspector.

(4) enlarges our visual acquaintance with the someone; also, by revealing the uncertainty with which he enters the door, further arouses our curiosity about what is to happen.

(5) sets up the confrontation and points up the opening question, thus starting the conflict, which is the main subject of the scene.

(6) alternating with (5), reinforces the opposition between the two characters. (Remember that these were practically the only shots used in the original run-through.)

(7) ends the first round of questioning with the inspector's rise and points up his determination (seen in closeup) to go for a second round.

(8) uses a camera movement in toward the suspect in order to reinforce the inspector's attack, and also in order to view the second round more closely than the first round, thus helping to build toward the climax.

(9) helps to make the second round more active and urgent by allowing the inspector freer movement. This movement varies the composition by carrying him away from the suspect into a one-shot. It gives more impact to his next question by getting the suspect out of the picture momentarily. This renews interest in the suspect when he does enter the picture again. It also obviously allows the inspector to move in on the suspect again.

(10) illustrates what has been explained in the three preceding sentences.

(11) uses a strong movement in depth to introduce and point up the filing cabinet, from which the document appears, which wins the round.

(12) is, so to speak, a squeeze play, with the inspector moving in on the victim from one direction and the camera moving in on him from the other. The converse camera movement has the effect of intensifying the inspector's movement, which, being straight toward camera, is already a strong one. The moves result in a tight two-shot, which permits the significant document to be as large as possible in the frame.

(13) is, of course, the take to a big image of the suspect's face, to give maximum force to his confession.

This example shows how changes of picture can support changes of meaning from moment to moment, adding not merely visual variety, but also a variety of understanding, which makes the viewer's experience more perceptive and more dynamic.

Camera Treatment for a String Quartet

Although not a critique of a student exercise, this final example is still apropos. It is a list of shooting principles that were used in video recording the performances of a string quartet:

Dissolve during the more legato and lyrical passages. During the more staccato and dramatic ones use takes.

In general, use takes to separate one passage from another. Within a passage, if shots of different picture content have to be taken, unify them with dissolves. Pan, truck, or zoom when the lead for sustaining the passage passes from one instrument to another. For crescendo and diminuendo, dolly or zoom in and out.

When you do dolly or zoom out to support a portion that is louder and more dynamic, boom up and shoot down as much as possible in order to fill the frame with the activity of the musicians, since a low angle shows too much of the motionless background. An alternative to dolly-backs and zoom-outs for very agitated portions is to zoom in close to single instrumentalists and then pan from one to another.

The symmetry of the frontal group shot does not seem as active as those shots taken from side angles.

The greater the contrast in musical content between one passage and another, the greater should be the contrast in shot content—in angle, for instance, or screen size of the visual subject matter.

For especially dramatic passages, try close-in shots with a wide lens from a low camera position. These will increase the contrast in size between foreground and background figures, supporting the dynamic contrasts in the music.

Chapter 18

Stimulating Responses

1   Stimulate your viewers. Make and keep them responsive to your program.

Think of yourself as working not merely on a program but on an audience. What passes through your cameras is only a means to an end. What you are really programming is a sequence of active responses in your viewers, in their minds, emotions, and motor mechanisms. Think, then, of the program you are directing as a series of stimuli designed to elicit audience responses.

2   These stimuli should be visual as well as aural.

The presence of a screen leads your viewers to expect stimulation for their eyes as well as their ears. Unless they have been warned in some fashion not to expect much visual stimulation and are prepared to feel rewarded primarily by what they hear, the lack of visual information will make them inattentive and apathetic.

3   The visual stimuli should satisfy two primary conditions.

3.1   They should be definite, positive, and pointed.

We tend to respond to only one stimulus at a time. The stimulus must be sufficiently pronounced to provoke a response and sufficiently definite to elicit the response intended. Therefore, as you were advised at the outset of this book, learn to perceive your program content as a series of changing points. Convey each point by means of its own separate picture statement, making that statement as positive as possible and as forceful as its significance warrants.

3.2   The visual stimuli should keep changing.

A constant set of conditions does not act as a stimulus; a stimulus is always a change. In a static visual situation (e.g., when a still photograph is on camera), the viewer's interest drains away as soon as the pertinent information has been exhausted. As a director, you must keep cranking up interest as you would an old spring-driven phonograph. To do this, keep giving the viewer new meaningful visual information. Keep showing him or her new things to notice and react to. Keep the subject and/or the cameras moving.

4   Induce visual change through your camera treatment.

4.1   Keep new visual subjects out of sight until their turn comes to enter the action.

Remember how, in Chapter 2, this was done with the guest violinist and also with his violin.

4.2   Find camera positions that provide maximum shot variety.

For an example, you may wish to look ahead to Chapter 24, "Making Floor Plans," noting Figure 24/9 (page 211) and the storyboard derived from it.

4.3   Between shots, when time permits, don't be reluctant to move cameras to locations that permit new shot possibilities.

This may become particularly desirable when a group of performers remains in fixed position for an appreciable length of time.

4.4   When animation is restricted to only a portion of the subject, shoot close enough to make that animation discernible.

For example, if a performer remains stationary and does not express himself with gestures, shoot close enough to at least reveal the changes in his facial expression.

4.5   As soon as the closeup of an inanimate subject has made its point, go back to the shot of a human being.

In entertainment television, this may happen in as little as three seconds. In instructional video, however, more time in closeup may be needed for a studied examination of the material.

4.6   To enliven a lengthy shot of a static subject, consider the possibilities of camera movement.

Can you zoom in to contract and concentrate the interest? Dolly out to expand the field of interest? Pan from one part of the subject to another? Arc around it for a progressively changing view? When contemplating such possibilities, however, remember that noticeable camera movements should have a reason that is evident to the viewer.

5 Prefer animated visuals to static ones.

For example, use pull strips on bar charts to make the bars mount one after another. Use them to make a route travel across a map. Use them (as mentioned in Chapter 1) to reveal in succession "The Five Rules of Water Safety."

Use magnetic boards, which allow the performer to add and remove pieces and move them from one place to another.

Instead of merely talking about inanimate objects, show them in action. How dull it was in one student exercise to watch the performer point out the parts of a violin as it lay inertly on a table. How much livelier (and more informative) to see the performer pick it up, pluck a string, tighten a peg, demonstrate the shoulder rest, etcetera. Similarly, to assemble a rifle or take it apart is more interesting than merely to point out the parts of the assembled piece.

When citing statistics, use of real objects can be more interesting than abstract charts. For example, to show that the wheat flour consumed in England comes 10 percent from Great Britain, 16 percent from the Sterling Areas, and 66 percent from the western hemisphere, one might slice a loaf of bread into the relative proportions.

5.1 Some ways of animating still pictures are more appropriate to film techniques and electronic animation.

Fast zooms or quickly changing shots of the details of a still visual, particularly one of small dimensions, are likely to require the use of a film camera on an animation stand or digital effects units used in the video editing room. For information, consult books on film and video animation techniques.

6 Introduce changes through performers' action.

Again remember: the audience isn't interested in camera shots. What it wants to see is something happening to the subject of a shot—and it's your responsibility to make this happen.

Even when performers remain in fixed locations, you can still work to give them changing and expressive business.

For example, in a toothbrush commercial as devised by a student director, the salesperson sat behind a desk doing nothing but hold the toothbrush while saying 1) that the previous act on this show had been a good one, 2) introduced the toothbrush, and 3) recited its claimed advantages. This was revised as follows:

SALESPERSON:

(SEATED SIDEWISE, LOOKING OFF-CAMERA) Boy, that was great, wasn't it! etc.

(TURNING TO CAMERA) I want to show you something else that's great . . .

(LIFTING TOOTHBRUSH FROM DESKTOP) . . . and here it is: the Dent-87 toothbrush.

(RUNNING FINGERS OVER BRISTLES) The only brush made out of genuine Toughlon, the fiber that stands up, springs back, and never wilts.

(RAISING ENDORSEMENT CARD BEHIND BRUSH) Dent-87 is backed by the Loomis Laboratory Seal—and do you know why?

(EXTENDING BRUSH TOWARD CAMERA) Let's take a closer look . . . etc.

Each line brings a visual change and new business. One way to judge a television script is to count the number of stage directions. Inside the parentheses of the above revision are the factors that make a good television performance instead of "radio on camera."

7   Induce visual change through performers' movements from place to place.

It is worth repeating: don't freeze your performers into blocked-out positions merely so they can be sitting ducks for your camera shots. Resist inhibiting them with too many technical directions. Instead, recognize and promote the important role human movement plays in communicating meaning and in maintaining interest through changing visual stimulation. Examples of this have been given, particularly in the "Drygas Commercial" and "Breaking the Suspect's Alibi" in Chapter 17.

7.1   Study the language of human movement and changing physical relationships.

For acquiring command of this language, theatrical experience is invaluable.

Do you know how actors control attention and regulate emphasis through movement and gesture?

Do you realize the difference between moving with breadth and moving with restraint? . . . between agitation and composure? . . . between quick movements and slow ones?

What does it mean: to rise? . . . to sink down? . . . to confront someone? . . .

to turn your back on someone? . . . to approach a person? . . . to move away? . . . to pursue? . . . to stop and turn?

Test yourself on these questions by providing stage directions for the following speeches. What are He and She doing in the course of their dialogue? When are they together? When apart? Do you see any occasions for confrontation? . . . evasion? . . . pursuit? . . . turnings toward or away? . . . halted movement? (The speeches, by the way, make no pretense to dramatic quality. They were written by a student expressly to serve in the classroom the same purpose as here.)

SHE: All right. Now we're alone, stop holding out on me.

HE: Holding out? I don't get you.

SHE: You know what I mean. What really happened last night? What went wrong at the party?

HE: Now wait a minute, baby. I can't tell you. I wasn't even there.

SHE: After all you've promised—and now you're lying to me.

HE: Oh look, darling. I'd tell you if I could. You know that.

SHE: I thought we agreed to be partners, but it looks like this partner doesn't count for anything.

HE: Jean, wait a minute. Let me explain.

SHE: You needn't bother to explain anything, Roger—because I know.

HE: Know what?

SHE: I know you were there because you left your lighter—and here it is.

HE: Oh . . . all right. I'm sorry. But it isn't what you're thinking. Now please relax and I'll tell you everything.

In the next chapter one possible solution to this is offered, and a floor plan and camera shots are derived from the performer's movements.

7.2   Performer movement is applicable to other kinds of programs besides drama.

In a televised lesson, for example, the instructor may move to:

. . . signify the change to a new aspect of his or her subject. Thus, having finished a demonstration at a wall map, the instructor moves away from the map to introduce a new train of thought.

. . . introduce new visual material. Thus, the instructor moves over to the microscope or to the chalkboard.

. . . emphasize a special point, as by moving closer to the camera.

. . . manipulate visual material, as when operating demonstration equipment.

. . . reflect his or her state of mind, varying from stationary positions for thoughtful concentration to animated striding as the instructor gets enthusiastic about his or her subject.

. . . impersonate personages in a story which the instructor cites to illustrate a point about the subject matter.

7.3   Movements by your performers can be induced by providing different locations for different segments of the action.

Example: In staging a panel program, an upper level is provided for the opening statements of the mystery guests before they descend to occupy the seats from which they answer the panelists' questions.

Example: The violin in the guest violinist program (Chapter 2) was placed where the host and guest would have to rise and move to it.

8   Induce visual change by lighting.

Example: The mystery guests in a panel program appear first in silhouette and are then lighted, one after another, as they speak their opening lines.

Example: A couple embrace in shadow. When the girl withdraws from the embrace, her head enters a beam of light, the radiance of which expresses her radiant feeling.

9   Visual changes must be motivated.

There is something annoyingly false about the performer who, while talking to camera, gets out of a chair for no apparent reason, perches on the desk for no apparent reason, then stands up and moves around with no particular place to go. Such arbitrarily induced variety is almost as bad as no movement at all, just as shots which are taken with no motivation but visual variety are almost as bad as no takes at all.

Notice that all of the examples of visual change that have been cited in this chapter have been supported by evident reason. For example, the host and guest have to move because the violin they wish to inspect is not where they are seated. The change from silhouetted to lighted mystery guests is in keeping with the situation that panelists and audience are in the dark concerning the identity of these guests.

9.1   A director can go only so far toward inducing visual change unless the program has been planned to provide for such change.

A performer cannot interact unless there are other program ingredients, animate or inanimate, with which to interact. Nor can there be any great amount of shot variety unless there is more than one visual subject to motivate a change of shots. The director cannot be blamed for failing to inject visual interest into a program during which a single performer does nothing but talk.

9.2   Responsibility for meaningful visual changes begins with the program creator—the writer or producer, for example.

To give the program a chance to be visually stimulating, this person should follow one or more of the following suggestions:

. . . Choose subject matter which inherently involves physical movement: a person doing things instead of merely talking.

. . . Otherwise, involve multiple visual subjects—at least two persons, for example, or one person and various inanimate subjects with which this person interacts—so that visual attention can be shifted from one subject to another.

. . . If possible, develop the program in segments, each of which involves a change of visual subject and a different approach to the program objective. For example, "Planning Your New Home" might be staged by having an architect talk to the camera for a half hour. The program has a better chance to sustain interest, however, if it is developed in segments such as:

Hostess shows audience a poor floor plan.
Hostess and guest architect.
Hostess introduces couple who are interested in building a new house.
Couple converse with architect.
. . . etc.

10   Besides moving your visual subjects, move the mind of your viewer.

When it is said that a show moves, it likely means that we have been moved—that our thoughts and perceptions and emotions have been activated and kept active. Good writers and producers know how to move the mind. Good directors should be able to do this with their camerawork.

How can the viewer's mind be moved?

10.1   The mind reaches forward toward the end of something incomplete.

One of the tried-and-true adages of show business is to "make 'em wait." Suspense and curiosity are mainstays of the successful performance. Your camera can arouse suspense and curiosity by showing a part of the subject before showing the whole, or by panning onto the subject to reveal it by degrees, or by showing it indistinctly first (back-to, or in the distance, for instance) before showing it nearer and clearer. Your lighting can do this also, by starting with the subject in silhouette.

The mind reaches forward when an action projects a consequence, and then a further consequence. Consider, for instance, the following shot sequence:

> Boy hits ball. (Where did it go?)
> Ball smashes window. (What will boy do?)
> Boy looks around and starts to run. (Who is coming?)
> . . . etc.

In editing, it is often effective to cut between an action and reaction or between a deed and its consequence.

10.2   The mind empathizes with the push-and-pull of opposing forces.

Feeling with a force and feeling the desire to resist it set up dynamic tensions in the spectator, which constitute a strong appeal in many kinds of shows and spectator sports. The spectator waits suspensefully for the resolution of the conflict. And when the forces are unbalanced, the lack of equilibrium creates in the spectator a state of unrest with an accompanying urge to see things set aright.

As a director, you can help to build these kinds of excitement by singling out and stressing the opposing forces with your camera. In this connection, review what was said in Chapter 16 about building tension and supporting the degree of force in the subject matter.

10.3   The mind moves when it makes relations, putting two and two together to draw its own conclusions.

Years ago, silent filmmakers discovered that the spectator could be given an active part in the creative process by making associations between successive shots. Shot 1 is a closeup of a woman weeping. Shot 2 shows a grave at her feet. That combination yields one kind of association. But if shot 2 shows an onion being peeled in her hands, the spectator forms an entirely different conclusion. This principle of editing is still an effective way to keep your audience actively involved.

The mind can also be activated by being given a chance to realize the bigger picture from a suggestive clue. To suggest is often more effective than to show the whole; and strong dramatic impact often results from finding mental short-cuts in the viewer's imagination so that one activates a whole stream of associations by a single stimulus. Sometimes this stimulus can be completely pictorial. Witness the film sequence in which young English newlyweds dangled clasped hands over a ship's rail, dreaming of the happy life ahead of them in Canada. The scene ended as, straightening up, they withdrew their hands to reveal the label on the life preserver behind which they had been standing: S.S. *Titanic*.

11 Once you have set the mind in motion, work to preserve its pace.

11.1   Good pace results from economy, from producing a maximum of result with a minimum of means.

In a well-paced program, each moment is filled with matter that counts. There are no waits, no wasted moments. This holds true in every form of show business. A good entertainer includes just enough to sell the act, sticks to the point, and quits before the audience has had enough. The entertainer knows what to do and does it without faltering or fumbling.

In a motion picture, the shot of a buoy passing tells that the ship has put to sea; thus the filmmaker makes the point with a minimum of means. By distillation and combination, the filmmaker seeks to tell the story with the utmost brevity and power. Beginning each scene as close as possible to its high point, the filmmaker cuts to the next scene as soon as the point has been made.

11.2   You, too, can work to eliminate dull and inexpressive moments from your continuity.

Among the causes of such moments are:

. . . performers having to clear off already used demonstration material before bringing new material into view, or having to erase material from a chalkboard before writing new material on it.

. . . performers having to walk unnecessarily far to bring into view the next visual subject, which they have already verbally introduced.

. . . delays in rolling taped segments or delays in commentary from the studio over silent footage because the commentator cannot see the studio monitor.

. . . holding too long on opening theme and titles after the announcer has whetted audience desire to see the program.

. . . empty, meaningless visual content traversed during a pan from one subject of interest to another.

. . . late shots, which oblige the performers to mark time until the shots are ready. In this connection, remember what you have already learned about "Keeping Up with the Action."

. . . unnecessarily long dollies-in and zooms when interest has contracted to a portion of the scene before the camera can concentrate the view. Remember also that a dolly-in or zoom-in from a demonstrator and the product to a closeup of the product will go faster if you compact the wider view as much as possible, for example, by keeping the product closer to the demonstrator's face, or by reducing the width of the sponsor's logo behind the demonstrator.

12 Moving the mind requires good timing: the picture must coincide precisely with the action.

Example: In a motion picture filmed with a single camera, the turning point came when a man picked up the wrong hat and got a sudden clue to a guilty person's identity by reading the initials on the hat band. For proper shock effect, a closeup of the initials was needed precisely when the act of recognition occurred. Zooming the single camera in for the closeup blurred this important effect.

Example:	Demonstrator:
CU DEMONSTRATOR LOOKING THROUGH TRANSPAK	(HOLDING PRODUCT UP TO FACE) The next time you go shopping, ask for Transpak.
TILT DOWN TO LEFTOVERS	(LOWERING PRODUCT) Transpak forms a seal to protect your leftovers . . .
PAN TO SANDWICHES	sandwiches for the kids going to school . . .
PAN TO LUNCH BOX	or your husband's lunch.

Here is a typical problem of suiting the picture to the words. The demonstrator must lower her product at precisely the right time to motivate a tilt down to the leftovers, following which the pans to the sandwiches and thence to the husband's lunch box must neatly coincide with the appropriate phrases. A second too late or too soon will be enough to destroy the proper accent.

Example:
IRATE YOUNG LADY: (TURNING FROM DESK WHERE YOUNG MAN IS SITTING AND STRIDING TOWARD DOOR) . . . And I hope that I never, never see you again—never ever! Good-*bye*!!! (SLAMS THE DOOR)

This is a problem in space-time relationships: the distance from desk to door must be nicely proportioned to the time taken by the young lady to deliver her exit line. The problem begins when you design your floor plan.

12.1   There is a proper moment, too, for every camera take.

No less important than what a picture shows is the time at which it occurs. Good directing requires that you develop your sense of sight, your sense of hearing, and—by no means least—your sense of timing. A book cannot help you much to develop that sense. Therefore it is all the more important to work on developing it for yourself.

Chapter 19

From Script to Camera Plan

Visual Development of the "He-She" Dialogue

This is the dialogue presented in the preceding chapter, for which you were invited to work out the characters' movements and business. One possible interpretation of this scene will be developed here, starting with the movements and business, then relating these to the cameras and the arrangement of the setting, resulting in a complete plan for visually communicating the action on the screen.

Movement and business

Note the parenthetical directions:

SHE: (CLOSING DOOR AFTER SOMEONE WHO HAS JUST LEFT, AND TURNING TO YOUNG MAN, WHO STANDS BESIDE HER) All right. Now we're alone, stop holding out on me.

HE: (MOVING AWAY WITH PRETENDED CASUALNESS TO RETRIEVE THE CIGARETTE HE HAS LEFT ON AN ASHTRAY) Holding out? I don't get you.

SHE: (FOLLOWING AFTER HIM TO PRESS THE POINT) You know what I mean. What went wrong at the party?

HE: (TURNING TO FACE HER) Now wait a minute, baby. I can't tell you. I wasn't even there.

SHE: (MOVING AWAY FROM HIM, WITH INJURED AIR) After all you've promised—and now you're lying to me.

HE: (FOLLOWING BEHIND HER) Oh look, darling. I'd tell you if I could. You know that.

SHE: (STILL EVADING HIM, AGAIN MOVING AWAY, USING "HARD TO GET" TACTICS) I thought we agreed to be partners, but it looks like this partner doesn't count for anything.

HE: (FOLLOWING MORE URGENTLY) Jean, wait a minute. Let me explain.

SHE: (HAVING TAKEN HER PURSE FROM A TABLE, EYES HIM DIRECTLY) You needn't bother to explain anything, Roger—because I know.

HE: (TRANSFIXED) Know what?

SHE: (REACHING IN PURSE) I know you were there because you left your lighter—(RAISING IT IN FRONT OF HIS NOSE) and here it is.

HE: Oh . . . all right. I'm sorry. But it isn't what you're thinking. (RESTING A HAND ON HER ARM TO URGE HER DOWN ONTO SOFA) Now please relax and I'll tell you everything.

(THE NEXT SCENE IS PLAYED SEATED.)

Analyzing the structure of the scene

So that the camera shots may point up the meanings in the scene with the proper degrees of emphasis, it is necessary to analyze the dramatic construction, asking such questions as the following:

What is the overall action of the scene?

Overcoming the boy's denials with incontrovertible evidence, the girl forces the boy to an admission.

Is there a climactic pattern to the action?

Yes, the scene develops with rising earnestness and intensity to the turning point, at which the girl produces the lighter.

Should some speeches be underlined more than others by the visual treatment?

Yes, the following are key lines, which should make a special impression on the audience:

"What really happened last night? What went wrong at the party?" (This is the clearest statement of what the girl wants to know.)

"Now wait a minute, baby. I can't tell you. I wasn't even there." (This defines the opposing position taken by the boy.)

"I know you were there because you left your lighter—and here it is!" (This is the turning point, at which the girl wins out.)

The first two speeches delineate the opposing forces that generate the action; the third speech resolves the action.

The camera shots and their rationale

Camera 1

1 dolly back

Still on 1

Take 2

2

SHE: (CLOSING DOOR AND TURNING TO THE YOUNG MAN) All right. Now we're alone, stop holding out on me.

A balanced two-shot, since so far the forces are equal. The girl commands attention by her turn from the door to the young man. Framing is reasonably loose in order to allow closer shots later for supporting climax.

HE: (MOVING AWAY) Holding out? I don't get you.

Heading back to his cigarette on an end table, the young man advances toward camera, the camera dollying back with him and leaving the girl in the distance. The movement is made roughly toward the camera, since a lateral movement by the boy would probably require losing the girl from the frame. The camera dollies back in order to keep the boy's screen size constant, since his line is not sufficiently important to be underscored by enlarging him.

SHE: (FOLLOWING) You know what I mean. What really happened last night? What went wrong at the party?

The girl's enlargement as she moves down to him emphasizes the importance of her speech.

HE: (TURNING TO FACE HER) Now wait a minute, baby. I can't tell you. I wasn't even there.

This speech is reinforced by a take to camera 2, which throws him into the "upstage" position.

SHE: (MOVING AWAY) After all you've promised—and now you're lying to me.

She moves toward camera 2. He follows up to behind her shoulder.

2

2 pan

Still on 2

Take 1

Take 2

HE: (FOLLOWING BEHIND HER) Oh look, darling, I'd tell you if I could. You know that.

SHE: (STILL EVADING HIM, MOVING TOWARD ANOTHER TABLE TO PICK UP HER PURSE) I thought we agreed to be partners, but it looks like this partner doesn't count for anything.

Camera pans right with her, losing the young man from the frame. Her sidewise cross breaks the pattern of the advancing movements previously employed. There is no need to keep both characters in the shot. Were the shot widened to include them both, they would be too small on the screen. Furthermore, eliminating the young man briefly serves to regenerate interest in him as he reenters the shot on his next speech.

HE: (FOLLOWING MORE URGENTLY) Jean, wait a minute. Let me explain.

Now they are facing each other directly and in stationary positions which, in contrast to the previous fluid movement, add tension to what is about to occur.

SHE: (HOLDING PURSE, EYEING HIM DIRECTLY) You needn't bother to explain anything, Roger— (UNFASTENING PURSE) because I know.

Since the previous two speeches have been devoted to picking up the purse and the young man's reentry into the shot, it is this speech during which the stationary confrontation is actually achieved.

SHE: (REACHING IN PURSE) I know you were there because you left your lighter—(RAISING IT)— and here it is!

A take to a closer shot, strongly favoring the girl and tight enough to throw considerable attention to the lighter as she raises it in front of his nose, serves to underline the turning point of the scene.

HE: Oh . . . all right. I'm sorry. But it isn't what you're thinking. (URGING HER DOWN ONTO SOFA) Now please relax and I'll tell you everything.

The beginning of a new trend of action is marked with a new, looser shot from camera 2.

The floor plan (Figure 19/1)

In devising the floor plan, the first relationship to be established was that between the door and camera 1's first location. Next came the placing of the end table where he had left his cigarette, and the adjacent armchair was added to justify having an end table in this location. Then camera 2 was located where it could favor the young man on its first take. There remained only to locate the table to which the girl moves to get her purse, and to place the sofa next to this table. The other armchair was added for set dressing. Still

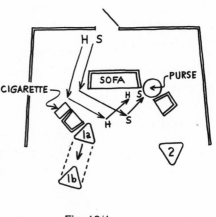

Fig. 19/1

other items would probably need to be included in the room for the same reason. Exact camera positions are yet to be determined, based on the specific lenses on your cameras. For this, you remember, a scaled floor plan needs to be drawn. Perhaps at this point you would like to take over and finish the project.

DUST 'N WAX Commercial

The following commercial was written by a student of advertising and turned over to a student of directing to realize on camera:

	DAUGHTER:
MOTHER AND DAUGHTER BY COUNTER FINISHING FLOWER ARRANGEMENT	The guests are going to think that you're an artist, Mom. The flowers look great.
	MOTHER:
MOTHER PICKS UP FLOWERS AND CAMERA LEADS MOTHER AND DAUGHTER INTO LIVING ROOM	Why, thank you. Let's put them on the coffee table and then get ready for the party. The guests will be here soon.

	DAUGHTER:
MOTHER AND DAUGHTER STEP-PING TO TABLE	Oh Mom, look—there are glass stains all over the table.
	MOTHER:
TIGHTER SHOT OF MOTHER AND DAUGHTER FACING EACH OTHER	Well, that's no problem. We can wipe them right away with spray-on DUST 'N WAX.
	ANNOUNCER:
TAKE TO A CU OF DUST 'N WAX. DISSOLVE TO DAUGHTER LOOKING AT CAN OF DUST 'N WAX AND MOTHER HOLDING FLOWERS	Smart mother, she knows about new DUST 'N WAX, the polish that sprays on for a quick shine. Spray-on DUST 'N WAX is so quick and easy to use. Anyone can polish furniture with it . . .
MS OF DAUGHTER SHAKING CAN	Just shake the can gently . . .
TIGHTER SHOT OF DAUGHTER SPRAYING WAX ON TABLE	Spray the wax on the furniture . . .
CU OF TABLE BEING WIPED	And wipe it off right away. There's no waiting, no rubbing.
	DAUGHTER:
DAUGHTER POINTING TO TABLE AND MOTHER HOLDING FLOWERS	Mom, look how it shines. This DUST 'N WAX worked so fast.
	MOTHER:
WIDER SHOT OF MOTHER AND DAUGHTER PLACING FLOWERS ON TABLE	And the shine won't scratch, either.
	ANNOUNCER:
DISSOLVE TO CU OF DUST 'N WAX	So for those last-minute shines on your furniture, get new spray-on DUST 'N WAX today.

The director's analysis of the script

The director reviews the commercial's general objectives.

The director should focus attention definitely on whatever elements of the scene carry the meaning at each moment of the action. What will appear in the frame? What will be excluded as negative, nonessential, or distracting?

The director's shots should support the degrees of force that are found in the script. Within a given shot, which element should be emphasized as most important? Within a succession of shots, which should make a stronger impression than others? (In a commercial, shots of the product or of what it can accomplish are usually expected to be more forceful than other shots.)

The director is also expected to punctuate each shot to mark and reinforce the divisions of the action or thought—not cutting during a passage that should seem continuous, nor, on the other hand, failing to change the picture statement when the action or thought takes a new turn.

With these objectives in mind, the director analyzes the script as follows:

(1) *Mother and daughter talk about the flowers and the party.* This is a shared conversation; therefore, include both persons, and from an angle that will favor them equally. Being merely introductory, the scene should carry little force compared to what is to follow; therefore, a relatively loose shot is appropriate.

(2) *Daughter discovers glass stains on the table.* This is the complication of the plot which is resolved by use of the product; hence it must be more strongly pointed up. The meaning is carried by the daughter and the table; to include the mother will weaken the spectator's concentration on the essential factors. Hence, let the daughter precede the mother toward the table and pan with her into a one-shot. Getting off the mother will also lend impact to her reappearance, which introduces the product.

(3) *Mother suggests DUST 'N WAX.* A cut here will lend impact, saying, "Look, this is new. This is important!" Emphasis should be on the mother. But rather than taking a one-shot, an over-shoulder two-shot will show the new physical relationship between the characters, making it clear that the mother is still in the kitchen area, where she can get the product from a cabinet. To avoid empty space between the figures on the screen, an angle shot is advisable. By showing their different distances from camera, this shot will also promote a feeling of depth on the two-dimensional screen.

(4) *Announcer ratifies mother's recommendation.* Vigorous emphasis on the product demands the most forceful shot yet. Hence, a take, and also an abrupt change of shot content and of scale, shooting the can as close as possible and further emphasizing it by putting it in sharp focus against a defocused background.

(5) *Mother brings product to daughter.* It seems better to substitute this action shot for the author's static prescription of "daughter looking at can and

mother holding flowers," which does not say much and does not explain how the daughter got the can that she is about to put to use. For the revised action, one can return to the previous over-shoulder shot. As the mother moves forward, she and the can she carries will grow in size and importance. Reaching the table, she can give the can to her daughter in exchange for the bowl of flowers.

(6) *Daughter demonstrates product.* Mother is not important here, so back to an angle that throws the emphasis on her daughter and the table. Since the table waxing is a continuous action, there is no reason to break it up with different shots. But the meaning gradually concentrates and climaxes on the spraying and wiping actions and their result: a polished table surface. This narrowing down can be achieved by a zoom-in.

(7) *Mother and daughter express satisfaction with the result.* A balanced two-shot will reinforce their mutual satisfaction; and the return from angular to symmetrical composition may, through stabilization, promote a feeling of resolution to the outcome of the plot.

(8) *Announcer's tag urges viewers to use product.* The can should be framed as in the previous closeup of it, since it's the same can—before untested, now a proven "hero." But this time, a take to it would be too abrupt, making it seem to be another suddenly occurring incident in the action. This time, mother and daughter have solved their problem, and their resultant satisfaction should linger a while, blending into and thus being associated with the product that has solved their problem. Hence, the product should be introduced by a dissolve.

All of the foregoing considerations (or others equally detailed) pass through the conscientious director's mind, although more swiftly and instinctively than would appear from the written analysis.

The director must now realize this visualization by planning a camera treatment.

Ultimately this results in the floor plan sketched in *Figure 19/2*. Some of the considerations that influenced this plan are as follows:

The setting must be accommodated to certain limitations in the production circumstances.

Directing classes normally have no budgets for scenery and little time for setting and striking it. Hence, the director uses existing studio drapes and, for further backing in the party area, a three-fold screen, which is quick to erect and remove. The director also uses an existing built-in kitchen with an island counter, where mother and daughter can complete the flower arrangement, and a cabinet from which the can of wax can be procured.

The director must check the alternation of cameras.

Thereby the director ensures that each camera will be available to take the shots expected of it—for example, that camera 1 will be available to take both closeups of the can on the pedestal.

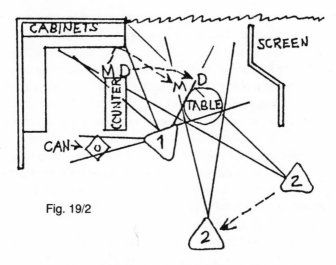

Fig. 19/2

The director must work out exact locations for the cameras and for their subjects.

Thereby the director ensures that each subject will be framed at the correct distance and from the proper angle. For example, camera 1 opens with a shot of mother, daughter, and flower bowl upstage of the counter, then pans with the daughter to the table. The camera distances from counter and table must be such as to permit the exact framing desired, both at the beginning and the end of the pan.

Time for camera deployment must be considered.

The can on the pedestal, which is taken in closeup, must be the same distance from camera 1 as are the mother and daughter in their opening shot. This will allow camera 1, after a quick pan over to the can, to zoom in quickly and reframe without having to refocus. To take the second closeup of this can, camera 1 must pan very quickly to its original location after having zoomed in on the table to look more closely at the polished surface. Placing the table at the same distance from camera 1 as the can will again save valuable time, since refocusing will not be required. There must also be time for camera 2 to move between shots from its opening location (aimed toward the kitchen) to its final location (aimed toward the drapes). As things worked out, both cameras were able to make these moves safely, but with little time to spare.

Both video and audio requirements must be kept in mind when selecting furniture.

For the opening scene, the director specifies a counter away from the wall, since a wall counter would have tended to face the performers away from the camera. The director also specifies a high counter in order to reduce the vertical distance between the flower bowl and the performers' faces, thus permitting a closer shot.

Whereas the writer of the commercial specified a coffee table to be polished, the director chooses a table of normal height. Otherwise, the daughter would have to stoop or kneel to do her polishing while the mother remained standing. Not only would this require a longer shot, making the performers smaller on the screen, but it would also raise the problem of balancing the audio levels between mother and daughter, since the daughter would be some distance below the boom microphone, which, to keep out of the picture, would have to remain above the mother's head.

In rehearsal, there must be work with the performers' actions.

For example, an abrupt stop and turn to her mother will help to visualize the daughter's dismay when she discovers the glass stains on the table. Business at the table must be timed to the announcer's lines. After the mother has given the can to her daughter and taken the bowl of flowers, she must retire sufficiently to be out of camera 1's shot of the daughter polishing the table.

Finally, the resultant commercial is intended to go like this:

FADE   UP—Mother, daughter, and bowl upstage of counter

DAUGHTER:
The guests are going to think that you're an artist, Mom. The flowers look great.

PAN WITH DAUGHTER TO TABLE

MOTHER:
(HANDING BOWL TO DAUGHTER, WHO CARRIES IT TO ADJOINING AREA)
Why, thank you. Let's put them on the table and then get ready for the party. The guests will be here soon.

DAUGHTER:
(STOPPING AND TURNING) Oh Mom, look—there are glass stains all over the table.

TAKE 2—Daughter and table in right foreground, mother in left background, still in kitchen

MOTHER:
Well, that's no problem. (GOING TO CABINET) We can wipe them right away with spray-on DUST 'N WAX.

TAKE 1—CU of can in limbo

ANNOUNCER:
Smart mother, she knows about new DUST 'N WAX, the polish that sprays on for a quick shine.

DISSOLVE TO 2—Same as previous shot, with mother advancing to camera left of daughter

MOTHER:
(BRINGS CAN TO DAUGHTER AND TAKES FLOWERS FROM HER) Spray-on DUST 'N WAX is so quick and easy to use. Anyone can polish furniture with it. . . .

Take 1—Daughter and tabletop (2 MOVE LEFT)

DAUGHTER:
(SYNCHRONIZES HER BUSINESS WITH ANNOUNCEMENT)
Just shake the can gently . . .

ZOOM IN TOWARD TABLETOP

Spray the wax on the furniture . . . And wipe it off right away. There's no waiting, no rubbing.

TAKE 2—Balanced two-shot, including tabletop

DAUGHTER:
Mom, look how it shines. This DUST 'N WAX worked so fast.

MOTHER:
(PLACING FLOWERS ON TABLE) And the shine won't scratch, either.

(1 BACK FAST TO CU CAN IN LIMBO)

DISSOLVE TO 1—CU can in limbo

ANNOUNCER:
So for those last-minute shines on your furniture, get new spray-on DUST 'N WAX today.

FADE TO BLACK

Chapter 20

"On-Location" Production

There was a time when all location production for television was shot on film, returned to the station or professional film lab for processing, physically cut apart, shortened, and then reorganized into scenic continuity by a film editor. Television cameras were simply clumsy devises designed to be mounted on heavy tripods and pedestals and only on very unusual occasions taken out of the studio.

By the mid-seventies broadcast-quality television cameras and video recorders that were portable (dinosaurs by today's standards) began being used to cover events that until then had been considered film situations.

Today almost half of all videotape shot for television is shot "on location" and more than 80 percent of that done with single-camera production.

While many comparisons can be made between film and video production on location, two considerations are the most noteworthy—time and money. When a video crew leaves the field, they may have already viewed the raw production materials and can be confident that creatively and technically the project is successful. The cost and reuse potential of videotape compared to film is significant. Ten minutes of videotape can cost as little as 10 percent of an equal amount of 16mm film and processing.

There are two basic styles of on-location video production, ENG and EFP.

1   ENG (Electronic News Gathering) is the video technique that provides almost all location news features, "man-on-the-street" interviews, coverage of police and fire stories, and so on that you see nightly on television news.

1.1   Hand-held cameras, which can be shot from the shoulder or mounted on lightweight tripods, with portable video tape recorders (either carried over the shoulder or directly mounted to the camera), powered by batteries, are the primary elements in ENG.

Other equipment includes a camera-mounted "shotgun" microphone for sound and a "sun gun" to provide illumination and a hand-held microphone for the reporter that is either cabled or wireless.

1.2   The entire production in the field is generally the work of only two people, the camera operator and the reporter.

At small stations the camera operator might also ask the questions and shoot cutaway coverage that is later voiced over in the studio. Larger stations and network teams may send additional staff such as a director, audio operator, and production assistants to help divide up the tasks and to provide other logistical support.

1.3   The events covered often are ones that unfold in front of the camera.

The function of the director may fall on the camera operator or reporter and those responsibilities include selection of the shots and scenes that will tell the story, the point of view that will be taken in the coverage, and the selection of those people at the scene to interview concerning the story. Many teams develop a loose formula of coverage that can be applied to a specific type of event, which speeds the process in the field. ENG is an approach to topical situations that attempts to provide a coherent reflection of those events in a very timely manner.

1.4   Interview and feature stories shot using ENG techniques allow time for more planning and direction.

In addition to the camera operator and the reporter, a staff director might be involved in this type of story coverage. When assigned a feature story or an environmental profile, the director has more control over the situation being shown before the camera, often including choices such as:

—time of day to shoot a specific part of the story
—location on which to shoot
—scouting several possible locations
—returning to a location several times
—shooting cutaways in advance or at a later time
—advanced selection of interview subjects
—working with prepared scripts and/or interview questions

1.5   ENG provides an air-ready production without the time necessary to process news film.

And since videotape is also significantly less expensive than film, a station can provide more visual news coverage on the same budget.

1.6   The ENG crew can feed the station, or for that matter the world, "live" television from the field.

With the advent of microwave and SNG (Satellite News Gathering) equipment and trucks, news coverage in the field has become instantaneous. While this provides some obvious advantages and some very real benefits, it also suggests many instances where some very uneventful coverage of "live" news is a part of a station's regularly scheduled newscast. The six o'clock evening news has often looked very much like this:

> ANCHOR: And now we have Ann Mahre standing by live at the courthouse. Ann, what's the verdict?
> ANN: Well, John, the jurors just broke for dinner without coming to a verdict and there's no one around again until eight-thirty. I guess we'll just have to wait and see what happens after dinner on this one. Back to you, John.

With the technology that makes live feeds now affordable to even small television stations, and the technological competition between stations heated, the use—and misuse—of live coverage will continue to grow.

2   EFP (Electronic Field Production) is generally more complex than ENG.

While there are areas of overlap in ENG and EFP, EFP by definition requires more extensive planning and highly controlled technical and creative situations. In EFP the director plays a roll not unlike the film director shooting a documentary or feature film. While EFP includes situations using big video trucks and multiple cameras, switched live, we will concern ourselves with the single-camera/recorder applications of EFP.

2.1   As in shooting a film, there is more directional involvement in EFP.

The director spends a great deal of time at the side of the camera operator, providing for a much more personal directing style, with closer interaction, than when the director is off in the control room and providing direction to multiple camera operators over an intercom system. In fact, many EFP directors skilled in the technical, as well as the creative aspects of production, shoot the camera as well, thus the director/cameraman has become a common job description in EFP.

2.2   Basically, the differences between ENG and EFP are in degree and intent.

EFP tends to be a more involved process, with complicated location logistics and generally requiring more production time. EFP might also involve more than one camera/recorder system to shoot the various aspects of a specific event, designed to be edited together at a later time.

2.3   In EFP the director is usually working with staged events, designed to play before a live audience or staged specifically for the camera.

The director in ENG primarily directs the camera; in EFP that responsibility includes to different degrees direction of crew and talent as well. This, in theory at least, provides for a more artful and theatrical television presentation.

2.4   EFP audio and lighting is more complex than in ENG.

Sound and light play a larger roll in producing a specific mood and feeling in EFP than the more basic audio and lighting approach used in many ENG situations. EFP is often elaborate enough to demand location searches, followed by scaled floor plans and camera/shot plots, multiple lighting units powered by generator units in the field, and audion using multiple wireless transmitters and battery powered audion mixing consoles. This contrasts with the single hand microphone held by the reporter (or the camera-mounted "shotgun" mike when the camera operator works alone) and the light provided by a "sun gun" or at best a portable lighting kit containing several small units that can be mounted on light-weight stands.

3   ENG and EFP share some common production aspects.

3.1   As a general rule, events covered in single-camera situations are shot in a series of short takes rather than being followed in their entirety.

Action on camera may be repeated several times in order to provide coverage from a variety of angles, using various compositions and subject actions.

3.2   Generally, both ENG and EFP subjects are shot "out of sequence" with the intention of later assembling them together in post-production electronic editing.

To shoot "in sequence" in many situations would require repeated setups and returns to the same location and also require that all the actors be present throughout the entire production process. Shooting "out of sequence" is the method used in all feature film productions and is common in single-camera video production on location, as well as studio production, particularly when television commercials are being produced.

3.3   Shooting on videotape for both ENG and EFP applications allows the director and the camera operator to review each shot recorded on the tape while the crew is still set up, confirming that action, creative intent, and technical standards have been met.

Everyone leaves the shoot location knowing that the objectives have been accomplished and the required technical standards met.

4   Directing on location provides less control.

The director may find that there is less control over the physical setting before the camera in an on-location shoot. A studio setting provides complete control over sound, lighting, weather, etcetera. On location, the director is faced with automobile traffic, airplanes, uncooperative people in the background, the sun going in and out of the clouds—the list is almost endless. Just when the director thinks everything is under control, a new situation develops. Staying cool in these situations is the proof of the experienced and confident director. Listed here are only a few of the many extra considerations that have to be taken into account when you direct on-location shoots.

4.1   The time of day that you shoot.

The light angles, levels, and the actual time of day can be controlled only in a limited way with the use of supplementary lighting, reflectors, color gels, and so on. This is especially important when the shooting takes place over a period of time and the scenes must match when intercut.

4.2   Direction of nonactors and extras.

On-location shoots often involve working with people not professionally trained as actors. These include workers on the assembly line, the company president, artists in their own environment, musicians on the street. The background settings also include many nonprofessional people, both selected extras and simply passers-by.

Plan extra time to block and rehearse the talent but pay special attention that you do not overrehearse them. The trick to good directing is to know when the talent is approaching their best performance, and to shoot before the energy begins to wain. While the ability to anticipate this moment is important to good direction in every situation, it is especially important when working on location with nonactors.

4.3   Know when to follow your shooting plan and when to throw it away.

Many a great opportunity has been missed by the director who was unable to discard the script or shot sheet and take advantage of a spontaneous moment or unplanned natural occurrence that often happens in the uncontrolled environments of on-location shooting. You can always shoot the scripted action afterward and then make judgments at a later date as to which will serve the story's needs the best. Take advantage of opportunity.

4.4 Take good notes.

The on-location environment is much more difficult to duplicate than that set up in the studio. If you feel that it will be important to match action and environmental elements, such as time of day, later in your shoot or at some future date, assign an assistant the responsibility of keeping track of every scenic element involved in the location shoot.

4.5 Plan ahead.

While preproduction planning is necessary on all productions, this is especially true of those shot on location. In addition to the normal script supervision, lighting, talent, and camera rehearsals, the on-location shoot has several additional requirements. Among the many that need special attention are permits, security and crowd control, dressing and makeup facilities, supplemental electrical, and when working internationally, incompatability of television and electrical standards. Don't get caught off guard because of poor planning and location scouting.

Finally, accept that there are some limitations on the control that you will have over a shoot on location. Plan as carefully as possible, keep your eyes open to unexpected opportunities, and enjoy the freedom that working outside of the studio provides.

Chapter 21

A Few Words About Editing

There are fewer and fewer programs being produced "live" or "live to tape" these days. Almost every program is shot in segments, on different locations, both in and out of the studio, over a period of time, and then edited together electronically. While multiple-camera production is still common in both the studio and on location, rarely is the entire program completed without some editing. Unlike physically splicing film, the videotape editorial process "dubs" scenes from the original recording generated with the camera onto another piece of videotape electronically. On this "edit master" that is being created, the scenes are laid into their proper relationship with each other, taken often times from a large number of different original recordings. Since the signal from the tape is "dubbed" to the edit master electronically, the original tapes are never physically or electronically altered in the editing process.

While this text is specifically about directing, and there are other works that address the editorial process, some advantages that you as a director may gain over live-to-tape production are included. Hopefully some of the ideas addressed in the following points will assist you in making better directing decisions.

1 Decisions about where to fade in, cut, dissolve, and so on do not have to happen in real time.

All the events already exist on an array of tapes previously recorded. The director is given time to consider different options and to experiment, time that would not have existed in a live-to-tape situation. Timing of transitions can be much more exact than when trying to perform them live. As an example, in editing, it is possible to sequence a series of events to happen very rapidly. It would be impossible to cut such a sequence together live in real time. Until the advent of videotape editing, those types of fast-cut sequences had to be shot on film and then turned over to the film editor.

2   Working to the script, the director and editor can assemble the story from many reels of original camera tapes shot out of sequence, over a period of time and on many different locations.

Shot selection can be made between many takes and different camera angles not provided for in multiple-camera live-to-tape production.

3   The basic story line and audio tracks can be cut together into the proper sequence for timing and then the director and editor can go back over the edit, inserting the cutaways, cut-ins, reaction shots, and so on.

Trying to pick up the product shot at the proper moment in the script on the live shoot is not easy, due not only to timing but to other aspects such as lighting, as well. Getting announcer voice-overs timed and dropped into exactly the right place, the music rolled on cue, and the sound effects exactly in place is often impossible. Remember some of the earlier studio exercises in this text as examples.

4   Many mistakes in the original production, as well as those noticed later in the edited version, can be corrected at the editorial stage.

If, for example, you directed your way into a corner during a multiple-camera shoot, you could simply cut, fix the problem, pick up the action again, and then later edit the parts together. The same is true in the edit you are working on. Something that you thought worked yesterday does nothing for you today. You look through the material previously shot, find a new option, and simply insert it into the edit in place of the previous choice.

5   The editorial process saves the director the problems of complex audio recording and mixing during the videotaping process.

Music and sound effects can be added later providing the director more concentration on the video aspects of the production and on the action taking place in front of the camera. Rather than trying to get a good mix of the announcer and the background sound while on a location shoot, both sound tracks can be recorded separately on the video tape recorder, and later in the editing room their relative levels can be experimented with and then mixed.

6   Some programs are better shot using a mix of single- and multiple-camera production that is later taken into the editing room for finishing.

While there are probably an infinite number of different ways to direct a multitude of videotaped events, there never seems to be just one way to cover any of them. The challenge to the director, in working with the producer and the writer, is to apply a mixture of all the possibilities, a plan that presents itself as appropriate to the event and practical in terms of the time, money, and equipment available. Far from all-inclusive, let's take a look at two real-life examples of those situations that face the television director almost on a daily basis.

Coverage of the 90-meter National Ski Jumping Championships

The Situation:

The EFP crew consisted of four camera/recorder teams, each assigned a specific element of the event coverage. One crew was responsible for shooting interviews, cutaways, and the crowd's reactions. The other three teams were each assigned a different position near the jump. Crew 2 covered the jumper on the in-run as he started down the jump. With some overlapping coverage to give the director some editorial latitude, crew 3's responsibility included the jumper coming down the last part of the jump, launching into the air and landing. Crew 4 had the responsibility of also covering the landing from down farther on the mountain and following the jumper to his final stop at the bottom. Sounds like adequate coverage to me.

The Problem:

Sixty jumpers made two jumps each, each one covered on three different tapes. Each of the shots lasted about eight seconds and were edited into a twenty- to twenty-four-second sequence. Each of the individual shots had to be separately color corrected because the individual camera/recorder systems differed slightly in their color reproduction since they could not be compared side to side with each other as they would have been in a multi-camera system where the engineer could shade each one so they'd match each other. Then the interviews and the cutaways had to be added, along with the opening commentary, music, and titles. If you're still with me, I think you may have figured that this was one incredible engineering and editing headache.

A Solution:

While it seemed to the director and the producer that money would be saved while on location by shooting four isolated camera/recorder systems rather than renting a multiple-camera truck for the day, the savings were more than offset by the cost in terms of time and money wasted in the editing process. Having a three-camera truck with color-balanced cameras switched live to tape covering the jumping, and a fourth camera/recorder shooting the interviews, cutaways, and crowd, would have been more effective in saving time, as well as in the long run, money. The crew would have left the event with all the jumping exhibition already edited together. All that would have remained was to select the sequences containing the desired participants, edit them together with the selected interviews, intercut the cutaways and the crowd, add the opening commentary and music, and be done with it.

Author's Note: The year this text is being published the National 90-Meter Championship was held in Steamboat Springs, Colorado. The coverage was provided by the same production company, using a multiple-camera truck. Postproduction was greatly reduced and the program was ready to be aired six days later.

"The Photographer's Eye" Television Series

The Situation:

This series of twenty-six 30-minute interview programs with world-famous photographers was to be shot in the studio using three cameras. The program design incorporated a casual interview of the guest by the series host and the intercutting of various photographs taken by the guest.

The Problem:

In order to properly set up camera framing of printed photographs and to transfer works shot as slides onto videotape, preserving the proper color correction and tonal range, a great deal of time and camera tuning would be necessary. While all this was happening, the guest and host would have to sit around and wait, wasting their valuable time.

The Solution:

The interview segments were recorded live to tape using the three-camera setup switched live. In order to make sure that all topics of interest were covered, the program taping involved about one hour of interview, later to be reorganized, prioritized, and cut to half-hour program length. In this manner the guest and host could take several breaks during the taping to compare notes and would then be allowed to leave promptly.

After the interview segments were recorded on tape, two of the cameras and their operators were released, saving valuable production dollars. Had the photographs been rolled in during the interview segments, these two cameras and operators would have had to "stand by" while not in use and that wastes money.

Under the direct supervision of the director, one camera was used to transfer the photos to tape. (In order for the host and guest to look at the pictures during the interview, nonbroadcast-quality work transfers of the images were made in advance of the studio session for playback on the studio monitors.)

Later, in the edit room, the interview segments were condensed and cut to length, with the proper images inserted at the appropriate places. This method allowed the director to have tighter control over the content than was possible if an attempt to record the program to length in the studio had been made. And the director, by not having to be concerned with getting the photographs inserted into the program at the exactly correct moments, had more time to pay attention to the content of the interview.

7   Consider time, resources, and money, as well as technical requirements, when deciding how to shoot a program.

Close work with the producer and writer will assist the director and help in decision making about how best to shoot a given production. There is always more than one method of coverage in any given situation. The selection of how much should be shot using multiple cameras switched live or live to tape, how much EFP technique might be needed outside the studio, and to what degree post-production editing will be necessary to complete the project all influence the time and cost associated with any program.

Chapter 22

Don't Forget Audio

Although this book mainly deals with visual communication, it should not leave the impression that video is more important than audio. To the contrary, much information and enjoyment reaches your audience through their ears.

Some directors become so involved with the look of their program that they ignore what it sounds like. In a way, this is understandable. The camera shots tend to demand primary attention because they change more frequently than the sound connections. Furthermore, it is usual for the director personally to guide the cameras through their paces, whereas for the sound pickup the director has the support of the audio engineer.

But this does not excuse the director from knowing what good audio sounds like and how to achieve it. In devising floor plans, blocking movement, and planning shots, the director must reckon with sound as well as picture. During setup and rehearsal, the director must realize when time is needed to remedy an unsatisfactory pickup. As interpreter of the program content, it is for the director to prescribe how sound production can best convey that content and to judge with a critical ear whether his or her standards have been met.

Certainly the most basic consideration in sound reproduction is that:

The audience should be able to hear clearly.

This requires that:

(1) The sound is sufficiently distinct. Speakers' voices are not muffled (as when they pass through a necktie to reach the microphone beneath it). Speech is not overridden by background noise, nor is it distorted by excess reverberation or by system noise, both of which will be discussed in due course.

(2) The sound is sufficiently loud—and loud enough consistently. It does not

keep fading during a speech or come through loudly when one person is speaking and faintly when the next person speaks. This does not mean that an excited speech should not be heard more loudly than an intimate one. It does mean that you should prevent unmotivated volume variations and make even the intimate speech loud enough to hear in your listener's living room. Wherefore this first instruction:

1   Keep the sound loud enough, without unmotivated volume variations.

This requires your attention to three factors: 1) how loud the original sound is, 2) how it reaches the microphone, and 3) how it is regulated by the volume controls. Taking these factors in order now, what can you do about them?

2   Get the performers to speak up.

Television usually requires normal conversational projection, not that of an actor in the theater projecting to the last row of the second balcony. Nevertheless, speech that is too quiet may require bringing the microphone closer than is feasible or raising the volume control to the possible detriment of sound quality.

When two performers are on the same microphone it is troublesome if one speaks more faintly than the other. Sometimes this can be remedied by placing the microphone closer to the fainter voice. Otherwise, continual adjustments of the volume control will be needed as the speakers alternate, and if the control operator does not know when the alterations are to occur, mistakes can lead to adjustments that occur too late.

Since a boom microphone rides above the performer's head, it requires the performer literally to speak up rather than too much downward toward the notes he or she may be holding or the properties that are being handled on a table surface.

If the boom must be farther from one speaker than another, you may have to ask the farther speaker to compensate by speaking louder. This situation can occur when one of the persons is seated, hence farther from a boom microphone, which must remain above the standing person's head. It can also occur with two standing persons when one is an adult and the other is a child.

The trouble with asking performers to compensate by speaking more loudly at certain times is that, unless they are seasoned performers, they may forget to do so, or else do so unnaturally. Hence, you may have to try other remedies. In the situations just cited, for instance, you might ask the adult to stoop down to the child, or elect to use a different means than the boom microphone to record the sound. You will thereby be fulfilling the next instruction:

3   Keep the performer in range of the microphone.

3.1   The microphone should be reasonably close to the subject and pointed as directly as possible toward the sound source.

3.2 The farther outside the angle from which the sound originates or is directed, the more faint its pickup will be.

The farther the microphone is from the subject, the higher the recording level must be set, possibly picking up more background and extraneous noise than desirable.

4 When action is a key element in your story, consider using a wireless microphone transmitter.

When you have a lavalier microphone hidden on an actor or a hand microphone used by a pop singer, a trailing cable is not only unsightly but seriously restricts the movement of the talent. The battery-powered wireless transmitter concealed on the actor's person or built into the hand microphone is the best solution to these problems. Even in a situation where the audio person working with a "shotgun" mike is on a football field, the wireless transmitter allows freedom of movement as well as saving the task of laying the thousands of feet of audio cable necessary to get the sound back to the press booth or remote truck where the audio and video are being recorded.

5 Cooperate with the audio control operator in his or her efforts to achieve acceptable volume settings.

The various sound inputs of your program pass through the audio console, where channels are opened and closed and volume adjusted by the audio operator. Except in the larger stations, the audio operator runs the turntables and audio tape recorders, the other sound reproducing devices, and is responsible for the setup of microphones in the studio.

5.1 Before setup time, provide all the information the operator needs concerning audio requirements.

The audio operator should know the various sources of sound in your program, how the setting will be arranged, where the talent will be stationed and will move within it, and the sequence of events as indicated by your script or run-down. (When preparing the script, by the way, make the audio cues sufficiently prominent for the operator to follow with minimum dependence on your verbal instructions.)

In accordance with this advance information, the operator should be able, before the start of facilities rehearsal, to select the appropriate microphones, install them where needed, and connect them to the channels that will allow the most effective control of their volume. The audio operator should also have located the desired starting and stopping places on the tapes and records to be played and determined the control settings that will transmit at the proper volume level. Next, the operator will be ready to set the levels of the performers' microphones.

5.2   As soon as the performers are ready, give the operator an opportunity to set each one's volume levels.

No matter how loudly a performer speaks, or how much on microphone, the transmitted voice will be too faint if the volume (or "gain") control is set too low. In setting a level, the operator finds the desirable setting for the average or normal degree of loudness delivered by the sound source, a setting that will still allow the quieter sounds to be intelligible and will also permit the louder sounds to be transmitted acceptably. With this setting established, the operator should have a minimum need to ride gain (i.e., to adjust the volume controls) during the performance.

Your part in setting the levels is to ask the performers to run through a sample of their lines or music. When only ordinary conversation is involved, a few random sentences will suffice from each performer; only be sure that the sentences are spoken at the volume to be used in performance. When the program involves music or drama, the operator will need a sample of the loudest and softest sounds that are to occur before the correct average settings can be established.

5.3   During performance, warn the operator of pronounced changes in volume before they occur.

This is especially necessary when the operator has not listened to a preliminary run-through of the program.

One example should suggest why your warnings are important. Assume that an instrumental band has been playing so loudly that the operator has turned down the volume control in order to keep the sound signal within the permissible range. Suddenly, the band stops and one of the musicians begins talking in an ordinary voice over the same microphone that had been picking up the much bigger sound of the band. The reduced setting for the big sound is too low to make the speaker sufficiently audible; hence, part of the musician's words will be missed before the operator has had time to react to the change and turn up the control. Had the director readied the operator, this need not have happened.

So far, this chapter has been devoted to just one of the director's responsibilities in the realm of audio—that of ensuring that the audience can hear the program with steady and consistent clarity. It is now time to consider another responsibility which, particularly in musical and dramatic programs, may demand a good share of the director's attention, namely:

**The sound heard by the audience should seem to be
a faithful reproduction of the event being televised.**

For example, does the orchestra sound larger than the voice of the person who introduced it? Can one hear the different instruments in their correct proportions? Is there sufficient distinction between passages marked piano and those marked fortissimo? Is a voice from the distance fainter than one close to the camera? Does the vocalist's tonal quality seem full and vibrant—or boomy and hollow as if coming out of a barrel?

The purpose of this section is to point out some factors that must be controlled in order to give favorable answers to questions such as those just asked. To start with the last of those questions:

6   Pay attention to audio quality.

The quality or character of a sound is determined by its component frequencies. The range and distribution of those frequencies determine what the sound sounds like—whether like a flute or a steamboat whistle, Mary's voice or Susan's voice—whether thin or full, tinny or harsh, or whatever.

Good reproduction of sound quality depends on 1) preserving the range and distribution of the frequencies in the original sound, and 2) protecting the reproduction from distortion by spurious frequencies.

6.1   The instruments used to transmit sound may alter its frequency pattern.

For example, a voice heard over the telephone does not sound as it does when you hear it directly. A transmitting instrument may alter sound either by failing to reproduce its total range of frequencies or by stressing some frequencies at the expense of others. Models and makes of microphones vary considerably in their frequency response. Consult with your audio engineer to obtain the ones most suitable for your purpose. For music reproduction, use the most responsive ones available. When using multiple microphones on the same pickup, select those with similar response characteristics lest the same audio input sound different on each. And when resuming a recording session after an interval during which the equipment has been struck, use either the same microphone or one matching that employed for the previous session.

Sometimes, of course, you may wish to simulate the sound of an instrument, that does not transmit a full range of frequencies. To represent the sound of a telephone or loudspeaker, your studio may be equipped with a variable frequency filter, which can cut off high or low frequencies, or both. This may also prove useful for the voices of robots or things that walk in the night.

6.2   Quality is influenced by the environment in which a sound originates.

Some sound waves from the source pass directly into the microphone; others reach it only after reflecting off surfaces such as the floor and walls. Reflections from distant surfaces, by taking a comparatively long time to return, will produce echo, whereas speedier reflections often enhance the original tone by adding reverberation. Radio and sound recording studios are designed to provide controlled reverberation for giving a vibrant, "live" quality to voice and music. Television studios are apt to be less reverberant since their walls, being designed to absorb unwanted operational noise, are less reflectant. Even so, you may be concerned with reverberation in the following instances:

The output of a microphone that is close to a reflectant surface sounds different from that of one with much space around it. When using table microphones, therefore, you may need to cover the tabletop with a sound-deadening material.

The degree of reverberation in a sound pickup should correspond with the supposed location of the program action. If at the seashore, for instance, reverberation would be minimal, whereas in a cave there might likely be echo. To simulate the latter location, your station may have an echo chamber through which the microphone output can be processed.

Different studios, or even sometimes different areas within the same studio, may differ in reverberation characteristics. Remember this and check it out if, for some reason, segments of a sequence you are recording piecemeal are assigned to different locations.

Sometimes an announcer is established on camera and microphone at a remote site to introduce action that is to occur there; then the rest of the commentary (which will be heard over the action) is recorded at the studio. In this case, there may be a noticeable difference in the reverberation characteristics of the two environments, and also a contrast between the quiet studio and the background sound of the remote location. This latter discrepancy is sometimes disguised by recording "wild" sound at the location and mixing it with the voice recorded at the studio.

6.3   *Quality varies with the physical relationship between sound source and microphone.*

The distance between sound source and microphone should be such as to minimize the pickup of unwanted sounds. A microphone that is too close to a mouth may put an undue emphasis on breathiness, sibilance, lip smacking, and tongue clacking; and one that is too close to a piano may register the action of the pedals or the rustling of sheet music being turned.

Furthermore, the distance between sound source and microphone also determines what frequencies are picked up from the desired sound. A close microphone transmits less of the reflected sound, and more of higher and lower frequencies in the direct sound. Such reproduction is said to have "presence," meaning that it contains the full (and presumably satisfying) range that characterizes a sound when it is sufficiently close to the hearer to establish its true quality. By contrast, when the microphone is too distant, the pickup will be thin, roomy, hollow and lusterless—and if the gain has to be raised to obtain sufficient volume, the pickup will also exhibit proportionally more undesirable background and electronic noise.

Audio reproduction of a large source such as the sounding board of a grand piano will vary according to which part of the source the microphone is near or is aimed at. Placing the microphone off the tail end of the piano will favor the treble frequencies, whereas placing it off the right end of the keyboard, perpendicular to the direction of the strings, will favor the bass. The pickup will also be influenced by the height and inclination of the microphone, by whether it is raised where it can "see" the strings, or lowered to aim at the underslant of the raised lid, or aimed down to pick up reflections off the floor.

When high fidelity is important, as when good music is being played by competent artists, take special pains with microphone placement. Heed the advice of competent audio specialists. Allow sufficient time for critical listening. Listen for the full range of frequencies in their proper proportions, plus the proper degree of desired reverberation—minus unwanted kinds of reverberation and irrelevant and disturbing factors either in the intended source or from sources that have no business intruding.

6.4 In certain circumstances, good audio quality may require pre-recording.

A string quartet with an international reputation was engaged for a series of programs on national television. For a number of reasons its members felt that their music would fall below their high standards if it were recorded during the video-taping sessions: they might be too tired by retakes to play well; their physical relationship to the microphone and to each other, being partly determined by shot requirements, was not the one to which they were accustomed; and the studio was not sufficiently reverberant to produce the desired vibrancy of tone. So they made audiotapes of their performances in their own sound studio. During camera sessions at the television station, the studio microphones were cut, and their own audiotapes, besides being fed to the video tape recorder, were played to them through the studio loudspeaker so that they could synchronize with them as they played for the cameras. Thus, their standards of audio quality were upheld by prerecording.

Prerecording is also used in song and dance shows, particularly for production numbers. Obviously, a singer who is moving and turning rapidly in various directions is very difficult to keep on microphone. Furthermore, it is a rare artist who can undergo such exertions and still produce commendable vocal quality. And in spectacles requiring wide shots, microphones may have to be at such distances that good audio pickup is next to impossible. All such difficulties can be circumvented by prerecording.

Brief mention should also be made of post-recording. This has its uses shooting at remote locations, where satisfactory audio is difficult to attain either because microphones cannot be suitably placed or because unwanted sounds (such as automobile and airplane traffic noises) cannot be avoided. Although, to produce visible lip movements, the performers go through the dialogue during the taping and it is recorded, the sound actually used on the program is rerecorded later at the studio. There the taped action may be played back over and over again through headsets while the performers work to synchronize their words with the lip movements on the screen.

6.5   Quality is difficult to achieve when the transmitted sound is desired to be very quiet or extremely loud.

Mention has already been made of the spurious noise generated by the recording system. The fainter the program sound is desired to be, the more it comes into competition with this system noise, producing what is called an unfavorable signal-to-noise ratio.

On the other hand, extremely loud sounds are liable to what is called "amplitude distortion." The audio control operator on your program also has to guard against distortion by keeping the needle on the VU meter from peaking too far into the red region of the scale. If the operator allows sounds to peak at more than $+1$ or $+2$ volume units, they may become distorted. For example, when recording sound on audiotape, the maximum volume you can record with good fidelity will depend on the power output of your amplifier. Normally, the amplifier's power output will increase proportionately to increases in the signal put into it—but if the input signal is increased in volume (i.e., amplitude) to the point where the amplifier is putting out as much power as it possibly can, further increases will produce the distortion.

To control against distortion generated by such unexpected loud sound levels, many audio systems in use today employ audio level compressors and automatic limiters. These devises are very helpful but should never be relied upon in place of good audio recording technique, but rather be used to assist the audio operator in situations of unexpected changes in sound levels.

This introduces another kind of problem in achieving an acceptable reproduction of the program audio content. Besides preserving the quality of the original sound, you must preserve the distinctions in its volume variations.

7 Work, within the conditions of the medium, to transmit the relative degrees of loudness in a sequence of sound.

Thus, you should try to ensure that the finale of the *1812 Overture* will sound appreciably louder than the announcement that follows it—and that actors' whispers will be softer and their shouts louder than their normal conversation—and that the performance of Ravel's *Bolero* will be heard as one steady crescendo from a faint beginning to an almost overwhelming ending.

7.1 But do not expect to transmit as much volume contrast as the program may contain.

There may actually be an enormous difference in volume between a speaking voice and the finale of the *1812 Overture* as heard in the concert hall. But the sound systems of home television receivers are not capable of reproducing this range—nor would most members of your audience enjoy the full impact of a hundred-piece orchestra in their living rooms. Also, they do not enjoy sudden, great increases in volume, as might naturally occur when a verbal introduction is followed by the brassy opening of a band selection. These are some of the reasons why broadcast music is not transmitted at a level greatly louder than that of speech.

Another reason for restricted volume range was cited a few paragraphs ago: soft sounds run into competition with signal noise, and loud sounds are liable to amplitude distortion. Therefore, there are audio control operators who resist letting the needle on their VU meter drop below 40 percent modulation or shoot beyond 100 percent into the red region.

The restricted range of the system can be a problem when one is trying to reproduce music or dramatic speeches that contain passages much softer or louder than the 40 to 100 percent bracket allows. Keeping the needle within the bracket compresses the sound at both ends, eradicating all distinctions within the softer passages on the one hand and within the louder passages on the other.

7.2 When faced with this problem of compression, there are some things you can do to improve the situation.

In some ways, you can try to keep the performance within the transmittable volume range. For example, you can avoid casting in an announcer's role the person who habitually blasts out the beginning of sentences or explodes consonants, driving the needle into the red at every other word. And when directing angry dramatic scenes, you can try to tone down the shouting, working with your actors to produce the illusion of extreme loudness by more projections and less lung power. When working with a band, you can sometimes get the musicians to hold back their peaks a little. But with concert and recital music, where every variation in volume has been introduced for a calculated aesthetic effect, your best course is to leave the performance unaltered and work with your audio engineer to reproduce it as faithfully as possible.

If your engineer is a 40-to-100 person, try to get him or her to give the needle a little more latitude. It has been known to peak at +1 and +2 volume units without causing serious distortion, and for the softest notes, it can drop at least briefly well below 40, provided that it stays moving.

Let your audio control operator hear the entire composition in advance of performance. Especially when music is concerned, an audio rehearsal is just as important as camera rehearsal, and maybe more so. Only by having heard the music will the operator know what volume variations have to be distinguished, and when they occur.

Thus forewarned, the audio operator should be able to make compensating adjustments when the music exceeds tolerable range. Knowing where a maximum peak occurs, the operator can imperceptibly reduce the volume for half a minute or so before the peak is due, thus giving it some more latitude in which to rise. Similarly, the operator can gradually sneak up the gain before a very faint passage is due. Thus, the audio operator can fit more into the audio suitcase, so to speak, than the suitcase was built to contain.

Correct reproduction of volume levels requires both an ear to the program sound on the audio monitor and an eye to the signal strength indicated on the VU meter. Without that meter, the engineer might have the volume on the monitor turned up enough to hear the soft sounds acceptably, yet actually be feeding too weak a signal to the audio or video recorder. Remember that the monitor does not indicate the signal strength. If it happens to be turned down, you might be tempted to complain that the transmitted sound is not loud enough when a glance at the meter would show that it is.

That the signal is peaking satisfactorily, however, does not really reveal how the program sounds to your audience. This can be estimated only by listening. Therefore, the good director will discourage unnecessary chatter in the control room so that, together with the engineer, their ears can be kept on the audio content.

These ears will be needed to judge not only volume variations, but also the balance between various sound sources.

8 Multiple sound inputs in a given sequence should be balanced to achieve a natural or intended proportion between their respective volume levels.

8.1   Balance can depend on three factors:

(1) It is affected by the distance between the sound sources and the microphone. For example, when two speakers are on the same microphone, the microphone is placed closer to the one with the weaker voice.

(2) When several microphone channels are used for the same pickup, balance depends on the relative volume settings of these channels. For example, if the two speakers just mentioned are on separate microphone channels, that for the weaker voice will be given a higher setting than the other channel.

(3) Remember that, in the first place, the desired balance may already have been established by the performers themselves. Musical groups, for example, may work long and hard to achieve a desired ratio of sound between their component sections. Hence this caution:

8.2   Take care lest you destroy the auditory balance of a musical group by rearranging it in the interests of pictorial composition.

Instrumentalists and the members of vocal choruses become accustomed to established physical arrangements where each person can regulate his (or her) own volume according to what he hears from his colleagues. Likewise, the group's conductor is accustomed to hear certain sounds coming from certain established directions. Rearranging the parts of an ensemble, then, should not be undertaken without its members' consent.

Incidentally, not only balance but also coordination between musicians may be injured if you rearrange them without prior consultation. For example, double pianists may be accustomed to facing each other in order to coordinate their playing by nods and eye signals or observation of each other's movements. To place them side by side or back to back may hamper their musicianship.

8.3   Microphone-performer relationships are important when televising bands and orchestras.

It is advisable to keep the more strident and percussive instruments farther from the microphone: thus, reeds in front, brass behind them, and drums in the rear. The piano is usually at one side so that the pianist can see clearly for purposes of accompaniment.

How many microphones should be used to pick up a large ensemble? On this question there are two conflicting theories. One is to avoid any interference with the balance created by the performers or established by a conductor. This calls for a single microphone in monaural television sound recording or for a stereo microphone or a pair of microphones when recording a stereo television audio track. In this manner you can pick up the aggregate sound much as it would reach the live audience's ears.

Opponents of this theory point out that when instruments (particularly soft-toned ones such as cellos or flutes) are heard in small combinations or solo passages, they may sound thin and faint, lacking presence because of their distance from the microphone. Also, the single microphone placement cannot always be located where it will pick up the balance between sections as the conductor hears it. Therefore, these critics advocate at least additional microphones to reinforce the solo instruments; and beyond this, some prefer to cover each section with a separate microphone channel, balancing these channels at the audio console. To avoid upsetting this balance, once achieved, the channels can be controlled by a single submaster, with the possible exception of those channels covering certain featured instruments, which may need to be controlled separately in order to make them stand out sufficiently against their accompaniment.

8.4   In balancing, protect an important sound source from being dominated by other sources.

For example, a vocal or instrumental solo should stand out against its accompaniment. To this end, one can sometimes succeed in getting the accompaniment to be played more softly; otherwise, one must resort to other solutions.

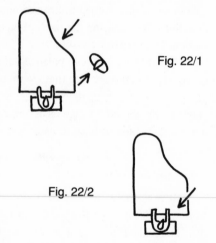

Figure 22/1 shows a common arrangement for a soloist with piano accompaniment. The two sound sources are picked up on separate directional microphones so that their volumes can be adjusted independently. Each microphone is pointed toward its own sound source, with a dead side toward the other source.

Fig. 22/1

In *Figure 22/2*, the pianist himself is singing or talking as he plays, with a single microphone directed toward his mouth. The microphone should be so mounted that it can be reasonably close to the mouth. An overhead boom may serve if it can be dipped low enough without appearing in the picture. When there is no objection to revealing the microphone, a lavalier may suffice, but better sound can probably be obtained using a stand-mounted microphone with superior response characteristics.

Fig. 22/2

When a soloist performs in front of an orchestra, a directional microphone should be used and controlled separately. It should also be placed so that it does not pick up the orchestra as strongly as it does the voice. If the performer can face at right angles to the orchestra, the orchestra will be on the dead side of the microphone, but if the performer must stand in front of the musicians, facing the same way they do, the microphone will be pointed toward them as well. In this situation, it helps to bring the soloist as far forward as possible and as close to the microphone as the performer's technique will allow. By this method, the background sound will be reduced due to an increase in physical distance between the musicians and the microphone and some of the sound will also be blocked by the performer's body.

8.5   Balancing should take account of audio perspective.

The voice of a distant person should not sound the same as that of a person in the foreground of the picture. Not only should the voice be fainter, it should also lack some of the high and low frequencies heard in a nearby voice. The easiest way to achieve the effect is to keep the microphone farther away from the distant speaker than the nearby one.

Two major considerations in sound reproduction have now been covered. The audience should be able to hear clearly; and what it hears should seem to be a faithful reproduction of the event being televised. Next, you are being asked to consider what the audience should not hear.

The audience should be protected from auditory disturbances.

This rule will serve to introduce a blacklist of things to avoid in audio production either because they impair intelligibility, distract attention, offend sensibility, misrepresent the subject matter, or disrupt the unity of the production.

9   The blacklist can start with some things that have already been discussed, including:

. . . sound that is unintelligible, either because it is too faint or too indistinct.

. . . unmotivated fading.

. . . sound of poor quality, due to insufficient frequency response, or the wrong amount of reverberation, or amplitude distortion, or an unfavorable signal-to-noise ratio.

. . . extreme, abrupt changes in volume level, which may oblige the viewers to either turn up or turn down the volume control on their sets.

. . . pauses while the microphone is moving from one sound source to another.

. . . volume that is inconsistent with the natural loudness of the source, or with its visible distance from the observer, or with its intended importance relative to other attendant sources.

. . . sound quality that is inconsistent with the auditory characteristics of the assumed environment.

. . . inexpert production of sound by the performers, insofar as the director may occasion this by requiring them to perform under unfavorable circumstances, or may unduly emphasize it, as by tolerating a microphone that is too close.

. . . the presence of irrelevant sound—offstage noise, piano pedal action, etcetera.

Although this is already a formidable list, still other causes of disturbance should be added to it. Some of these will fit into categories already established, but nevertheless deserve to be singled out for special emphasis. In addition to the foregoing, therefore:

10   Anticipate and prevent, or be alert for and prevent:

10.1   Distracting noises made by performers:

Paper rustling, dish rattling, pencil tapping, and so on, carried on too close to a microphone, usually either by performers seated in front of a table microphone or holding things too near a lavalier microphone.

The clunking of lavalier microphones against buttons and tie clips or the edges of desk and countertops.

10.2   Wind noise:

Outdoors, your audio engineer should select a type of microphone with minimum sensitivity to wind, and may also need to equip it with a wind-shielding cover.

10.3   Mechanical noise:

This is picked up when, as examples, a camera operator or assistant moves the audio/camera cables across the floor too rapidly, an announcer or on-camera player taps a ring he or she is wearing against a hand-held microphone, or the dolly wheels on the tripod squeak when moving a camera.

10.4   "Wow":

This word describes the sound of a phonograph record or a film or tape sound track that is fed into a program before it has attained its proper speed. Your cues for film, videotape, and recorded sound should be delivered early enough to allow whatever time the relevant mechanisms need to attain speed. Also, because of the delay in attaining speed, it is advisable when picture and recorded theme are to be faded in together (as in the beginning of a program) to cue music before picture, e.g., "Music, fade up on 6."

10.5 *"Out of sync":*

This is when prerecorded or post-recorded sounds fail to synchronize with the picture, as in a song being sung by a performer on tape, where the words do not correspond with the lip movements.

10.6 *Microphone interaction:*

An effect resembling echo sometimes results from a time delay when two microphones are used for the same pickup, one picking up the sound immediately, the other after it has reflected. A filtered effect (as if some of the frequencies have been filtered out) may be heard when two microphones are close together, as when lavaliers or table microphones are picking up persons who are next to each other. This can be prevented by riding down the gain of one microphone while the other is in use.

10.7 *Feedback:*

Feedback occurs when part of the output of a system returns to its input. In audio production, this is liable to occur when program sound is fed through a loudspeaker into a studio with an open microphone, either to let an audience hear the program or to let performers hear a recorded musical accompaniment. To prevent the excruciating howl that can result from this signal interference, considerable attention may be needed to adjusting the volume of the loudspeaker and to the relative positioning of loudspeaker and open microphones.

10.8 *Various errors by the audio control operator:*

A sound cue is delayed or missed altogether. The wrong microphone is opened. A microphone is left open when it should have been cut, thus conveying information the audience is not intended to hear.

Such errors often result from a failure of communication between the director and the operator, particularly when there has been no audio rehearsal and when the operator's written instructions (as on the script or rundown) are deficient, or not sufficiently prominent, or not clear.

11   ENG and EFP audio considerations.

In addition to the considerations of microphone usage discussed in this chapter, ENG and EFP demand that you consider the following additional needs when working outside the studio:

11.1 *Recording audio in the field often involves noisy locations.*

Using lavalier microphones close to the performer's body and supercardioid "shotgun" microphones help to isolate background sounds and when used properly will contribute to a better signal-to-noise ratio.

11.2   Shooting on location almost always involves wind.

Wind screens and, in extreme conditions, a zeppelin are almost always necessary for these outdoor shoots.

11.3   Working distances may be greater in the field than in the studio.

The wireless microphone transmitter will help cover the distances as well as save the effort necessary to hide the exposed audio cable in long shots.

11.4   When more than one or two microphones are to be used, you will need to take along a battery-powered microphone mixer.

12   Two errors that are nontechnical in nature also deserve inclusion in a list of auditory annoyances:

12.1   The program lacks a sense of auditory completion.

Specifically, this refers to the closing musical theme that is interrupted in progress as a program fades to black. To give the ear as well as the eye a sense of finality, the director should see that the audio operator backtimes the recording. For example, knowing that the program is to end at 29:30, and having determined that the track on which the closing theme is recorded lasts one minute and thirty seconds, the operator will start playing the track at 29:30 minus 1:30, or, in other words, at 28:00. The theme does not have to be heard when the track is started, since the operator can keep the volume faded down until the director cues music.

12.2   Recorded music and program content do not harmonize in character.

A particular example is the bombastic opening theme that precedes comparatively sedate content.

This completes the blacklist—and also those suggestions about audio production that fall within the limits of a book for beginning directors. There is much more for you to learn about the subject than has been presented here. You should become familiar with many kinds of music, which you can draw upon for themes and establishing background moods. You will want to experiment with the use of music and sound effects to create mood, atmosphere, and locale, and to tie assorted segments together in the interest of continuity. To prepare yourself for directing music programs, you should learn all you can about instruments and the structure of music. As a director of drama, you will need to cast your actors with an ear to vocal contrast and their capacities for oral expression. You must be able to help them express the meanings of the script by nuances of inflection, tone, and volume; by emphasis and underemphasis; and by changes of vocal pace. And for general purposes, you will want to seek further technical knowledge in books and articles on audio production, not only for television, but also for the related media of radio, phonograph records, audiotapes, and motion pictures.

In the meantime, keep in mind the summary advice:

When the cast of your program contains artists who express themselves in sound, consult with them about what they are trying to achieve and how you can help them achieve it.

Rely on your audio technicians, orient them to your requirements, and provide them with sufficient opportunity to achieve those requirements.

Remember that the best arrangement for picture may not be the best one for sound.

Besides looking, keep listening. Don't forget audio!

Chapter 23

The Three *E*'s

This book began by reminding you that the television director is an interpreter, charged with conveying faithfully the meanings of whatever action passes through the microphones and cameras. To help you become a good interpreter, you have been furnished with many principles—so many, perhaps, that you may find it difficult to tie them all together. If so, it may help you to realize that, underlying all these principles, there are essentially three important objectives:

1 Like every other communicator, you must make your communication:

Evident—clear to the vision and understanding.
Engrossing—fully occupying the mind and attention.
Effective—producing the intended effect.

These three *E*'s should govern every program you do and every shot you take.

2 Your program material will be evident when:

. . . the viewers recognize what they see on the screen.
. . . they are oriented to the relative locations of the visual elements in the scene.
. . . they can relate these visual elements to derive the intended meaning from them.
. . . they can relate the pictures in time sequences to derive the intended meaning from them.
. . . they realize whether each new shot is a continuation of what has been happening or is the beginning of a new train of action.
. . . they discern the pattern of the subject matter and the units that make up that pattern.
. . . they sense the relative importance of each ingredient.

3   Your program material will be engrossing when:

. . . the viewers' attention is kept stimulated by new experiences.

. . . their minds are kept from being frustrated by not seeing what they want to see when they want to see it.

. . . they are stimulated by some engaging activity, e.g.:

> the tensing and releasing of their emotional energy,
>
> the mental association of pieces of information,
>
> the sensing of forces in conflict,
>
> the urge to attain a goal,
>
> the urge to set things aright,
>
> or a motor activity, such as moving in time to rhythmic stimuli.

4   Your program material will be effective when:

. . . the viewers respond to it in the manner intended.

. . . they learn—or are entertained—or are persuaded to some action, whether writing their Congressman or buying a commercial product.

. . . they feel the mood of the love scene, the suspense when the bases are loaded, the danger faced by the circus aerialist. They admire the dexterity of the trumpeter and the coordination of the orchestra.

. . . they notice and react as it was hoped they would to every stimulus the director exposes them to.

5   You can define your job in terms of stimulus and response.

A group of directors at a professional meeting were once amused to hear a behavioral psychologist define their role as "management and control of the stimulus field." On second thought, however, the directors understood and so should you.

Think of each picture you show as a stimulus, designed and controlled by you to produce in your viewers a calculated response.

It follows that, within each picture, the viewers' attention should be focused on what the psychologist would call "relevant cues," i.e., those ingredients which will give your viewer an understanding of what is going on and the reaction to it which you expect of them at that moment.

More colloquially, you want them to get the point. So you show them what will make them get that point. This is where Part One started, and also where it ends.

Part Two: ACCESSORY APTITUDES

Part One is solely concerned with principles of communication. It has aimed to develop an aptitude which, beyond all else, it is important for a director to cultivate: that of finding the meaning in the action to be televised and then devising pictures that will communicate the meaning.

But there are other aptitudes the director must cultivate as accessories to this major one in order to realize the pictures he or she has visualized. To have these pictures properly staged and lighted, the director should be able to make floor plans. To have the right shots readied and taken at the proper moment, the director needs to develop his or her skill in calling shots. And to coordinate all of the activity that goes into preparing and executing the production of these pictures, the director must be a model of efficiency.

These aptitudes have such a bearing on the director's ability to realize his or her objectives that it seemed unwise to omit them simply because they did not fit smoothly among the chapters on communication principles.

Therefore, they have been retained, but placed in their own separate part. Thus segregated, they may be studied in any order and, if the reader desires, read concurrently with Part One. And without disturbing the continuity of Part One, any chapter in Part Two may be ignored by the reader who considers that he or she is already proficient at the aptitude it discusses.

Chapter 24

Making Floor Plans

1 Floor plans serve two purposes:

(1) They allow you to work out the location of scenic elements, performers, and cameras well in advance of camera sessions, when time is too precious for random experimentation. By experimenting on paper, you can try out many solutions until you have found the best one. By drawing the plan with accurate measurements, you can ascertain in advance that your scheme will work.

(2) This accurate drawing will furnish necessary information to the technicians who are to erect and light your settings, install microphones, and set cameras in their opening positions.

To help you devise your own floor plans, you are going to be shown some simple plans, which have been used for staging student production exercises. The first of these (*Figure 24/1*) is for "News and Weather Briefs."

2 The plans use symbols and labels.

The triangles with rounded corners indicate pedestal or tripod mounted cameras. The long dash lines show the angles of view included by the principle camera shots, the numbers within or near these angles designating the focal-length setting on the lenses to be used for these shots. Other symbols locate the microphone, stands for holding graphic materials, furniture, background, a studio monitor to be watched by the news anchor, and even the key locations (a, b, and c) to be occupied by the news anchor, which will be helpful information for the persons who will light the show.

Examples of other symbols used in floor plans are shown in *Figure 24/2*.

NEWS AND WEATHER BRIEFS
Scale ⅛" = 1'0"

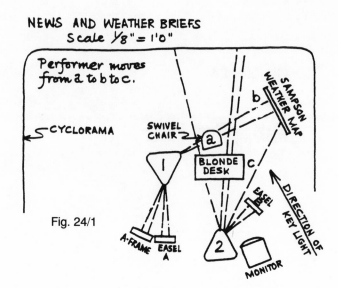

Fig. 24/1

Before making plans at the studio where you work, find out whether there are special symbols used there. Also learn the names by which particular pieces of furniture and scenery are identified there, since labels such as "A-frame," "blonde desk," and "Sampson weathermap" will indicate the specific items you have in mind.

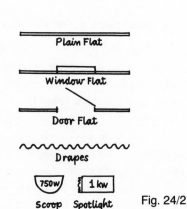

Fig. 24/2

3 The plan is drawn to scale.

Objects on the plan are outlined as if someone had traced around them while they were occupying their proper positions on the studio floor. Since it would obviously be impractical to draw these outlines at their actual size, the plan is drawn to some convenient reduced scale. Every foot of actual size is reproduced by some smaller unit of measurement, large enough to show necessary details yet small enough to fit the paper available. For this unit, directors often use ¼". To fit the pages of this book, however, the scale (as you can read on the plan) is ⅛" = 1'0". This means that every eighth-inch on the drawing represents one foot at actual size. Thus, the desk outline measures ¼" by ½", which is equivalent to ²⁄₈" by ⁴⁄₈", showing that the actual size of the desk is 2' by 4'.

You can save time in laying out floor plans by carrying commonly used dimensions in your head. For example, an interior door opening is often 2'6" wide, a straight chair is about 18" square, and a person's shoulder span is approximately 28". If you know that the sides of the base of your camera pedestal measure 36", you will plan enough space between the table and the sofa for the camera to dolly between them.

Draw to scale not only the scenic objects, but also the distances between them. Only when all relationships have been scaled can you be reasonably sure that the shots you intend are possible and that the scene will be set as you intend it.

4 Lens angles can be tested on the floor plan.

When you have scaled the distance of your camera from a given subject on the floor plan, you can test how much of the subject will be included by various lens angles. As you should already know, the angle of view embraced by a lens depends on its focal-length setting and on the diameter of the face of the pickup tube in the camera being used.

There are various guides for drawing these angles on your floor plan. With a little ingenuity you can make a device with straight edges that are pivoted and calibrated to open up (like scissor blades) to the desired angle. Or, with the aid of a protractor, you can draw each separate angle on cardboard, or better, on transparent plastic, and then cut it out, retaining either the cut-out piece or the remaining

"jaw." Or, as in *Figure 24/3*, you can simply draw a clump of angles on a sheet of paper, which you can slide around under your plan. This requires drawing your plan on paper sufficiently translucent so that you can see the angles through it.

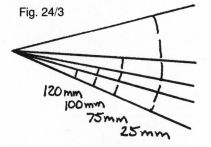

Fig. 24/3

120 mm
100 mm
75 mm
25 mm

The angles in *Figure 24/3* are horizontal angles, which can be used to determine what width of field you will have at a given distance from the lens. The height of the field will be three-quarters of the width. This fact was used to establish the proper distance of camera 2 from the news anchor's swivel chair on the plan (*Figure 24/1*) for "News and Weather Briefs."

The first things the director drew on this plan were the swivel chair and the desk in front of it. Then, knowing that a camera with 1" image pickup tubes would be used, and choosing a 50mm setting on the lens for the shot, the director laid a $13\frac{1}{2}°$ horizontal angle for that lens setting on the plan, and adjusted it until the width it framed, where the news anchor's shoulders would be, measured approximately 32". The height of the field at this point would be three-quarters of 32", or 24". This would be sufficient to include some headroom and a little of the desktop. So the angle was traced onto the plan in that position. As you can see by measuring the plan, this placed the front of camera 2 about 9′ from the back of the newsman's chair.

5   The floor plan is derived from the script.

The locations of virtually all the other elements in the setup were derived from the calculations just described. But to see how these other elements fit in, you will need to read the script for the program, for the floor plan is derived from the script and is devised to carry out the intentions of the script.

That this script is student-written and reflects an undergraduate's sense of humor makes it no less useful as a basis for floor planning.

Numbers in parentheses along the left margin indicate which camera, 1 or 2, the director plans to assign to a shot. In the audio column, the time for beginning each shot has been indicated by the symbol (X).

(2) CARD: Horse and buggy	*MUSIC:* *THEME UP & UNDER (OUT AFTER BOOTH ANNOUNCE-MENT)*
(1) CARD: News and Weather Briefs	BOOTH ANNCR: The National Association of Local Livery Stables brings you (X) "News and Weather Briefs," reported by Horace Trotter. (X)
(2) DISS TO: MS NEWS ANCHOR AT DESK	TROTR: (AT DESK) AD LIB OPEN-ING NEWS STORY, ENDING: . . . And now for the news in pictures. READ BRIEFS ON:
(1) PIC: Man in apron	MAN IN APRON
(2) PIC: Shotputter	SHOTPUTTER
(1) PIC: Spaghetti baby	SPAGHETTI BABY
(2) MS NEWS ANCHOR PAN HIM TO MAP	(X) And that's the news. (RISE & MOVE TO MAP.) Now for
(1) CU WESTERN HALF OF MAP	the weather from coast to coast. (X) In the West, sun and blue skies from Frisco to Fargo . . .
PAN TO EASTERN HALF	but in the East, tornadoes, ty-phoons, and thunder showers. (MOVING TOWARD CAM-
(2) NEWS ANCHOR, MOVING TOWARD CAMERA	ERA (X) That's the national picture. Now here's the local

(1) CU TOP WEATHER BOX   BOOTH   prediction . . . (X) Today's fore-
   (Weather)   ANNCR: cast for this vicinity: cloudy
  TILT DOWN   with clearing skies toward eve-
   (Temperature)   ning . . . Maximum tempera-
  TILT DOWN   ture 57, minimum temperature
   (Pollen)   48 . . . Pollen count six thou-
(2) MCU NEWS ANCHOR   sand, two hundred two. (X)

MUSIC: *THEME IN UNDER*
TROTR: Before we say goodbye, here's
     a closing thought from our
     sponsor.

(1) CARD: Sponsor ID   BOOTH   (X) When you're thinking of
(2) CARD: Horse and buggy   ANNCR: riding, remember: (X) a horse
     stands head and shoulders
     above any car on the market!

MUSIC: *UP TO TIME*

6   How the director devised the floor plan.

The studio cameras take all the graphics in the program, those on stands outside the playing area as well as the weather map within it. Where graphics follow one another, the director preferred, for the sake of clean transitions between them, to show them on alternate cameras rather than flipping through a sequence of them on a single stand. Early in the director's considerations, therefore, camera numbers were tentatively marked on the script by him to test whether the specified shots would alternate properly between the cameras. For example, the "horse and buggy" card is used twice; would it come up both times on the same camera? Fortunately it did. Fortunately also, all shots of the news anchor could be taken by the same camera, thereby allowing the audience a consistent view of him and considerably simplifying the problem of camera placement, since only one camera need be located where it could cover him effectively. It's a blessing when the scriptwriter, as in this case, has been educated to the director's problems.

6.1   In devising a shooting plan, the director first considered the news anchor's actions.

It is usually wise to begin by working out, at least tentatively, the performer's actions before deciding too firmly about the camera locations, since these actions, after all, are the subject of the program and the cameras are only the reproducers thereof. In the interests of effective reproduction, the actions may be modified to accommodate the cameras, but not at the expense of becoming less animated and less convincing.

As shown by the script, the action in "News and Weather Briefs" is simple: the performer delivers the news while seated behind his desk, then rises and walks to the weather map, then approaches the camera for his closing statements.

You have already seen how the shot of the desk was set up. There seemed to be no reason why the rest of the action could not be taken from the same camera location. In a show that moves as fast as this one, and is also to be shot by student camera operators, unnecessary camera deployment may entail being late for a shot or off position for it. Therefore, the director located the weather map where it, and the news anchor standing beside it, could be taken without moving camera 2. Since this shot required wider framing than the shot at the desk, the map was located farther from the camera than the desk, eliminating any errors that the camera operator could make while zooming out. To keep the map from showing during the presentation of the news, it was placed outside the desk shot, but not so far outside that the news anchor would not have time to reach it during his brief line, "Now for the weather from coast to coast."

Having fixed the location of the map, the director could now locate camera 1 for its closeup of the map. To avoid perspective distortion, this shot should be perpendicular to the map. To remain outside of camera 2's shots, camera 1 must be on the opposite side of the desk from the map, but not so distant that it cannot get a close shot of a section of the map when the lens is zoomed in.

No problem is caused by camera 2's last shot of the news anchor. The news anchor is to approach the camera for this, moving away from the map to signify that the weather reporting has ended. For informality, the director has him walk up to one end of his desk and perch on it. Giving him this point of reference also keeps him from ending up too close to camera.

6.2   Now it is possible to locate the stands on which the title cards and news pictures will be displayed.

Here the primary consideration is speed—speed for the camera to move between an easel and its other shots. To avoid unnecessary delay for zooming and focusing lenses, the easels are placed where the graphics they hold can be framed at the same focal length used for shots of the performer. To minimize the distance the camera must pan when getting on and off the graphics, the easel for camera 2 was situated just outside of that camera's shot of the map.

For camera 1 there were required both an easel (for three titles and pictures) and an "A-frame" on which to mount the "weather boxes." In locating these stands, a necessary consideration was available labor. Besides the floor manager, there was only one assistant. The assistant could be used for changing the graphics on camera 2's easel. Those on camera 1's easel would have to be changed by the floor manager, who would also have to cue the news anchor from a position close to the camera the news anchor would be addressing. Since a picture change occurs almost coincident with the news anchor's opening cue, it seemed necessary to locate camera 1's easel where the floor manager could stand between it and camera 2.

6.3   The plan also suggests a direction for the key light.

Much television lighting operates on the premise that the illumination of a scene should seem to be coming from a principal direction. The light moving from this direction, called the "key light," is usually originated by spotlights, and spotlight beams can cause troublesome shadows. By specifying that these beams travel parallel to the weather map instead of toward it, the director aims to keep shadows of the news anchor off the map.

It is easier to keep unwanted shadows off backgrounds if the backgrounds are kept at some distance behind the performers. This also facilitates backlighting the performers and enables you to control the brightness of backgrounds by lighting them independently of the playing area. For these reasons, the director plotted to keep the news anchor well in front of the cyclorama. The director also ensured that the weather map would not obstruct backlighting aimed on the performer.

6.4   In this situation you might use a lavalier microphone.

Since the news anchor gets up and moves around and even turns away from camera for a moment, sound is better recorded on a microphone that moves with him. Since the distance covered is short and the anchor's movement covered in a medium shot, it is also possible to conceal a trailing cable from the lavalier microphone without having to incur the additional cost of an expensive wireless transmitter.

One final element specified on the plan is a video monitor. This is placed where the news anchor can view the news pictures on it while reading the stories they portray.

Three Answers

The next floor plan to be considered is for a studio production exercise called "Three Answers." This program is opened by a host who, having cited some

problem or situation deserving of comment, propounds a question regarding
it. With the host are three guests who
will answer the question in turn. The
host calls on guest #1, who gives his
opinion. The host comments briefly on
this answer, then repeats the question
for guest #2. The process is repeated
with guest #3. Then the host summa-
rizes, thanks the guests, and closes the
program.

The floor plan is shown in *Figure
24/4*. Consult it while reading the following rationale for its design.

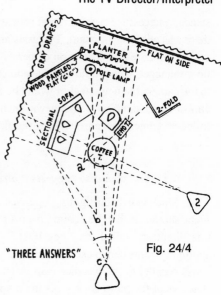

"THREE ANSWERS"   Fig. 24/4

7   First, the director establishes performer relationships.

How should the performers be arranged to support the action of the program? In this instance there are two entities to be related—the questioner and
those questioned. These entities require some sort of visual separation, but since
they are not in conflict, there is no reason for diametrical opposition; hence, the
director visualizes an L-shaped relationship.

Since the director desires a mood of relaxed informality, desks or tables are
avoided, seating the host in an armchair and unifying the guests by placing them
all on the same sofa. The director chooses an angled sofa to bridge the corner
between host and guests, blending them into a closer relationship.

The group needs to be as compact as possible. The wider the shot needed to
establish the total group, the smaller its members will be on the screen and the
more difficult it will be to discern their facial expressions. For the best control over
the audio situation, the director chooses to mike each person individually with his
or her own lavalier microphone.

8   The director places the cameras.

Camera 2 has been angled to show the guests from as nearly full face as
possible when they turn toward the host. Camera 1 has been angled to favor the
host and also to take establishing shots of the group. Letters "a," "b," and "c"
indicate that the camera will begin on the host only, then dolly back and simultaneously pan to the three guests, and finally reach a spot from which it can include
both host and guests. By shooting the sofa from an angle to overlap the guests, it

can obtain larger images of them than from the front, where they would present a wider spread.

The distance of camera from subject and the choice of the camera lens angle are interdependent considerations. For camera 1's opening shot, the director chooses to start on a 25mm lens setting because its generous depth of field will facilitate staying in focus while dollying, and its relative wide angle of view will embrace the entire group in a shorter distance, while at the same time requiring less studio space to withdraw into than if one started on a more telephoto-lens setting. From this distance (location "c") it can frame the host's chair, when zoomed into 75mm, when one-shots of the host are being alternated with one-shots of the individual guests. To make these alternating shots consistent in framing, perspective, and focal characteristics, camera 2 is placed at approximately the same distance from the guests as camera 1 is from the host, and will also take its one-shots at 75mm. From this distance it can also, if desired, zoom out to 50mm and include the host and the guest nearest him, or zoom out farther to 25mm to include the entire group. Both cameras, then, have base locations from which they can adequately cover all their shots within the range of their zoom lenses without having to move the cameras.

9   The director considers scenery and set dressing.

The staging for "Three Answers" evinces a concern for economy, both of money and of the time needed to set and strike. Most of the background is composed of already hanging drapes. The standing pieces are all from stock, and the few there can all be justified either for suggesting locale or for helping to achieve good pictorial composition.

Several of the pieces serve both purposes. The wood-paneled flat suggests a contemporary interior and encourages the studio drapes to read as drapes across a broad living-room window. Compositionally, as can be noted in *Figure 24/5*, the flat also serves, by backing the guests, to unite them visually and to distinguish them from the host, who is backed by the drapes.

Fig. 24/5

By simulating a portion of interior wall in the shot from position "a," the two-fold economically suggests a room. As a compositional factor, it brings the eye forward instead of letting it follow the bottom line of the drapes diagonally back and out of the picture. Similarly, in the shot from "c," the coffee table pulls the eye forward. Its mass helps to balance off the guests on the other side of the frame. It adds visual interest where there would otherwise be too much empty floor. The broad horizontal plane of its top opposes the vertical lines of the figures and helps to weigh down the composition, gravitywise, to the floor. The table also serves as a center around which the arc of the guests is curved.

Besides helping to form this arc, the angled sofa also prevents having the guests spaced with too military a regularity; note that the two men overlap, but the girl is separated from them. The still wider gap between girl and host is filled in with the vertical line of the pole lamp in the distance. All of these vertical directions are knit together by the horizontal lines of the furniture and the top of the planter.

An impression of the three-dimensional space is created by the curve of the performers, the diagonal planes of walls, furniture, and bodies, and by an axis that runs from the coffee table, as the nearest element, to the pole lamp, as most prominent distant element. This impression would be further enhanced, of course, by light and shadow and by focus differentiations, which are absent in the purely linear illustration. Also missing from the illustration is the distribution of color values. Perhaps you would like to experiment with how these should be distributed.

10   Vertical relationships in the picture are influenced by the floor plan.

It is possible to leave the considerations just discussed to a scenic artist, but it is unlikely that an artist will achieve a perfect solution unless your floor plan shows the relationship between performer locations and camera locations. The elevations of television settings must be designed to suit the shots, complementing rather than interfering with the appearance of the performers in these shots. For example, if the pole lamp was arbitrarily located, it might appear on camera directly behind a performer and seem to grow out of the top of his or her head. Its proper location can be determined by projecting on the floor plan a line that starts at camera 1 and passes between the host and the guest nearest to him. On this line, a short distance from the planter, is the spot where the pole lamp should be. By similar projections you can locate where the ends of the flat and the two-fold should occur.

If you have already completed the scenery and furniture locations on your floor plan and are experimenting with camera locations for certain shots, you can use this same method of projecting lines to determine where, in a given shot, elements in the background will appear in relation to the performers in front of them. For example, using the plan for "Three Answers," lay a ruler between camera 2 and the left end of the 6'6" flat. Where will the edge of the flat appear in camera 2's shot of the performer nearest the host—to the right or left of her head, or immediately behind it?

Microquiz

For a last example of floor planning, please identify yourself with the director of a program called "Microquiz." A plan for this program is to be contrived from advance data supplied by its producer.

According to this data, a husband and wife will be interviewed briefly and then invited to guess the identity of pictures shown on a rear-projection screen. The projector is to be operated through remote control by the program host. Its projection lens angle requires that it be twice as far behind the screen as the screen is wide. Both host and guests must be able to see the slides. The television audience must see the slides and must see the program participants both separately and in various appropriate combinations. The shot changes are likely to be frequent. Two cameras will be used.

What is the best interrelationship of cameras, participants, and rear projection screen?

11 There is more than one possible relationship.

From the previous floor plans shown to you, it might seem that the solution of a given planning problem will come readily to the director's mind. This is not necessarily so. The director may have to think through various arrangements, possibly sketching them on paper, and evaluating each against the requirements until he or she hits upon the one most likely to serve. There is more than one way to shoot a show. Don't always stop with the first solution that occurs to you. There may be a better one still in your head.

For example, *Figures 24/6* through *24/9* show four possible ways to shoot "Microquiz." Each will be analyzed in turn.

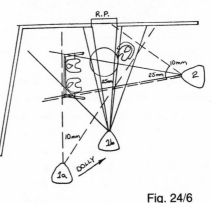

Figure 24/6

Here, the host is in an armchair, his guests on a sofa. Camera 1 starts back where it can establish the entire group at its 10mm lens position. For the quiz, it dollies into a position where it can include the host and the screen at 10mm, or if zoomed in to 25mm can pan be-

Fig. 24/6

tween the host and the screen. Camera 2 is placed where at 10mm it can take in the whole group, at 25mm the two guests, and at 50mm each guest separately.

What problems might arise from this arrangement? The rear projection screen may be placed so close to the performers that its images will be diluted by spill light from the performance area. Moving it back, however, will probably require enlarging the images, which will make them less brilliant. It may be possible to restrict spill light by cross-keying, i.e., by lighting the guests from the direction of camera 2 and the host from an instrument behind the guests, so that the light beams run more or less parallel to the rear wall rather than toward it.

Audio pickup in this solution may not be satisfactory unless each performer wears a lavalier microphone. Otherwise, since there are no surfaces to support table microphones, it will be necessary to use a boom microphone, and for this the performers are rather too widely separated.

Figure 24/7

This is an attempt to solve the audio problem just discussed. Although the performers are in much the same relationship as before, they have been moved closer together and seated at a table, which permits the use of table microphones. To view the host as nearly full face as possible, camera 1 has been stationed close to the desk—so close, indeed, that it may disturb the concentration of the guest nearest to it.

Fig. 24/7

Figure 24/8

This attempt is probably not as promising as the preceding one, since it catches the host in profile at best—although he might be given a swivel chair to facilitate turning toward the camera for his opening and close. Camera 2 is placed so as to be able to zoom between closeups of the screen and wider shots that include the performers.

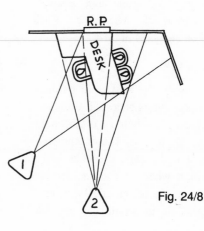

Fig. 24/8

Figure 24/9

In this arrangement, audio pickup is feasible and there is less danger of light diluting the projected images since the performers have been moved to one side of the screen. Both host and guests can be shown relatively face-to, and the cameras are sufficiently distant to prevent their intruding on the performers' concentration. Unlike the two previous plans, no specially constructed table is required.

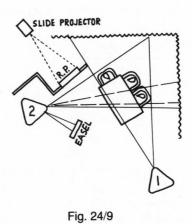

Fig. 24/9

Perhaps, then, this scheme has possibilities. Before deciding on it, however, the director tests it against a representative portion of the program action to see what kind and variety of shots it will provide.

1 (LS) HOST OPENS STANDING AT R.P. SCREEN. AS HE WALKS TO TABLE AND SITS, PAN WITH HIM AND ESTABLISH THE COMPLETE TABLE, INCLUDING ALREADY SEATED GUESTS.

2 (CU) PAN FROM ONE GUEST TO THE OTHER AS THEY ARE INTRODUCED.

1 (MS) HOST. PAN LEFT TO SCREEN WHEN HE INTRODUCES FIRST PICTURE.

2 (MS) BRIEF CUT-AWAY: BOTH GUESTS LOOKING TOWARD SCREEN.

1 (MS) SCREEN. PAN RIGHT TO HOST WHEN HE SAYS THAT TIME FOR VIEWING SLIDE IS UP.

 2 (CU) PAN GUESTS AS EACH GUESSES.

 1 (LS) SCREEN AND HOST AS HOST TELLS CORRECT ANSWER.

 2 (MS) BOTH GUESTS, FOR THEIR REACTIONS; THEN PAN LEFT TO HOST AS HE TURNS TOWARD SCREEN TO INTRODUCE SECOND SLIDE.

 1 (CU) SCREEN.

2 (LS) ALL THREE LOOKING AT SCREEN, OFF LEFT.

 1 (MS) HOST AS HE CALLS TIME AND ASKS FOR GUESSES.

 2 (CU) PAN GUESTS AS EACH GUESSES.

1 (LS) ALL THREE, AS HOST GIVES CORRECT ANSWER
... etcetera

This test demonstrates that the setup is capable of providing meaningful shots. And although the game follows the same routine over and over, the setup provides a sufficient variety of shots to enliven what might otherwise prove to be a very monotonous visual sequence.

Even so, you may be able to work out an even more satisfactory solution.

At any rate, when working on floor plans, don't settle for the first solution that occurs to you. Try several until you are sure you have found the most promising.

In evaluating a plan, don't think of it merely as outlines of scenery, furniture, and camera positions. View it, rather, in terms of shot possibilities such as those sketched above. These are the end toward which your floor plan is the means. The plan is only as good as the pictures it enables you to present to your audience.

Some Further Considerations

12 Relate your plan to studio conditions.

Most of the factors you have been invited to consider when designing a floor plan have been concerned with communicating the meaning and action of a program to its audience. The design may be modified, however, by some considerations not connected with the program, but rather with accommodating the production to the studio where it will take place. Thus, you may need to take into account:

. . . the location and needs of other setups that must occupy the studio at the same time.

. . . the possibility, when doing live programming, that cameras, microphones, and even some of the lights used on your program will be needed on a previous or following program, with a minute or less in which to make the transfer.

. . . studio traffic patterns—the need to keep entrances and passageways clear and to provide access to your area without crossing in front of cameras or interfering with other studio activities.

. . . the location of studio outlets for camera, microphone, and video monitor cables, or for supplying utilities such as water, gas, or 220-volt electrical power to equipment used on your program.

. . . the location of overhead pipe grids, battens, and traveler curtain tracks, so that your plan does not call for scenic pieces and lighting instruments where it is not convenient to suspend them.

. . . the possible desirability of being able to view both your performance area and camera deployment area through the window of the control room.

13 Try to economize time and money.

When planning your setup, minimize setting and striking time where possible by using already hung pieces, such as drapes and cycloramas. Minimize construction by using stock pieces when feasible. Condense as much as possible the area to be backed by scenery and lighted. Restrict technical operations, scenic embellishments, and special effects to whatever can be accomplished during the allowed preparation time. Submit your plans to the technical departments early enough to be carried out during their normal production schedule. Provide all of the information needed by these departments so that time will not be lost through guesswork or the need to seek you out for further details. Avoid last-minute revisions.

14   In summary, the satisfactory floor plan should:

(1) Establish meaningful physical relationships between the performers, and between them and whatever properties and scenic elements may be engaged in the action.

(2) Provide for performers' movements that are meaningful, animated, and convincing.

(3) Ensure that shots are so alternated between cameras that each camera can show what is expected of it.

(4) Locate the cameras to get each shot with the proper angle and framing.

(5) Prevent camera delays due to unnecessary camera repositioning.

(6) Permit effective lighting, with no undesirable shadows.

(7) Permit good audio pickup.

(8) Allow the available technical crew to function effectively.

(9) Locate furniture and scenic elements where they will support and enhance the pictorial composition of each intended shot.

(10) Relate to conditions in the studio to be used.

(11) Reflect a concern for economy of money and people power.

By governing where your subjects and cameras will stand and move, the floor plan determines to a large extent what shots you can get and how these shots will look. But the floor plan in turn should be determined by what shots you want to get and how you want them to look. Hence, a great deal of what you learn about television picture making—not only from what you have read here, but also from your future reading and thinking and experience—will ultimately be reflected in your floor plans.

Chapter 25

Efficiency

Although you may have designed superbly communicative television pictures, you have to rely on others for the designs' realization. The performers, the service departments which assemble your production materials and facilities, studio and control room crews which operate the facilities—all must be oriented to their objectives and guided in the achievement of them, each separate contribution being coordinated with all of the others to make a perfect whole. And this perfection must be achieved with due regard to always existing limitations of time and resources.

The realization of your pictures, therefore, depends on how well you direct the activities of people and make the most of the limitations within which they work. It depends upon your qualities as an administrator and efficiency expert.

This chapter traces the course through which your efficiency must operate, from the initial conception of your production through the facilities rehearsal. To promote efficiency, this chapter asks you to observe certain practices, the first of which is:

1   Work closely with the service departments.

1.1   Give them sufficient time and information to do a job that will reflect credit on them and on you.

As soon as you know your program objectives and how you propose to accomplish them, you will need to supply various kinds of information to the departments that will carry out your production requirements. If your program is a new and reasonably important venture, it would be advisable to hold a production conference involving, besides yourself, the producer and client's representative (if any), and representatives of staging, lighting, engineering, art, and any other department contributing to the production. This conference provides an opportunity to:

   . . . arrive at a mutual understanding of the production purpose, format, and style.

   . . . determine the facilities needed and the time and space in studio required.

   . . . schedule dates and times for rehearsals and actual broadcast or taping sessions.

   . . . discuss the budget and desirable modifications in it.

   . . . iron out any disagreements or technical difficulties.

Whether or not a general conference is held, you can profitably hold individual conferences with members of the various departments to work out the specifications for everything you require. To confirm and record these requirements, you should use the prescribed forms for submitting floor plans of your setting, ordering titles and other graphics, clearing music, and obtaining various other materials and services.

Films, slides, tape, and other materials that you may procure from outside sources will need to be in the hands of appropriate personnel by prescribed times. There will also be a deadline for your script or program rundown. If there is a standard format for these, it is to your advantage to follow it, since the operators on your program will be familiar with this format and can therefore follow it with minimum chance for error. There also may be required a cover sheet listing properties, music, and sound effects, tapes to be inserted into the program, and the films and slides to be projected. Such lists allow operators to check whether the items are all on hand and to have them arranged in the proper order.

1.2   To increase the possibilities of getting the services you need:

Meet the deadlines of the service departments. Remember that your program is not the only one on their assembly line.

Be certain that all responsibilities are allocated. Let there be no occasion to say, "I thought you were going to do that!"

Anticipate and provide for everything. If you need a tractor in the setting, will it fit through the studio door? Can the ice cream be kept refrigerated? Is there a 220-volt outlet for operating the clothes dryer? How long will it take to light the glossy automobile? Will you be allowed by fire regulations to start its motor in the studio?

If you contemplate any unusual electronic or scenic effects, check with experts regarding their feasibility and test them well before camera rehearsal.

Take nothing for granted. Check the progress of preparation and procurement. Be sure that everything is going to be ready and to conform to specifications.

2 Save studio time by advance preparation.

Come to the studio with as much of the production organized as possible, knowing exactly what remains to be done and how you are going to do it. Studio time is too precious to use for determining what the performers will do and say or what kind of shots the director will take.

Except in the case of routine and extremely simple programs, work with your performers outside of the studio, rehearsing in a mock-up of the setting and checking your shots with a viewing device. Establish the timing of the performance, including an estimated allowance for fades, dissolves, musical bridges, and other transitional material.

For personnel not present at these outside rehearsals, it is sometimes expedient to prepare written instructions in order to minimize the time taken by verbal instructions during studio rehearsal. Besides shot plots for the camera operators, one can write out cues and instructions for other operators, such as the audio engineer, curtain puller, or lighting control person. You can also include directions in the booth announcer's script: "Pause until camera has dollied in. . . . Wait for next painting to show on monitor," etcetera.

3 In studio, accomplish as much as you can before the cameras are ready.

For example, you may be able to:

. . . check the scenery and lighting setup.

. . . see that the technical director has film, slides, and videotape readied in the proper sequence.

. . . see that the audio operator knows the cues and has located the proper starting places on records and audiotapes.

. . . check to see that all electronic graphics and titles are correct.

. . . work with the floor crew on manual operations such as the flipping of easel pictures.

. . . work with the performers to accustom them to studio conditions, relating their business and action to the actual furniture and scenery, solving their problems with the wearing of lavalier microphones, wireless transmitters, and so on.

. . . see that the floor manager and the performers have a mutual understanding about the meaning of the floor manager's signals and when they are to occur.

. . . hold a complete dry rehearsal of dialogue and action if time permits. Sometimes it may be possible to have the camera operators watch this before they have to operate their cameras.

4 Assuming that you have some camera rehearsal, make the most of it.

Ideally, for perfecting any new production involving considerable movement by performers and cameras, there should be enough camera rehearsal time to allow a continuous run-through. This will give both talent and technicians practice in sustaining a coordinated performance and will allow a final check on total running time. Following this run-through, there should be a sufficient interval before broadcast or recording to make last-minute corrections, restore various items to their starting positions, and rebalance the cameras.

Before the run-through there should be a stop-and-start or blocking rehearsal to set each major shot and transition, taking them sequentially, one by one. It is to this blocking rehearsal that the following suggestions apply.

4.1 Save time.

Start the rehearsal punctually.

Know precisely what you want to do and move briskly along from one objective to another. Your plans should be definite but flexible. If a camera has to be worked on, be ready to do something that mainly involves the still serviceable cameras, or work on a performer's interpretation, or an audio effect, etcetera.

By thorough advance preparation you should have forestalled the need for any major changes. Just one change may entail many others. Changing a table position may necessitate relighting. Relighting may entail moving the furniture and performers out of the way. Meanwhile, the clock keeps ticking.

Make your instructions precise and phrase them in terms of action. To a performer, for instance: "Chris, first look toward the map. Now move—that's it, clear across to Maine. Now stop and point. Good!" Or to a camera operator, "Bill, you need to zoom in more quickly, and into a tighter shot; all we want is the keyboard, not the whole accordion. Ready? Go! In . . . in . . . tilt down more, and in . . . in . . . and stop! That's the idea. Let's try it once more now to smooth out the jerky tilting." (Note that Bill is told the objective of his zoom-in. Compliance can be speeded up when a person comprehends what is to be done, and why.)

There's usually no need in a blocking rehearsal for performers to run through all their dialogue. If the shot doesn't change, interrupt them and move on to the next change.

On the other hand, do involve a performer whenever his or her movement or dialogue affects the shots you are setting up. Thus, obviously, the performer must rise and walk if you are to perfect the tilting up and panning with the action. Less obviously, perhaps, the duration of a speech may affect a pictorial transition: what the master of ceremonies says to introduce the panelists may determine the amount of time a camera has in which to dolly back and pan to the panel.

As mentioned previously in this book, you can sometimes expedite matters by working part of the time on the studio floor in direct communication with the performers. Also as previously mentioned, you should proportion your time so that overconcern with one problem does not rob time from others of equal importance.

Your job is to keep everything going. You cannot do this if you lose yourself in concerns others can handle for you. Delegate authority, so that you have lieutenants working on several concerns at the same time. Identify those things others can be working on while you're busy rehearsing something else. Get things started early in the rehearsal so they'll be ready by the time you need to weave them into the show.

5   Your watchwords are STOP, LOOK, AND LISTEN—not FAITH, HOPE, AND CHARITY.

. . . Well, charity, maybe, but not the other two. Never take anything on faith and hope that it will work. Demand to see and listen to it. This is the only way to be sure that people understand what you want and that you are capable of achieving it. And before the actual performance, check to see that everything used in rehearsal has been restored to its proper starting position and is ready to go.

Throughout rehearsal, look and listen critically. Remember what was said in Chapter 11, "Concealing Mechanics," about professionalism being, in the main, a painstaking attention to details.

On the other hand, there are times when it doesn't pay to stop and correct every small mistake. If rehearsal time is short, come to it knowing which things are the most critical or difficult, and restrict your attention to them. Furthermore, constant stopping can become discouraging and irritating to your personnel. It is often more important to give them the feel of the whole, to let them practice sustaining the continuity of the performance, than to get lost among the pieces and never put them together.

When you do discuss problems with a person, don't point out too many problems in the same breath—unless you want to overwhelm, confuse, and discourage your talent, as well as have most of the corrections forgotten.

6   Maintain the morale of your team.

6.1   You are their servant as well as their boss.

Give them the information they need when they need it. Restrict your demands to what they and their equipment can reasonably accomplish.

6.2   Show them that you respect their abilities.

Give them a chance to exercise these abilities. Make clear what is needed, but don't try to do their job for them. Keep yourself open to their suggestions—

without, of course, letting anarchy set it. Find a way to recognize their contributions without cheapening your praise through overspending it. Make them feel it's their show, too.

6.3   Beware of exploiting your own ego.

Crew people tend to resent the director who always uses the first-person pronoun: "Give me a closeup of so and so," or, "I want to see you pan left." People on the studio floor tend to resent the unseen presence who dominates them over the studio intercom system without giving them an opportunity to discuss their problems face to face.

6.4   Control yourself.

Never use the intercommunication system to publicly disparage an individual. Make every effort to stay calm and collected and to set an example of confidence. Anxiety is contagious; don't spread it.

6.5   Remember that idleness breeds restlessness and apprehension.

Be considerate of people's time. If, through unforeseen difficulties, they must be kept waiting, explain the situation briefly to them and give them a break, asking them to return to the studio at a certain time when you know you'll be able to work with them.

Much more might be said about the technique of supervision, but perhaps you have read enough to realize your need to become proficient at it. Your ability to design effective television pictures will count for little unless you can get your performers and technicians to bring those pictures to life on the screen.

Chapter 26

Calling the Shots

During most television performances the director calls the shots—gives the verbal directions that regulate what the technicians do and when they do it.

There are exceptions, mainly in the larger studios. In some instances the technical director may cue the camera operators following a shot plan established by the director in rehearsal. Or an assistant director may get the cameras ready for their shots, with the director calling for the shots to be switched and guiding the cameras while they are feeding the program. Lighting cues may be delegated to the lighting director, and audio cues to the audio director. When programs have been fully scripted and camera plotted, the camera operators and other technicians may follow written instructions with a minimum of verbal cues from the control room.

But in many situations today the director is likely to work where his or her verbal instructions will coordinate the work of many persons: camera operators, audio control operator, floor manager, booth announcer, projectionist, videotape operator, and technical director among them. Even when the director does his or her own switching, the director may be expected to call the takes so that all technicians will know what picture changes are occurring without needing to keep their eyes glued to a monitor.

Therefore, if you have not already done so, you will need to become proficient at shot calling—so proficient, indeed, that you can relegate the routine aspects of it to your subconscious, as with typing, bicycling, or driving a car, to free your attention for the thoughtful and creative aspects. Although you can reach this stage only through actual and repeated practice, the following pointers may help to guide and speed your learning.

1 Take it easy and learn by degrees.

You might start with a short, easily improvised sequence in which a host asks a guest one question:

CHEST SHOT, HOST	HOST:	INTRODUCES SELF AND PROGRAM. HE HAS A GUEST TO QUESTION. ASKS QUESTION.
ZOOM OUT TO 2-SHOT		
CHEST SHOT, GUEST	GUEST:	ANSWERS.
CHEST SHOT, HOST	HOST:	COMMENTS ON ANSWER, CLOSES PROGRAM.

If you have never called shots before, begin by just seeing whether you can fade a camera in and out on the host, without even having him say anything. Don't worry too much at this stage about memorizing the correct terminology for your directions. It's more important to think about what, at each stage, you have to get done:

Think this:	*. . . and therefore say:*
I must alert people we're about to begin. The technical director (T.D.) must preset the fader bank to come up on the proper camera.	STAND BY. READY TO FADE UP ONE.
Now, have the T.D. come up on it.	
That's all, so ready the switcher to end the show.	READY TO FADE TO BLACK.
Have him do it.	FADE TO BLACK.

Next, try repeating the same thing, but having the host speak his introduction. For this, in addition to what you did before, you need to 1) get the microphone opened, and 2) have your floor manager cue the host that he's coming on camera and microphone. And in order to end the show, you'll need to know in advance the last words the host plans to say.

Think this:	*. . . and therefore say:*
Alert everyone.	STAND BY.
The T.D. must be ready.	READY TO FADE UP ONE.
The audience must hear the host.	OPEN MIKE.
Alert the host that the camera's coming on.	CUE HIM.
Now he's ready to have his picture taken.	FADE UP ONE.
The show will end when he finishes speaking, so ready the T.D.	READY TO FADE TO BLACK.
(Listening) He's ending his speech.	FADE TO BLACK.

When you've mastered this, add the zoom-out that brings the guest into view. Start the zoom when the host mentions having a guest with him and go to black as soon as the zoom is completed. To avoid a wait at the end, ready the technical director for the fade-out while the camera is still zooming.

Your directions will be the same as before until after you've said, "Fade up one," Then:

Think this:	*. . . and therefore say:*
He's going to mention the guest.	READY TO ZOOM OUT.
He's starting to mention him.	ZOOM OUT.
The end's coming up.	READY TO FADE TO BLACK.
(Watching monitor) The camera's zoomed out far enough.	HOLD THE ZOOM.
That's all.	FADE TO BLACK.

Finally, you'll be able to add the second camera, taking it when the guest begins to speak. Then you'll take back to the first camera for the host's conclusion. Since the camera has zoomed out into a two-shot, however, you will have to get it zoomed back in for a closing one-shot of the host while camera 2 is on. The whole sequence, then, will go something like this:

Think this:	*. . . and therefore say:*
I must have the camera ready.	OPENING SHOTS, PLEASE . . . 1, CHEST SHOT OF THE HOST AND READY TO ZOOM OUT . . . 2, CHEST SHOT OF THE GUEST.
(Watching monitors) That doesn't look quite right.	2, A LITTLE MORE HEADROOM, PLEASE.
(Watching clock) It's almost starting time.	STAND BY.
The T.D. must be ready.	READY TO FADE UP 1.
Audience must hear.	OPEN MIKE.
Alert the host.	CUE HIM.
Show the host as he starts to talk.	FADE UP 1.
Guest's coming up soon.	READY TO ZOOM OUT.
(Listening) Host is starting to mention guest.	ZOOM OUT.
(Looking) Is 2's shot of the guest still OK? 1 has zoomed far enough.	HOLD THE ZOOM.
(Listening and watching) Guest's about to speak.	TAKE 2.
1's shot is finished. What's 1's next shot?	1, ON YOUR SHOULDER SHOT OF THE HOST.
(Listening) Guest's finished his answer.	TAKE 1.
End's coming soon.	READY TO FADE TO BLACK.
(Watching and listening) Host is finished, verbally and visually.	FADE TO BLACK.

Once you've been able to do all this, you're well on your way. If it seems complicated at first, remember that with practice it will get to be second nature to you. Most of it will roll out without your consciously thinking about it.

2   Shot calling is not reading words off a script.

Some beginners write what they're supposed to say and then try to read it aloud during the performance. This rarely works. If you lose your place on the page, you probably won't know what is supposed to happen next. Even if you do manage to follow along the page, you won't know what is happening to the program since you aren't looking at the pictures or listening to the sounds or feeling with your sense of timing when the changes should occur.

Directors usually do mark their scripts with symbols or brief reminders that tell them at a glance what's coming next. But these should be only reminders. Mainly, you should know what's supposed to be happening, following a thought sequence like that in the "Think this" columns above. Start by grasping the overall pattern of events—for example: "Host first . . . zoom out to include guest . . . guest alone . . . then host alone." With this in mind, you'll likely find that during the performance, if you really watch and listen to what's going on, each present occurrence will remind you of what's to follow it. Seeing the host, you'll remember that he has a guest with him whom you'll have to include by zooming out. The zoom-out to include the guest will remind you that next the guest gets a shot to himself. Listening to the guest's answer will remind you that the host will comment on that answer—and so on.

And as you watch and listen, you'll also be able to do the other things: see that the next shot is properly set up, see that the present shot looks right, refer occasionally to the clock, evaluate the quality and volume of the audio, sense the pace at which to guide a pan or zoom or dissolve and the time at which to call a take or cue in music.

Remember, then: calling directions is not just reading, or even speaking. It's thinking, feeling, watching, and listening.

3   Make your directions brief and to the point.

Say: "1 on the girl," not: "Camera 1, please pan left and get ready for the shot of the girl."

Unnecessary words can make an instruction less intelligible. They waste time that the technician needs for getting ready to do what you want done, and which you need for giving other directions at times when the cues come thick and fast. Too many words also communicate less urgency than is needed to keep a crew on its toes.

4 Use the vocabulary of your particular studio or station.

Terminology is not completely standardized throughout the country. Be sure that your terminology is understood at the facility where you report for work. Highly original phrases may not be understood, or understood as quickly as they need to be. Nevertheless, personnel at most stations should understand such variants as:

Zoom out—Zoom back
Dolly back—Pull back
Ready music—Standby music
Fade in 2—Fade up 2—Fade 2
Fade to black—Go to black
Tilt up—pan up
Truck left—Track left
etcetera

5 Know when to give ready or standby cues.

These are normally given in the following circumstances:

5.1 Before air time to alert everyone to the start of the program.

The floor manager will relay this cue to persons in the studio without headphones.

5.2 To any operator who has been out of action for some time, including:

. . . the booth announcer, who, usually having nothing to do on the program for some time after the opening announcement, may become lost in other concerns.

. . . the tape operator, before a videotape sequence is called for. The tape operator may be across the room, rewinding tapes or setting up another recorder.

. . . a camera operator who has not been used for the past several shots.

. . . the audio operator, for opening a microphone. Although the audio operator may have been involved constantly in riding gain, opening a new microphone is a different operation, which may not be a part of the operator's present thought pattern.

5.3 For any operation that requires some preparatory action—thus:

Before playing a disc recording, the operator must have the stylus in the proper groove, the turntable motor on, one hand on the disc, and the other on the volume control.

Before dollying a pedestal or tripod, the camera operator must have the wheels lined up in the desired direction and be ready to push or pull as the case may be.

Before making a dissolve, super, or introducing a special effect, the technical director must preset the special effects generator (SEG) and have his or her hands on the fader levers.

5.4   To better prepare the camera operators for the next shot.

Some studios, for example, require ready cues before camera takes. During a program shot with three or more cameras, the cues identify which of the idle cameras is to be used next. On the other hand, during a brisk alternation of shots, it is difficult to include ready cues and still take the shots on time.

6   Practice starting your cues to finish at the necessary time.

Commands for takes should finish a fraction of a second before the takes are wanted in order to allow for the technical director's reaction time. Tape must be rolled before it can be switched into the program. After starting, the videotape machine may require several seconds to get up to proper speed. When these are used for inserts, the cue to roll them may need to be given as early as two sentences before speech from the studio is to cease. The director should know what these final sentences are to be and remind the performer to deliver them verbatim so that, recognizing them, the director can give the roll cue at the necessary time.

7   Several cues may be needed simultaneously.

Sometimes a number of operations may coincide or follow one another so swiftly that the director has not time to deliver all the cues for them in their standard form.

Getting to studio from opening titles over which music has been played would theoretically require you to say, "Music out, open mike, cue talent, dissolve to 2." This can be condensed to, "Mike, cue, dissolve." (In this instance, the audio operator understands that the music is to be taken out when the dissolve occurs.) In any situation where several cues would make too much of a mouthful, you can arrange in advance with each operator to act on a single cue from you, such as the word "dissolve."

There may be some operations which, by custom in your studio or station, you will not have to cue at all. For example, the audio operator may automatically be expected to close the studio microphones whenever the program moves to some other source of sound (such as sound on tape) that requires no audio from the studio.

8   There is a preferable sequence for some sets of cues.

When a turntable takes longer to get up to speed than the technical director does to fade up the opening picture, give the music cue before the fade cue. It is customary to say, "Music, fade in one," rather than, "Fade in one, music."

Also say, "Mike, cue, dissolve," when going to a performer at the start of a studio sequence. Do not say, "Dissolve, mike, cue." To bring the camera up on your talent before the microphone has been opened may miss the starting word if the performer takes the cue from the tally light instead of from the floor manager. Do not say, "Mike, dissolve, cue." To bring the camera up on your talent before being cued is liable to catch the performer in the process of taking the floor manager's cue. Therefore, say, "Mike, cue, dissolve."

9   Follow these suggestions for giving directions to camera operators:

As soon as a camera goes off the air, specify its next shot. Make it habitual to think, It's off; what does it do next? Thus, your directions will run: "Take 1; 2 closeup on the bowl . . . Take 2; 1 hold your shot . . . Take 1; 2 on a cover shot . . ." etcetera.

In addressing the off-air camera, give its number before stating what it is to do. Thus: "2, pan over to the mayor." There are two reasons for this precaution: 1) if you do not start with the number, the camera operator who is on the air may assume that the direction is for him or her—panning to the mayor, for example, off the camera operator's present subject; and 2) when more than one camera is off the air, their operators, if obliged to wait in order to learn which of them you are addressing, will lose time that should have gone to carrying out the instruction.

When setting up shots of people, you are likely to get more accurate framing if you ask for a "shoulder shot" or "waist shot" rather than a "closeup" or "medium shot."

How much verbal information you give the camera operators about setting up their shots will depend upon how much they already know about their assignment. To the degree that they have been thoroughly rehearsed, you will need to be less explanatory. If they have shot sheets taped to their cameras, you may simply refer to the shots by their numbers: for example, "2, ready with shot 6."

As explained in Chapter 10, "Keeping Up with the Action," make it clear to the camera operators in advance when you wish them to find shots for you and when you wish them to wait for your instructions. When they are finding shots for you, keep your eyes on the monitors and give them your reaction to whatever they are offering you.

10 The tone and tempo of your directions will influence the crew's responses.

By the tone and tempo of your directions you can communicate a feeling of snappy efficiency, or easy relaxation, or some other desired psychological set. How you speak can be used to guide the pace and rhythm of a dolly or pan, regulate the speed of a dissolve, control the crescendo and diminuendo of music, or make a take occur at the proper moment. When guiding operators who are in the control room with you, such as the technical director and the audio operator, you may wish occasionally to supplement your voice with the snap of a finger or the movement of an arm such as an orchestra conductor might employ—provided, however, that these are helpful and are not done merely to dramatize your role.

11 Study the following example of cues for a complete short program.

Commands of execution are in capital letters. Preparatory commands are indented and in lowercase.

As previously mentioned, terminology varies between one station and another and between one director and another. You are not being asked to adopt the following phraseology word for word, but rather to understand its general style and purpose:

DIRECTIONS	SCRIPT	
Opening shots, please. Ready music, ready to fade up on effects (character generator)		
MUSIC—FADE UP EFFECTS.	CG (title)	*MUSIC: THEME UP & UNDER*
OPEN ANNOUNCE MIKE. MUSIC UNDER—ANNOUNCE.		BOOTH ANNOUNCER:
Ready host's mike.		From the Flagstaff Museum it's Bob Daniels with
Ready to dissolve to 2.		. . . Nature Quiz!
		MUSIC: OUT
MIKE, CUE HOST, DISSOLVE TO 2.	MS BOB	BOB:
CHANGE CG.		INTRODUCTORY REMARKS, DISCUSS PENGUINS.
Ready to key in effects.		
KEY IN EFFECTS.	CG	ENDING:
LOSE EFFECTS.	(host name)	And now let's watch
Ready to roll tape,		some penguins in their
Ready to dissolve to 7.		native habitat.
ROLL TAPE.		

	TAPE (3:16)	SOUND ON TAPE.

DISSOLVE TO 7, SOUND UP.
    2, we'll be dissolving back to you on a long shot of Bob. Be ready to pan from him to the guest.
    . . . 1, get a closeup of the mystery object . . . ready to dissolve to 2. Tape ends in 10 seconds—stand by. . . .		

MIKE, CUE HOST, DISSOLVE.
2, PAN WITH HIM—GOOD!
 	
1 steady . . .
TAKE 1
    2, zoom in on the guest.
    Ready to key in CG effects.
	LS BOB
	PAN
	WITH
	HIM TO
	GUEST
	CU
	MYSTERY
	OBJECT
		BOB:
		EXPLAINS QUIZ.
		MENTION GUEST & WALK OVER TO CHAT WITH HIM BRIEFLY. THEN: Now let's see if you know what this is. (AD LIB) . . . and meanwhile we'll let the audience in on the secret. . . . Are you ready to guess?

KEY EFFECTS Ready to lose CG effect. Ready to take 2 quickly.	CG (name of object)	
LOSE EFFECTS . . . TAKE 2 Change CG graphic. 2, ZOOM OUT TO INCLUDE HOST.	CU GUEST	GUEST: GIVES HIS ANSWER.
	BOB & GUEST	BOB: AWARDS NATURE CLUB POINTS. THANKS GUEST.
2, PAN WITH HIM Ready to dissolve to CG titles.	PAN BOB INTO 1-SHOT	BOB: MOVES AWAY, BACK TO HIS OPENING POSITION. EXPLAINS HOW AUDIENCE CAN SUBMIT QUESTIONS.
DISSOLVE TO CG Ready music. Ready to dissolve to 2. MUSIC UNDER.	CG (address)	Write to this address . . . (READ IT) . . . and be sure to include your name. *MUSIC: THEME IN UNDER*
CUE BOB, DISSOLVE TO 2. Ready to disolve to CG.	BOB	BOB: DISCUSS NEXT SHOW. ENDING: See you then on . . .

DISSOLVE TO CG, MUSIC UP.	CG	Nature Quiz!
Announcer, stand by . . .	(title)	*MUSIC: UP, THEN UN-*
Ready to roll CG credits.		*DER FOR:*
ROLL TITLES, MUSIC UNDER,	CG	ANNOUNCER:
CUE ANNOUNCER.	(credits)	Nature Quiz is written and
		produced for the Flagstaff
		Museum by Bob Daniels.
MUSIC UP		*MUSIC: UP TO TIME.*
Ready to fade to black.		
FADE TO BLACK	BLACK	

APPENDIX

As mentioned in the Introduction, this book was partially compiled from handouts issued to television-directing classes. With one exception, these handouts could be classified either as Principles or as Accessory Aptitudes. The ones that could not are offered here as an adjunct, which many students seemed to find useful.

Selecting Lenses

Here are some of the factors you may need to consider when selecting a specific focal length for a given shot:

Framing

The area included in the frame depends on:

(1) *The focal length on the lens*—The longer the focal length, the narrower the angle, the less the area included, but the bigger your subject on the screen. And (vice versa) the shorter the focal length, the wider the angle, the more area included, but the smaller your subjects are on the screen.

(2) *The distance between camera and subject*—The shorter this distance, the less area included, but the bigger your subjects are on the screen. The greater the distance, the more area included, but the smaller your subjects are on the screen.

So you can frame your subject at the same size either by using a short lens with the camera close, or a long lens with the camera farther away. Which of these solutions you choose depends on:

Physical limitations: Are your cameras confined to a distant location— across the street or way back in the bleachers? Then obviously you must use the longer focal lengths. Is the studio so small that you can't place the camera very far from the action? Then you must favor the shorter focal lengths. When you can back the camera up, do you risk shooting unwanted subjects such as other cameras, or area outside the setting? Then you should move the camera closer and use shorter focal lengths.

Keeping up with the action: Can you use the ending zoom range effectively from the distance at which you have placed the camera—or must you move it between shots, thus risking a possible delay?

Avoiding disturbances: Will the camera be so close to the subject that it will bump into furniture on the set? Or disturb the performers' concentration? Or get into another camera's shot? Or throw camera shadow on the subject? Or feed operational noise into the microphone?

Size of closeup desired: Although closeups are commonly associated with the longer focal lengths, the biggest possible closeup of a tiny subject can be taken by an extreme wide-angle lens, since the subject can be focused very close to this lens. At such proximity, however, depth of field is very shallow and perspective distortion is pronounced; hence, only very flat and shallow subjects can be shot in this manner.

Perspective

When two subjects are at different distances from the camera, difference in screen size between them can be increased by using a shorter focal length with the camera in close. In *Figure A/1*, A is twice as close to camera as B; hence, he will be twice as large as B on the screen.

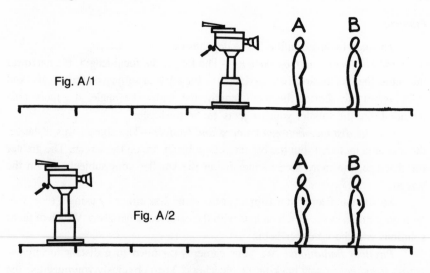

Fig. A/1

Fig. A/2

Vice versa, the difference can be evened out by using a longer focal length farther from the subjects. In *Figure A/2*, A is four-fifths of the distance to B and will consequently be only one-fifth larger than B on the screen.

Which of these two extremes you use depends on your purpose. *Use a short (wide-angle) focal length on the lens to:*

. . . distort a face for a comic or grotesque effect.

. . . accentuate the force of a movement toward camera. This makes the subject enlarge rapidly and seem to cover the distance swiftly.

. . . add more dominance to a foreground figure in relation to one farther away. The difference in screen height between the two figures can be increased by using a low camera position.

. . . add variety of size and height to your pictorial composition.

. . . give the illusion of greater depth to your subject or to the setting.

. . . bring miniature subjects or scenery in the foreground into apparent scale with an actual figure in the background.

. . . keep a subject framed when both subject and camera are in motion.

Use a long (narrow-angle) focal length on the lens to:

. . . equalize the importance of two subjects at different distances from the camera.

. . . make the appearance or action of the distant figure more apparent (e.g., when shooting past the catcher to the pitcher in a baseball game).

. . . give the feeling of compression (e.g., to make a row of tenement houses seem very crowded together or a traffic jam even more congested than it is.)

When a long and a short focal length on the lens both frame the same width at the plane of the performer, the short lens will include more background because of its wider angle. Therefore, if your background is too low or too narrow, or if backlights are causing halation at the top of your picture, try using a longer focal length.

When both focal lengths show the same foreground framing, a short lens will see farther behind obstructions than a long lens. Do you want to uncover the heads of panelists who are arranged one behind another? Note how the short focal length does this in *Figure A/3*.

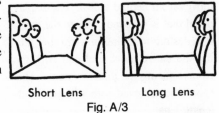

Short Lens   Long Lens

Fig. A/3

Focus

Depth of field can be increased by using a shorter focal length (if the camera remains at the same distance from the subject as with the longer lens previously used).

Both extended and limited depth of field have advantages.

Extended depth of field keeps foreground and background subjects in equally sharp focus at the same time. It makes following focus easier during advancing or receding movements either by the camera or by the subject.

Limited depth of field can be used to place more emphasis on the subject than on the background. It can be used to soften a background which is too "busy" or has imperfections such as cracks between flats or painted-looking stippling, or needs to look like sky rather than cloth.

Vertical Angle

The closer the camera, the more steeply it must tilt to frame a subject that is lower or higher than the lens. This consideration is important when the camera is mounted at a fixed height, as on a tripod.

Do you want to avoid seeing too much of a seated performer's pate or a standing performer's chin? Use a longer focal length so that you can pull the camera back and shoot at a more gradual incline.

Do you want to look down to reveal the contents of a bowl? Use a short focal length in close.

Space-Time Factors

The wider the lens angle, the more quickly you can dolly from long shot to closeup, or vice versa. There are two reasons for this. Because depth of field is greater, it is easy to maintain focus while moving briskly. Because of the wide angle, the camera can take a full shot of the subject at a closer distance; therefore, there is less distance for it to cover when dollying in for a closeup.

The wider the lens angle the more quickly you can dolly back with an advancing performer. Example: You take a one-shot of an entering character, then pull back as he advances to join another person already on the set.

Example 1 (see *Figure A/4*): The camera is to pan with a performer who moves from behind a desk to a display panel that is perpendicular to the desk. It is desired to maintain a hip shot during the entire move and end with the camera facing the panel squarely. This cannot be achieved with a longer focal-length lens.

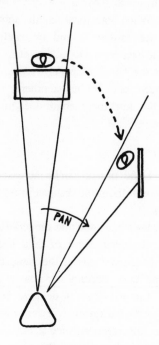

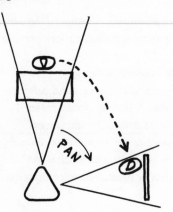

Fig. A/4

Example 2 (see *Figure A/5*): A
performer moves to a chair and sits, the
camera arcing with him to maintain
him in a two-shot with his companion.
On the short focal-length lens the arc is
of limited distance and can be traversed
quickly enough to keep up with the performer's action. On a longer focal
length, the camera would still be arcing
long after he had sat down.

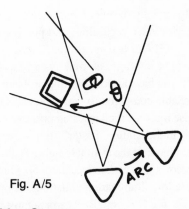

Fig. A/5

The Portable Video Camera

The portable video camera is designed to be shot from the shoulder or
mounted on a lightweight tripod and is powered from a 12-volt DC battery source.
The director armed with the following knowledge will be better prepared when the
time comes to plan his or her next shoot.

(1) *The lens*—While studio cameras can function fairly well with a zoom
ratio of 6:1 or 10:1, the ENG and EFP camera requires a lens with a relatively high
wide-angle-to-telephoto zoom ratio. A good wide angle of view is necessary for
shooting in confined locations, and, when an interview is being conducted by the
camera operator, a fairly long telephoto angle of view is necessary to accommodate
shooting subjects at considerable distance, commonplace when they are in an
outdoor environment. Since these longer focal-length lenses require the use of a
good fluid-head tripod to hold the shot steady and few of the working surfaces in
the field provide for camera dollying, the zoom lens must have the ability to cover
long distances from a fixed location.

Lenses with zoom ratios of 12:1 and 14:1 are common in both ENG and EFP
situations. Assuming that your widest lens position is 10mm and you have a 12:1
zoom ratio, the maximum telephoto focal length on that lens is what? If you came
up with 120mm, you're correct. Assume that the widest lens position is again
10mm and the telephoto maximum is 140mm, what is the zoom ratio? The correct
answer is 14:1. I think you get the picture. For special events such as sports in large
stadiums, lenses are available with much greater ratios that allow for a wide shot as
well as for extreme telephoto closeups on the field of play. Conversely, zoom lenses
can be found that have wide-angle positions greater than 10mm for use at extremely close distances, in very confined spaces, and for when the camera is being
hand held by a moving camera operator.

(2) *Automatic iris controls*—Since there are no studio engineers to remotely
control the amount of light reaching the pickup tubes in the camera, this function

helps greatly to reduce mistakes over a wide range of exposure that can produce inferior video recordings and possible camera tube damage.

(3) *Fast lens speeds and a long range of exposure control*—In ENG the light levels in interiors, as well as early morning and late afternoon, are quite low. In EFP you have remote lighting problems such as greatly reduced amounts of power available compared to what you can call upon in the typical television studio. For those reasons, the lenses on portable cameras tend to be "faster" than those used only in the studio. "Faster" simply means that at their maximum lens opening they let in more of the available light. Typically, a portable broadcast video camera will employ a lens with a maximum opening of f1.2 to f1.4, which will perform well in these low illumination situations. Along with the ability to work under low light levels, the ENG and EFP camera must be able to work in extremely bright daylight situations. For that reason the lens must also be capable of being "stopped down" considerably. Minimum lens openings of f22 are common. Additional light control is incorporated into these cameras in the form of a filter wheel built in behind the lens that allows the camera operator to dial in a neutral density filter.

(4) *Unlike the studio camera that operates under one specific color temperature light source, the ENG and EFP cameras must work equally well under a variety of lighting situations, including indoor tungsten lighting and daylight.* Color-correction filters, as well as a neutral-density filter, are provided for on this built-in filter wheel.

(5) *Studio cameras mounted on tripods or pedestals have large viewfinders designed for use by a camera operator standing behind the camera.* Cameras used for ENG and EFP have to be able to be used from the shoulder and therefore have 1.5″ viewfinders that are mounted on the side of the camera. The small viewfinder not only allows the camera operator to hand hold the camera, but, used with the associated rubber eyecup, helps to eliminate glare and reflected light associated with shooting in daylight from washing out the viewfinder picture. These viewfinders also have various types of function indicators built in that provide the operator information on battery condition, exposure measurement, recorder status, and so on.

(6) *Portable cameras rely on a high degree of automation.* Without an engineer in the field to shade the camera, perform color balancing, registration, and so on, portable cameras are designed to perform these functions electronically via switches and buttons. Periodically, the engineer takes the camera into the shop and fine tunes these automatic functions to assure that the camera will continue to work at its best in the field.

(7) *Portable cameras used in ENG and EFP have mounting attachments that allow for the use of lightweight tripods.* These cameras, having little mass when compared to their studio counterpart, truly need a tripod employing a fluid head if

the camera moves produced are to be of high quality. Quick release mounts are common, making it possible for the operator to easily switch between tripod and shoulder-mounted shooting situations.

(8) *Both ENG and EFP employ the use of compact, lightweight, portable video tape recorders that operate on 12-volt DC batteries.* The ENG trend is toward a camcorder system where the camera and recorder are a single unit, such as the Sony Betacam system. In EFP, with its more complex camera production and audio needs, we are more likely to find a separate camera and recorder. Often the choice between the two in either application is simply a preference of the station, engineering department, or the camera operator.

Microphones

While this text is designed to help you develop your skills as a director and much of the technical applications are best left to the studio technical staff, a fundamental understanding of the various microphones and their applications is probably appropriate here.

(1) *The first element to consider in any sound recording situation for video is the selection of microphone pickup pattern and its physical design.* Microphones come in several basic pickup patterns.

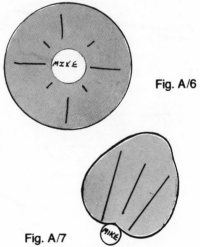

. . . omnidirectional (*Figure A/6*). This is a general-purpose microphone design that picks up sound coming from all directions. This type of pickup pattern is often applied to locations such as a tabletop for a panel discussion where several people share the same microphone.

Fig. A/6

. . . directional or cardioid (*Figure A/7*). This microphone pickup pattern has a high sensitivity in front, less from the sides, and its highest sound rejection from the rear. A directional microphone is a good choice for use in

Fig. A/7

hand-held voice or music recording where a specific sound source is to be recorded and a high degree of rejection of other environmental sounds is desirable. Many studio boom microphones are of this design.

. . . supercardioid (*Figure A/8*). This is a directional microphone pickup pattern with a very narrow angle of sound reception. This microphone pickup pattern is often used in field recording because of its excellent ability to reject sounds that it is not pointed at. Extreme care must be exercised to keep

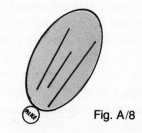

Fig. A/8

the performers "on mike," and loud sounds behind the performers must be avoided as the supersensitivity of this microphone design will pick these sounds up as well.

Microphones also come in a variety of physical designs as well as pickup patterns.

. . . hand microphones. These are most often seen in the hand of a news reporter on location and vocal music performers, but may also be found mounted on stands for talk shows and stationary recording of sound from musical instruments. Hand-held directional microphones are sometimes mounted on studio booms (*Figure A/9*) when a production involves a large playing area and the sound of several actors is picked up on a single microphone. In today's television applications the boom mount is generally confined to studio applications. A modification of the boom that is used on location is called a "fishpole" (*Figure A/10*) and can be

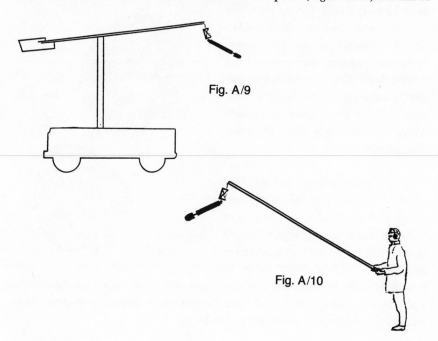

Fig. A/9

Fig. A/10

moved in and out of the playing area by an audio assistant. Hand microphones with an omnidirectional pickup pattern are usually confined to applications such as panel discussions or places where a single microphone must pick up the sound of several players at the same time. In a studio or conference setting the omnidirectional hand mike works well and economizes the equipment needs. However, in noisier locations such as on the street, it is difficult to discriminate between wanted and unwanted sounds.

. . . the "shotgun" microphone. This type of microphone is of the supercardioid design and can also be used on a boom or fishpole when an even greater degree of sound discrimination is necessary. Other applications of this microphone design include sideline coverage of live sound from football games. The "shotgun" microphone is often mounted inside a windscreen or zeppelin due to the sensitivity of the microphone to wind noise.

. . . the lavalier microphone. A lavalier microphone is either hung around a player's neck or clipped onto an element of the performer's apparel with a tie tack devise. For all frankly televised performances, the public has become accustomed to seeing microphones worn by performers and, indeed, may not even be aware of these mikes when they are covered by clothing sufficiently to be unobtrusive. It is difficult to avoid muffling of the sound pickup, however, when the sensitive end of the microphone is covered by a dense fabric. A lavalier microphone can be either omnidirectional or directional in its pickup pattern.

Lavalier mikes are ideal for seated commentators and guests, as the performers are always "on mike," even when they turn back and forth in conversation. Microphone cables attached at the waist or run down a pant leg are no problem when only limited movement is necessary. Another advantage of the lavalier mike is that when there's more than one person on the set you have independent control over each person's volume level. Because of the proximity to the mouth of the player, the lavalier microphone helps you keep background sounds at a minimum. In an interview situation it is also possible to place a lavalier mike on the person with the softest voice and, standing the interviewer and interviewee close together, pick up excellent sound. In situations where a concealed or inconspicuous mike is desirable, the lavalier works extremely well.

INDEX

Actors *see* Performers
Advertising *see* Commercials
Amplitude distortion, 184
Animation, 64–65, 126, 146–147
Arbitrary angles, 98–99
Arc, 115–116
Asymmetrical balance, 58, 64
Audio *see* Sound
Automatic iris controls, 235–236

Background areas, 47, 55, 94, 112–113, 116–117
Balance, 57–58, 187–189
Brightness, 36–38, 54, 64

Camera
  angle, 23–27, 31, 40–41, 66–67, 97–99, 119, 234
  areas of responsibility, 74–75
  compressing settings, 77–78
  consistency, 28, 94–100
  cover shots, 74
  crossings, 23
  eliminating extra-quick shot changes, 75
  and floor plans, 206–207
  keeping plan simple and consistent, 28
  keeping subject in focus, 30–31
  keeping subject in frame, 29–30
  keeping up with action, 71–82
  movement, 8, 42, 76–77, 78–79, 85–87, 99, 124–125
  on-location production, 166–171
  and performers, 59–60, 72–73
  planning, 12–20, 72–73, 155–165
  poor work, 63
  portable video, 235–237
  preventing masking of subject, 28–29
  rehearsal, 217–218
  relating action to proper, 27–28
  response to color temperature, 46
  revealing angles, 23–27
  sequence of subjects in same location, 75–76

Camera (*continued*)
  showing viewers what they want to see,
    71–72
  spatial relationships, 90–93
  and subject matter, 120–126
  and visual changes, 146–147
  and visual transitions, 101–119
  see also Lens; Mechanics,
    concealment of
Clarity
  and brightness levels, 36–38
  mixing up images, 38–39
  revealing camera angles, 23–27
  of structure of material, 6
  visual, 23–39
Climax, 130, 139
Closeups, 32–33, 40–41, 80, 106
Coffee tables, 60
Coherence, pictorial, 48–56
  arrangements, 48–51
  emphasizing elements in proportion to
    importance, 51–55
  environment of important elements, 53,
    54
  leading toward important elements with
    lines, 53
  and lens field of view, 55–56
Color
  adjacent and background areas, 47
  contrast range, 46–47
  effect of, 69
  fidelity, 44–47
  hue, 36, 43, 50, 64
  primary colors, 45–46
  reflective characteristics, 47
  temperature, 46
Commercials, 121–122, 129, 136–137,
    159–165
Composition
  linear, 68–69
  picture, 57–59, 116
Conference setup, 24
Consistency, 94–100
  in backgrounds, 94
  and camerawork, 97–99
  in illumination, 94–95
  location of subjects on screen, 95–96

  relating pictures to preceding ones, 94
  and screen size, 95, 99
  in segments, 99–100
Contact lens commercial, 136
Content *see* Program content
Contests, 136, 209
Contrast range, 46–47
Cover shots, 74
Cues, 225–230
Cutaways, 102
Cut-ins, 103

Depth of field, 55, 233, 234
Details, 66
  framing for, 31–35
  needlessly fine, 39
  and program content, 122
Diagonals, 65
Dialogue, 149, 155–159
Director
  advance preparation, 217
  calling the shots, 221–230
  cues, 225–230
  directions to camera operators, 227
  and editing, 172–176
  efficiency, 215–220
  and floor plans, 199–214
  as interpreter, 120–131
  morale of team, 219–220
  objectives, 194–195
  on-location production, 166–171
  and sound, 177–193
  stimulating responses, 145–154
  tempo of directions, 228
  vocabulary, 225
  watchwords, 219
  working with service departments,
    215–216
Dissolves, 103–106, 124–125
Dollying back, 91, 113–114
Dollying in, 111–113, 119
Drygas commercial, 136–137
Dust 'n Wax commercial, 159–165

Editing, 172–176
Educational television *see* Instructional
    television

Efficiency, 215–220
EFP *see* Electronic Field Production
Ego, 220
Electronic Field Production (EFP), 100,
    168–170, 236–237
Electronic News Gathering (ENG), 100,
    166–170, 236–237
Elongated subjects, 52
ENG *see* Electronic News Gathering
Establishing shot, 92
Exposure control, 236
Expressiveness, 66–70, 130
Extras and nonactors, 170

Facial expressions, 23
Fade-out/fade-in, 105–106
Field size, 118
Figure unity, 123–124
Film, 38, 95
Flare, 63
Flesh tones, 47
Floor plans, 159, 162, 199–214
    and camera placement, 206–207
    derived from scripts, 202–203
    devising by director, 203–206
    drawn to scale, 200–201
    economizing time and money, 213–214
    and lens angles, 201–202
    and performer relationships, 206
    purposes, 199
    scenery and dressing, 207–208
    and studio conditions, 213
    symbols and labels, 199–200
    vertical relationships in picture,
        208–209
Focus, 30–31, 55, 68, 80, 233
Foreground elements, 43, 52, 112–113
Form, preservation of, 40–47
Framing
    changes, 80
    closely around meaningful elements, 51
    for important details, 31–35
    keeping subject in frame, 29–30
    and lens selection, 231–232
    loose vs. tight, 67
    maneuvering subjects, 80–81
    of moving subject, 113

poor, 58–59
and visual transitions, 117

Glare, 62
The Glass Menagerie, 137–139
Graphics, 61, 203
Groupings, 50

Halation, 63
Hard lighting, 68
"He-she" dialogue, 149, 155–159
High key illumination, 68
Hues *see* Color, hue

Idleness, 220
Illumination, 30
    artificial, 46
    and clarity, 36–38
    color of, 44–45
    consistency in, 94–95
    and Electronic Field Production, 169
    extreme changes of, 37–38
    faulty, 61–63
    glare, 62
    hard vs. soft, 68
    high vs. low key, 68
    key light, 205
    modeling light, 43–44, 64
    natural, 46
    reflected, 47, 62–63
    too little, 46
    tying composition together, 49
    and visual changes, 150
    see also Brightness
Inanimate subjects, 146–147
Instructional television, 120–121
Interpretation
    and director, 120–131
    examples, 132–144
    objectives, 194–195
Iris controls, automatic, 235–236

Jump cuts, 95

Key light, 205

Lavalier microphones, 191, 205, 239

Lens
  angles tested on floor plans, 201–202
  extreme-angle, 41
  fast speeds, 236
  field of view, 55
  flare, 63
  focal length, 30–31, 80–81, 231–235
  portable video camera, 235–236
  selecting, 231–235
  wide-angle, 119, 234
  zoom, 8, 42, 76, 235
Lighting see Illumination
Linear composition, 68–69
Lines, 49, 53, 65, 69
Liveliness, 64–65
Low key illumination, 68

Mechanics, concealment of, 83–89
  avoiding camera movement without
    evident reason, 85–87
  avoiding new shots without evident
    reason, 83–85
  avoiding repetitive devices, 87
  elaborateness of undertaking, 89
  inept operation by crews, 88
  insisting on perfection, 88–89
  restricting technical virtuosity, 87–88
Microphones
  boom, 61–62, 178
  directional (cardioid), 237
  distance from sound source, 182–183
  hand, 169, 238–239
  interaction, 191
  lavalier, 191, 205, 239
  omnidirectional, 237
  and performers, 178–179, 187–188
  physical design, 238
  pickup patterns, 237–238
  quality, 181–183
  "shotgun," 167, 169, 179, 191–192,
    239
  supercardioid, 238
  wireless transmitter, 179, 192
"Microquiz," 209–213
Mind, of viewer, 151–153
Modeling light, 43–44, 64
Moving vehicles, 96, 114

Music
  camera treatment for string quartet, 144
  guest violinist, 9–17
  guitar-playing ballad singer, 135
  piano, 133–134, 188
  recorded, and program content, 192
  solos, 188–189

News coverage, 166–168
"News and Weather Briefs," 199–205
Noise, 184, 190
Note-taking, 170

On-location production, 166–171
Out-of-sequence shooting, 169

Panning, 37, 91, 109–111, 119
Pantomime face panel quiz, 136
Performers
  animation and naturalness, 65
  awkward or distracting movements, 61
  and camera, 59–60, 72–73
  expressiveness, 130–131
  and floor plans, 206
  giving sufficient time for changes,
    79–80
  grooming and dress, 60
  inappropriate action and unattractive
    appearance, 59–60
  introducing changes through actions,
    147–150
  movements, 148–150
  nervous tension, 61
  physical relationships between, 69–70
  rehearsing, 81–82
  and sound, 178–179, 187–188
  unsightly parts of body, 60–61
Perspective, 67, 189, 232–233
Phosphores, 45
"The Photographer's Eye," 175–176
Piano, 133–134, 188
Pictorial continuity, 71
Picture statements
  changing, 4, 7–8
  clarifying structure of material, 6
  composition, 57–59
  distractions and discomforts, 57–65

dividing action of program into, 3–4
examples of, 9–20
forcefulness of, 127–130
keeping new things happening, 5–6
moment-by-moment questionnaire,
    21–22
planning, 3–8
planning camera treatment, 12–20
and program content, 4–5, 122
punctuating, 5–6
subject of, 3–4, 6–8, 66
Poetry reading, 132–133
Police stories, 139–144
Portable video camera, 235–237
Postrecording, 184, 191
Prerecording, 183–184, 191
Profiles, 96–97
Program content
    concealing mechanics, 83, 85
    and director as interpreter, 120–144
    and recorded music, 192
    and spatial relationships, 90
Prompters, 59, 119
Properties, 61

Receding planes, 42
Rehearsal, 81–82, 217–218
Response stimulation, 145–154
Reverberation, 182

Scenery, 49, 61, 207–208
Scrambled superimposures, 38–39
Screen size, 95, 99
Settings, compressing, 77–78
Shadows, 62
Shapes, 49
"Shotgun" microphone, 167, 169, 179,
    191–192, 239
Shot sheets, 73
Side angles, 33–34
Signal-to-noise ratio, 184
Silent films, 152
Ski jump coverage, 174–175
Slides, 33, 38, 95, 105
Small subjects, 51–52
Soft focus, 68
Soft lighting, 68

Sound, 177–193
    balance, 187–189
    compression, 185–186
    distortion, 184
    disturbances, 189–191
    and editing, 173
    and Electronic Field Production, 169,
        191
    and Electronic News Gathering, 191
    feedback, 191
    lack of auditory completion, 192
    multiple inputs, 186–189
    noise, 184, 190
    "out of sync," 191
    postrecording, 184, 191
    prerecording, 183–184, 191
    quality, 181–184
    recorded music and program content,
        192
    reverberation, 182
    volume, 178–181, 185–189
    see also Microphones
Space, 41–44, 64–65, 114, 208
Spatial relationships, 90–93
Special effects, 107–108
Spencer, Herbert, 128, 130
Spotlights, 44
Static subjects *see* Inanimate subjects
Structure, of material, 6, 122–123
Subject matter *see* Program content
Subjects
    and consistency, 95–96, 99
    inanimate, 146–147
    introduction of, 92, 110
    long, 52, 115
    maneuvering, 80–81
    moving, 111
    of picture statements, 3–4, 6–8,
        66
    small, 80, 113
    stationary, 115–116
    succession of separate, 115
    and visual transitions, 101–102,
        109–119
"Sun gun," 167, 169
Suspense, 126–127, 143
Symmetrical balance, 57–58

Takes, 105, 111
Technique *see* Mechanics, concealment of;
    specific techniques
Tension, 61, 126
"Three Answers," 205–208
Three-dimensional space, 41–44, 208
Tilting, 91, 109–111
Time of day, 170
Truck, 114–115

Vertical angles, 98, 119, 234
Video engineers, 38
Visual changes, 122–123, 126, 146–151

Visual clarity *see* Clarity, visual
Visual stimuli, 145–146
Visual transitions, 101–119, 125
Volume, in settings, 43
Volume, sound *see* Sound

Wavelengths, 44–46
Wind, 190, 192
Wipes, 107
Wireless microphone transmitter, 179, 192

Zooming, 37, 91, 117–119
Zoom lens, 8, 42, 76, 118, 235